Biographical
Dictionary of
Public Administration

BIOGRAPHICAL
DICTIONARY OF
PUBLIC ADMINISTRATION

PATRICIA MOSS WIGFALL
and
BEHROOZ KALANTARI

GREENWOOD PRESS
Westport, Connecticut • London

Library of Congress Cataloging-in-Publication Data

Wigfall, Patricia M., date.
　　Biographical dictionary of public administration / Patricia Moss Wigfall and
　Behrooz Kalantari ; foreword by Paula Quick Hall.
　　　p.　cm.
　　Includes bibliographical references and index.
　　ISBN 0–313–30203–0 (alk. paper)
　　1. Public administration—Biography—Dictionaries.　I.　Kalantari, Behrooz.
　JA61.W54　2001
　016.351'092'2—dc21　　　99–046154
　　[B]

British Library Cataloguing in Publication Data is available.

Library of Congress Catalog Card Number: 99–046154
ISBN: 0–313–30203–0

First published in 2001

Greenwood Press, 88 Post Road West, Westport, CT 06881
An imprint of Greenwood Publishing Group, Inc.
www.greenwood.com

Printed in the United States of America

The paper used in this book complies with the
Permanent Paper Standard issued by the National
Information Standards Organization (Z39.48–1984).

P

In order to keep this title in print and available to the academic community, this edition
was produced using digital reprint technology in a relatively short print run. This would
not have been attainable using traditional methods. Although the cover has been changed
from its original appearance, the text remains the same and all materials and methods
used still conform to the highest book-making standards.

To my mother, Fakhr-eIran, who is always on my mind.
—B. Kalantari

To my family—Switzon, Mag, J. T., and Switz—with special thanks to J. T.,
for her invaluable assistance. I am deeply grateful.
—P. Wigfall

CONTENTS

FOREWORD

A relatively young academic discipline, public administration enables us to view governments and the extended family of non-governmental organizations from many perspectives. The diversity of views reflects the range of academic and socio-cultural backgrounds of those who define and develop the discipline. An often neglected aspect of theory is its source. Hypothetically irrelevant and transparent, the background of the writer may be critical to our understanding of the views offered, particularly in analyses that seek broad theoretical explanations.

This work is important not only as a resource for better understanding the *content* of the discipline. It also enhances the opportunity for studies of the people who are, themselves, legitimate and politically relevant subjects of analysis. This biographical reference contributes significantly to our ability to address interdisciplinary questions: Who studies and defines the field? How do those individuals come to hold and express their views? How do they gain legitimacy as scholars and spokespersons for public administration? To what extent and in what ways do these scholars represent the population groups about which they write?

To the authors of this volume, we are indebted. Kalantari and Wigfall have culled from numerous sources information which we now find in this one book. They give us a convenient means of placing ideas in the context of their human origins. Organized by name and indexed by subject, this reference enables us to examine, individually and collectively, the sources of the body of knowledge and perspectives called public administration. This is undoubtedly a major contribution to the field.

Paula Quick Hall, Ph.D.
Chair, Political Science Department
Bennett College
Greensboro, North Carolina

INTRODUCTION

As public organizations strive for greater efficiency and social recognition, the field of public administration has been faced with the challenge of rebuilding public trust and reengineering itself. Consequently, there is constant pressure in the field to improve its image and cultivate new ways to deal with future opportunities. Therefore, it is necessary that our students of public administration develop a solid grasp of fundamental theories. Developing a deeper understanding of the foundations of public administration and recognition of those who galvanized it can lead to greater understanding of the field. Unfortunately, in most public administration programs, there is more emphasis on studying theories than on those humans who created them. Therefore, teaching public administration usually takes place in a vacuum with disregard for the broader context from which those theories emerge.

Another major difficulty, especially for new students of public administration, is their exposure to many ideas from a variety of disciplines that represent the educational training, perceptions, skills, and values of their authors. Students are usually left with a psychological dilemma to connect with the contributors at an individual level in order to synthesize their ideas. Therefore, a holistic approach to learning is appropriate to produce effective results.

This work is a manifestation of the need to respond to the students' demands and a commitment to quality education in public administration. Although some dictionaries are available with descriptions of terms, a comprehensive collection of the biographies of major authors is seriously lacking. We hope that this modest attempt will fill the present vacuum and urgent need in the discipline of public administration.

The authors have been teaching public administration to a mixed audience of undergraduate and graduate students for several years. With the need for a compact reference collection in mind, the authors produced this biography of the original pioneers, as well as their contemporaries, who represent the public administration discipline. We do not recommend that students rely solely on this biographical dictionary for their studies. The *Biographical Dictionary of Public Administration* is not a substitute for the original works that it glasses; it is instead a tool for initial navigation of public administration fundamentals.

This work is a first step in a more comprehensive understanding of our field through a historical picture of the lives and accomplishments of its major personalities. It is of interest to beginners as well as advanced graduate students. Owing to the interdisciplinary nature of public administration, a great deal of open-mindedness on the part of students is essential in order to absorb the ideas presented to them by scholars from varied disciplines. Each entry seeks to highlight each contributor's personal, social, educational, and philosophical dimensions. The *Biographical Dictionary of Public Administration* can be read one entry at a time, as necessary, or comprehensively. Each entry is a distinct crystallization and has its own style and structure to engage readers who prefer reading cover to cover. This book is especially recommended to be used as a complementary source to the main public administration texts.

The selection criteria to include each entry was a difficult one. However, in selecting the entries, we attempted to cover a wide spectrum of contributors in differing areas of public administration, including organization theory, personnel, and budgeting. The main criterion that was used to include specific persons in this collection was the significance of their contribution to the development and evolution of the discipline. Besides the relevance of their ideas to the discipline, the frequency that their names appeared in major public administration texts and journals has also been a determining factor for inclusion in the collection. Despite the fact that contributors to the body of work in public administration are predominantly from other disciplines, the utmost effort has been made to include only those aspects of their contributions that are relevant to the discipline.

Perhaps due to the nature of the discipline, most contributors belong to the field of organizational theory as compared to other areas of public administration. Also, entries appear in different lengths, which is not indicative of the significance of the person's contribution but is more a reflection of author preference as well as availability of material.

The organization of each entry is very similar, beginning with each contributor's short personal history, followed by his or her major contributions to the public administration discipline. Owing to the scarcity of details on the personal lives of some individuals, a number of the entries lack information such as date of birth, place of birth, date of death, and place of death. To differentiate each subject's original works and the works that are produced by others about him or her, the end-of-entry bibliography for each is divided into two sections: "Works by [Subject]" and "Works about [Subject]." The first section contains works useful to students of public administration, so it is selective in nature. The latter section includes books and articles that are sources of additional information regarding the subject's contributions to the public administration discipline.

This work also includes an index, designed to facilitate retrieval of topical information and the authors of those ideas.

The authors hope that this limited offering sparks an interest in the production of more extensive work in the area of public administration and the individuals who have pioneered in this field. We hope that this effort helps to elevate student ability to conceptualize, describe, and explain the ideas presented by these theorists. We would appreciate the readers' feedback on the quality and usefulness of this work, along with suggestions for improvement, which will be utilized in future endeavors.

THE DICTIONARY

ALLISON, GRAHAM TILLETT (b. March 23, 1940, Charlotte, NC), political scientist; university professor

Graham Allison was born to Graham Tillett and Virginia (Wright) Allison. After attending Davidson College from 1958 to 1960, he entered Harvard University, where he received an A.B. in 1962 and a Ph.D. in 1968. He also received a B.A. and M.A. from Hertford College and in 1964 a B.A. and M.A. from Oxford College.

Allison's career began at the John F. Kennedy School of Government at Harvard University in 1968 as an assistant professor. At the same university, he served as associate professor from 1970 to 1972 and professor in 1972. He also served as the school's dean from 1977 to 1989. Allison served as a fellow at the Center for Advanced Studies at Stanford University from 1973 to 1974.

Included in the government positions he has held are membership on the secretary of defense's Policy Board, special adviser to the secretary of the U.S. Department of Defense from 1985 to 1987, and in 1993 assistant secretary of defense for policy and plans.

The underpinnings of Allison's model of presidential decision making in explaining decision making in the 1962 Cuban Missile Crisis rest on three explanatory theories: the rational actor, the organizational process model, and the bureaucratic politics model. According to Allison, each paradigm offers different, although not mutually exclusive, explanations for foreign policy formulation.

Describing executive policy making in the Cuban Missile Crisis as bureaucratic politics, Allison suggests that executive decisions follow political gamelike interactions—bargaining, compromise, and conflicts—among specialized subbureaucratic units—with their own interests, biases, and skills, to influence decision making at the top. Model III, then, suggests that decisions of foreign policy result from bargaining and compromise among heads of organizational units.

Allison theorizes that rational decisions, which are embodied in Model I, are often sacrificed for those that protect agency turfs, professional connections, and agency resistance to change. Model II, according to Allison, assumes that foreign policy strategy develops from organizational processes, such as the routines of bureaucratic agencies.

His analysis of foreign policy suggests that foreign policy mirrors the goals of and competition among the bureaucratic organizations responsible for international decisions.

In his comparative analysis of public and private management, Allison posits that managers in both sectors share similarities and differences. He suggests that differences such as greater scrutiny, longer tenure of service, and a noneconomic mission in the public sector, may be more important.

BIBLIOGRAPHY

Works by Graham Tillett Allison

Allison, G. T. *Conceptual Models and the Cuban Missile Crisis: Rational Policy, Organization Process, and Bureaucratic Politics.* Santa Monica, CA: Rand Corporation, 1968.
————. *Essence of Decision: Explaining the Cuban Missile Crisis.* Boston: Little, Brown, 1971.
————. "Public and Private Management: Are They Fundamentally Alike in All Unimportant Respects?" Public Management Research Conference. Brookings Institution, Washington, DC, November 1979.
Allison, G. T., and R. P. Berschel. "Can the United States Promote Democracy?" *Political Science Quarterly*, Spring 1992, 81–98.
Allison, G. T., A. Carnesale, and J. S. Nye, eds. *Hawks, Doves, and Owls: An Agenda for Avoiding Nuclear War.* New York: Norton Publications, 1985.
Allison, G. T., and P. Szanton. *Remaking Foreign Policy: The Organizational Connection.* New York: Basic Books, 1976.
Allison, G. T., and G. F. Treverton, eds. *Rethinking America's Security: Beyond Cold War to New World Order.* New York: Norton, 1992.
Allison, G. T. and W. Ury, eds. *Windows of Opportunity: From Cold Wave to Peaceful Competition in US–Soviet Relations.* Chewelah, WA: Ballinger, 1989.

Works about Graham Tillett Allison

Ball, D. J. "The Blind Men and the Elephant: A Critique of Bureaucratic Politics Theory." *Australian Outlook*, 28, April 1974, 71–92.
Bendor, J., and T. H. Hammond. "Rethinking Allison's Models." *American Political Science Review*, 86, 2, June 1992, 301.
Chong, D. H., and R. Lindquist. "The 1952 Steel Seizure Revisited: A Systematic Study in Presidential Decision Making." *Asia Quarterly*, 20, 4, December 1975, 587–605.
Kellerman, B. "Allison Redux: Three More Decision-Making Models." *Polity*, 15, 3, Spring 1983, 351–367.

Welch, D. "The Organizational Process and Bureaucratic Politics? Paradigms: Retrospect and Prospect." *International Security*, 17, 2, Fall 1992, 112–146.

ALTSHULER, ALAN A. (b. March 9, 1936, Brooklyn, NY), political scientist; dean; city planning expert

Alan Altshuler attended Cornell University, earning his B.A. in 1957 and M.A. from the University of Chicago in 1959 and Ph.D. in 1961. While completing doctoral work, he taught political science at Swarthmore College. Following degree conferral, Altshuler served as visiting professor of political science at Makere University College in Kampala, Uganda. Altshuler's post in Africa is an anomaly in his professional career, since his primary remaining positions are domestic—at his alma mater of Cornell from 1962 to 1966, the Massachusetts Institute of Technology from 1966 to 1983, New York University from 1983 to 1988, and Harvard University from 1988 to the present.

Born to Leonard Altshuler and Janet Sonnenstrahl in 1930s Brooklyn, New York, Alan Altshuler brought to his career an implicit concern for urban affairs and city planning. Next to the work of Woodrow Wilson—who first advocated the separating of politics and administration/professionalism in government service—the city is perhaps the greatest influence on Altshuler's scholarship.

During the 1960s, following his study of urban renewal in Minneapolis and St. Paul, Minnesota, Altshuler clarified his opposition to comprehensive planning. He launched four critiques of comprehensive planning based on his understanding of its impossibility due to these factors: (1) There is an assumption within comprehensive planning that public interest is not politically willed but awaits discovery; (2) the basis for measuring public interest is the hierarchy of collective goals constructed by the comprehensive planner; (3) comprehensive planners are assumed to have (but possibly lack) technical knowledge; and (4) comprehensive planners typically have yet to gain experiential knowledge prior to their strategy development. In particular, Altshuler, in *The City Planning Process*, noted that communities with high black populations were razed for freeway construction, whereas white communities were stabilized through curative revitalization efforts. Isolating displaced goals and corruption as key problems, Altshuler explained that "the promises of making these areas better will not be fulfilled if these games continue" (35).

During the 1970s, Altshuler's interest in city planning and racialized social dynamics manifested as a book-length campaign for minority input in the planning process, arguing "participation in the planning process is the only way that blacks and minority concerns can be addressed. . . . Blacks must be given the opportunities to voice their concerns in the planning process." The 1970s also saw Altshuler in public service roles as chairman of the Massachusetts governor's task force on transportation from 1960 to 1970, as director of Boston's Transportation Planning from 1970 to 1971, and as secretary of transportation for the Commonwealth of Massachusetts from 1971 to 1974.

By the mid-1980s, Altshuler's public notoriety was in full swing. In 1986, Altshuler was considered one of six New York citywide possibilities for the new chairman of the Mayor's City Planning Commission. While teaching public policy and urban planning at Harvard University in 1993, Altshuler coauthored *Regulation for Revenue: The Political Economy of Land Use Exactions* with José Gomez-Ibanez and A. M. Howitt through the Brookings Institution and the Lincoln Institute of Land Policy. Their study (a concise financial analysis of development) calls for use of exactions over growth controls—the lesser of two evils.

BIBLIOGRAPHY

Works by Alan A. Altshuler

Altshuler, A. "The Goals of Comprehensive Planning." *Journal of the American Institute of Planners*, 31, 3, 1965, 186–197.
———. *A Land-Use Plan for St. Paul.* Indianapolis, IN: Bobbs-Merrill, 1965.
———. *The City Planning Process: A Political Analysis.* 1965. Ithaca, NY: Cornell University Press, 1967.
———. *Community Control: The Black Demand for Participation in Large American Cities.* New York: Pegasus, 1970.
———. *The Politics of the Federal Bureaucracy.* New York: Dodd, 1968; New York: Harper and Row, 1976.
———, ed. *Current Issues in Transportation Policy.* Lexington, MA: Lexington Books, 1979.
Altshuler, A., J. A. Gomez-Ibanez, and A. M. Howitt. *Regulation for Revenue: The Political Economy of Land Use Exactions.* Washington, DC: Brookings Institution; Cambridge: Lincoln Institute of Land Policy, 1993.
Altshuler, A., J. Womack, and J. Pucher. *Equity in Urban Transportation: Final Report.* Washington, DC: Department of Transportation, Research and Special Programs Administration, Office of University Research, 1979.
———. *The Urban Transportation System: Politics and Policy Innovation.* Cambridge: MIT Press, 1979.

Work about Alan A. Altshuler

Innes, J. E. "Planning Through Consensus Building." *Journal of the American Planning Association*, 62, 4, Autumn 1996, 460–473.

APPLEBY, PAUL H. (b. September 13, 1891; d. October 21, 1963, New York), journalist; New Deal public administrator; university professor and dean

Appleby began his journalism work during his childhood by publishing a juvenile paper. Later he entered Grinnell College and upon his graduation published a newspaper in Montana; eventually, in 1924, he became the editor of the *Des Moines Register and Tribune* and after four years started his own newspaper in Virginia. He left publishing in 1933 to work in the public sector and became executive assistant to Secretary of Agriculture Henry A. Wallace. Appleby continued his public service until 1947 when he moved to New York to work for the state government.

Appleby's public service provided him with a good understanding of the workings of bureaucracy and helped him to develop his own theories of public administration. His writings reflect his life's work as a public servant. In 1947 he accepted the deanship of the Maxwell Graduate School of Citizenship and Public Affairs of Syracuse University. In that position Appleby was able to develop practical knowledge into theories of public organizations. Later on, in 1955, he returned to public service, becoming budget director for the state of New York for two years.

Appleby wrote several books and articles that cover a wide range of issues within public administration. Appleby's efforts to fuse the real working of the public sector with the theories of public administration emerge in his discourse *Big Democracy* (1945), where he sets the tone for differentiating public sector from private sector in their substance. He deeply acknowledges the public sector's uniqueness. He argues that the public and private sectors are different with respect to their goals, operations, and environment. He claims that public is different from private because its business is the business of government and "government is politics," and public administration is policy making. Appleby questions the dichotomy between politics and administration and argues that in reality they cannot be separated.

Appleby is recognized as the first advocate of differentiating between public and private sectors and creating a dichotomy between them. In his view, "administrative or executive process" is heavily involved with other governmental processes including the legislative, judicial, and party maintenance that make it anything but political. Therefore, he rejects the idea of the dichotomy between administration and politics that had had a strong following since the publication of Woodrow Wilson's work, "The Study of Administration," in 1887. Appleby examines the operation of government as a seamless web of many decisions that are the outcome of the interactions among different political forces. Therefore, the lines of separation between different branches of government are very blurred, and it is almost unrealistic to ignore the fusion of politics and administration in this environment. Appleby contends that public policy is the final product of the political process, and bureaucracy is the last component of the process of policy making. This makes bureaucracy a major component of the political process. By association, public administration is more political than administrative.

Appleby posits that the main function of public administration is to create a balance between its administration function and its political environment. In his judgment, the bureaucratic political environment, including its partisan politics and the influence of pressure groups, produces a healthy environment that checks bureaucracy and holds it accountable to the needs of citizens.

Therefore, public administration must cease looking to business for guidance. The business of government is mixed with politics, whereas business administration emphasizes profit maximization, influenced by the forces of the market, competition, and supply and demand. On the contrary, government operates in a political environment dominated by political compromise and gives and takes with many rules and regulations dominating the process. To understand the operation of the public sector, one needs to understand the political process. Appleby uses the Constitution to ground his argument that even constitutional arrangements provide a holistic approach to public decision making and determining public policy. He explains that although the Constitution advocates separation of powers, it also provides the opportunity for different branches to check on each other's operation and influence each other's decisions.

Finally, Appleby insists that public organizations should abide by stricter ethical standards than those of business organizations. This is simply due to the public nature of government institutions. Therefore, in his opinion, business ethics and public ethics are two different areas and cannot be mixed. With regard to morality, Appleby is more concerned with the effects of the administrative system on employees' morality rather than their individual morality. Thus, he determined that faulty institutional arrangements are the major threat to administrative morality. He contends that political intervention as well as sound organizational structure are necessary to ensure accountability in the public sector.

Appleby warns against the influence of special interests on bureaucracy and a condition whereby an elite minority exerts undue influence on the decision-making process. To ensure political sensitivity and responsiveness in regards to the needs of the citizens rather than to those of the elite few, he believes that governmental structure should be centralized to guarantee political responsibility and responsiveness. Therefore, his main emphasis is on the public organizational structure as opposed to the individual public servant. As for the public morality of public officials, Appleby believes that mental attitude and moral qualities should be the main ingredients of any public official.

BIBLIOGRAPHY

Works by Paul H. Appleby

Appleby, P. *Big Democracy*. New York: Knopf, 1945.
———. *Policy and Administration*. Tuscaloosa, AL: University of Alabama Press, 1949.

————. *Morality and Administration in Democratic Government.* Baton Rouge: Louisiana State University Press, 1952.
————. *The Reminiscences of Paul H. Appleby.* Microform, 1957.

Works about Paul H. Appleby

Cooper, T. L., and N. D. Wright, eds. *Exemplary Public Administrators: Character and Leadership in Government.* San Francisco: Jossey-Bass, 1992.
Martin, R. C. *Public Administration and Democracy: Essays in Honor of Paul H. Appleby.* Syracuse, NY: Syracuse University Press, 1965.
Maxwell Graduate School of Citizenship and Public Affairs. Addresses at the installation of Paul H. Appleby as dean. Syracuse University, May 11, 1947.
O'Donnel, M. E. *Readings in Public Administration.* Boston: Houghton Mifflin, 1966.

ARGYRIS, CHRIS (b. 1923, Newark, NJ), university professor; management consultant; trainer; pioneer in organizational development; consultant

Argyris's training was in psychology. He received his Ph.D. from Cornell University in 1951. Later he taught industrial administration at Yale University (1951–1955) and joined Harvard University to teach education and organizational behavior. After 1971 he was special consultant on human relations in industry to the secretary of state, the Department of Health, Education and Welfare, the National Science Foundation, the U.S. Commissioner of Education, and the Air Force Personnel & Training & Research Center. He also served as special consultant to several countries around the world.

His major contribution concerns the relationship between the individual and the organization. He concentrates on the needs of individuals and the needs of organizations. He strongly argues in favor of individual growth and development in organizations. He believes that there is a pattern of ignoring the basic needs of individuals in favor of organizational goals in most organizations. He argues that organizational structure has a direct effect on the development of individual employees and criticizes practices in organizations that inhibit organizational growth and development.

Argyris contends that when individuals grow in organizations, in the final analysis, organizations will benefit. He points out major incompatibilities between the growth needs of the individual and requirements of formal organizations. He also discovers some of the trends that have created certain expectations from individuals that are contrary to their evolutionary pattern of development. For example, employees are provided minimal control over their work, promoting passivity and submissiveness, and a dependent employee is detrimental to an individual's growth and self-actualization. Accordingly, such organizational practices as task specialization, unity of command, and span of control tend to be contradictory to the needs of individual employees. Argyris concludes that in most organizations, individual and organizational needs are seldom congruent.

According to Argyris, when organizations inhibit organizational growth, individuals behave differently to cope with those circumstances. They might leave the organization, become apathetic and disinterested in organizational goals, or feel frustrated and depressed. Consequently, explains Argyris, top-level administrators misdiagnose these defensive mechanisms and perceive the employees to be lazy and uncooperative. Therefore, they blame the employees for disloyalty and waste. Unfortunately, the top leaders concentrate only on their own needs and the organization's goals.

Argyris suggests several strategies for bringing about change to deal with the unhealthy situations that exist in organizations. He advocates change through learning, training, and utilization of an "interventionist" in the organization. The role of this outside agent is to bring necessary changes into the organization and to play the role of teacher/educator for the members of the organization. He suggests four areas in which organizations can use interventionists: organizational structures; improving interpersonal competence; development of personal and psychological maturity; and developing techniques of programmed learning. Argyris contends that learning should have two major focuses—learning about the organization and learning about one's self. He suggests the use of laboratory training, an unstructured small-group situation (T-Group), and survey research and feedback techniques to expose organizational dynamics and learn from them.

In his approach in bringing about change in organizational structure, he explains different structures that can be used for organizations and elaborates on their strengths and weaknesses. These include the pyramidal structure; the modified formal organizational structure; power according to function contribution; and finally, the matrix organization.

Argyris questions the organizational structure that relies on authority and control to achieve its goals. He contends that the authority exercised in this kind of setting hinders an individual's growth and development. He argues that individuals change and grow along an evolutionary pattern. For example, people grow from passivity to activity; dependence to independence; inflexible to flexible behavior; shallow interests to deep interests; short perspective to long-term perspective; accepting subordination to desiring equality or superiority; and lack of control to self-control. Treating employees like children interrupts their evolutionary cycle, reestablishing the stage of employee depression with its concomitant lack of job interest and dematurity. The final outcome of such an environment is lower productivity and a hostile workforce, and it leads "to human and organizational decay." In general, Argyris has contributed greatly to the theories of human relations in organizations by advocating change and development.

BIBLIOGRAPHY

Works by Chris Argyris

Argyris, C. "Successful Patterns for Executive Action." *Harvard Business Review*, 1957.

———. *Understanding Organizational Behavior*. Homewood, IL: Dorsey Press, 1960.

———. *Interpersonal Competence and Organizational Effectiveness*. Homewood, IL: Richard D. Irwin, 1962.

———. *Integrating the Individual and the Organization*. New York: John Wiley & Sons, 1964.

———. *Organization and Innovation*. Homewood, IL: Richard D. Irwin and Dorsey Press, 1965.

———. *Intervention Theory and Method: A Behavioral Science Review*. Reading, MA: Addison-Wesley, 1970.

———. *The Applicability of Organizational Sociology*. Cambridge: Cambridge University Press, 1972.

———. "Personality and Organization Revisited." *Administrative Science Quarterly*, 18, 1973, 141–167.

———. "Some Limits to Rational Man Organization Theory." *Public Administration Review*, May–June 1973, 253–267.

———. "Organization Man: Rational and Self-Actualizing." *Public Administration Review*, July–August 1973, 354–357.

———. "People: Managing Your Most Important Asset." *Harvard Business Review*, 1990.

———. *Organizational Learning II: Theory, Method, and Practice*. Reading, MA: Addison-Wesley Longman, 1996.

———. "What Is a Learning Organization?" *Harvard Business Review*, 1997.

———. *Knowledge Management*. Boston, MA: Harvard Business School Press, 1998.

———. *Effective Communication*. Boston, MA: Harvard Business School Press, 1999.

Argyris, C., and C. L. Cooper, eds. *Concise Blackwell Encyclopedia of Management*. Cambridge, MA: Blackwell Publishers, 1998.

Works about Chris Argyris

Bell, D. E., H. Raiffa, and A. Tversky, eds. *Decision Making: Descriptive, Normative, and Prescriptive Interactions*. New York: Cambridge University Press, 1988.

Crainer, S. *The Ultimate Book of Business Gurus: 110 Thinkers Who Really Made a Difference*. New York: AMACOM, 1998.

Crocker, J. D. "A Resource Manual, Influenced by the Model II Organizational Concepts of Chris Argyris: For the Board of Elders of an Independent, Conservative, Evangelical Church in Indianapolis, Indiana." 1981.

Crow, Thomas Allen. *A Review and Comparison of the Management Theories of Douglas McGregor, Rensis Likert and Chris Argyris.* 1965.

Denhardt, R. B. *Theories of Public Organization.* Belmont, CA: Wadsworth, 1993.

French, W. L., and D. Hellriegel, eds. *Personnel Management and Organization Development: Fields in Transition.* Boston, MA: Houghton Mifflin, 1971.

Friedman, P. G. "An Evaluation of Chris Argyris' Theory of Organizational Behavior as Applied to Speech Education Majors." 1971.

Garvin, D. A. *Becoming a Learned Organization.* Boston, MA: Harvard Business School Press, 1997.

Hesselbein, F., M. Goldsmith, and R. Beckhard, eds. *The Organization of the Future.* San Francisco, CA: Jossey-Bass, 1997.

Howard, R., ed. *The Learning Imperative: Managing People for Continuous Innovation.* Boston, MA: Harvard Business School Press, 1993.

Jackson, C. N., ed. *Contracting for Organization Development Consultation.* Alexandria, VA: American Society for Training and Development, 1988.

Lundstedt, S. B. "Contributions of Chris Argyris to Organizational Theory." Chapel Hill: University of North Carolina, 1966.

Natemeyer, W. E., and J. S. Gilberg, eds. *Classics of Organizational Behavior.* IL: Moore Publishing, 1978.

Pettigrew, A. M., ed. *The Management of Strategic Change.* Oxford, UK: Blackwell, 1987.

Quay, R. H. *On Leadership and Organizational Theory: A Checklist of the Works of Chris Argyris, Fred F. Fiedler, and Victor H. Vroom.* Monticello, IL: Vance Bibliographies, 1980.

Rothermich, A. E. "An Interpersonal Communication Training Program for Physicians in a Family Practice Residency: Trial of a Methodology Based on the Concepts of Chris Argyris." Salt Lake City, UT: author, 1976.

Srivastva, S., and associates. *Executive Integrity: The Search for High Human Values in Organizational Life.* San Francisco: Jossey-Bass, 1988.

————. *The Executive Mind.* San Francisco, CA: Jossey-Bass, 1983.

Whyte, W. F., ed. *Participatory Action Research.* Newbury Park, CA: Sage, 1991.

Woodman, R. W., and W. A. Pasmore, eds. *Research in Organizational Change and Development: An Annual Series Featuring Advances in Theory, Methodology and Research,* vol. 1. Greenwich, CT: JAI Press, 1987.

BAILEY, STEPHEN K. (b. May 1916, Newton, MA; d. March 1982, Lincoln, MA), political scientist; World War II veteran; fellow

Bailey attended Hiram College, where he received a B.S. in 1937. He attended Oxford University as a Rhodes scholar and received a B.A. in 1939 and a M.A. in 1943 from that university in England. In 1946 he was accepted at Harvard University to complete his graduate studies in political science. He received his M.A. from Harvard in 1946 and a Ph.D. in 1948.

He taught political science at Princeton and Syracuse universities for several years and then joined Harvard University to teach educational policy and administration. He later taught at Oxford University as a

Fulbright scholar. He also worked as a public employee for several years in Connecticut and was a member of the New York State Board of Regents. He was part of the Hoover Commission's study on the presidency and served in the U.S. Navy during World War II. In 1950, he received the Woodrow Wilson Foundation Award for the best publication in government.

Bailey has written extensively on the legislative process and how the complex process of democracy works. He argues that American democracy relies on human intelligence and requires a great degree of flexibility. He argues that the guarantor of the survival of the American system lies primarily in its responsive nature. It reflects the will of the majority and gives its citizens the right to hold public officials accountable for their policies. He emphasizes the importance of the ethical dimensions of public administration and government. He notes that the public interest is a complex concept to explain. He studied the workings of Congress for many years and made some suggestions to strengthen its role in the realm of policy making. According to Bailey, lawmaking responsibility in Congress is so dispersed that it is hard to hold a specific person accountable for his or her actions. Therefore, a great deal of cynicism surrounds the Congress. He emphasizes the importance of establishing accountability in public organizations and recommends that Congress improve its internal machinery. He studied the workings of Congress during the 1970s and made predictions concerning the dominant behavior of Congress the two decades to come. His predictions have proven to be very close to reality twenty years later.

Bailey is recognized for several important contributions to the field of public administration. They include organizational behavior, utilization of technology, and ethical behavior and considerations in public organizations. He argues that in order for public administration to develop its theoretical underpinning, it has to deal with four theoretical frameworks—descriptive, normative, assumptive, and instrumental. Descriptive theory is concerned with the description of different structures, relationships, and tasks within the organization. Normative theory concerns itself with the values that public administration practitioners and theorists should strive for. Assumptive theory refers to the reality of any situation in public organizations with no interference of "values" in the process. Instrumental theory promotes the idea of developing useful managerial techniques and tools in order to implement the policies more effectively and efficiently.

Bailey believed that public administrators, as guardians of public trust, need to develop a clear understanding of the moral consequences of their profession. He also investigated the relationship between morality and public administration and the qualities of the moral behavior of bureaucracies as well. He contends that there are three moral qualities that are essential in determining the degree of adherence to morality in public organizations: optimism, courage, and fairness tempered by charity. He refers to optimism as the willingness of public servants to face the ambiguity of moral situations and try to deal with them. Courage is the ability to face problems and be decisive in times of crisis. Finally, he believes "fairness tempered by charity" implies that public officials should strive for justice in their relations with the public.

In addition, he argues that public administration should pay considerable attention to the legal aspect of the field. Therefore, he emphasizes the role of administrative law in the public administration field. He also believes in the importance of education in society and argues that his concept of education lies beyond formal institutions. In his judgment, the purpose of education is to stimulate learning through reading, personal experience, observation, and peer interaction.

In cooperation with Edith Mosher, Bailey conducted a study of program development at the U.S. Office of Education. Their main focus was on the process by which the agency was trying to increase its funding and on the effort to bring some measure of change and innovation to the conduct of its affairs. The results of their study indicate that public agencies are able to bolster support through incremental and pluralistic means.

BIBLIOGRAPHY

Works by Stephen K. Bailey

Bailey, S. K. *Congress Makes a Law*. New York: Columbia University Press, 1950.
————. *Congress in the Seventies*. New York: St. Martin's Press, 1970.
————. *Educational Interest Groups in the Nation's Capital*. Washington, DC: American Council on Education, 1975.
————. *The Purpose of Education*. Bloomington, IN: Phi Delta Kappa Educational Foundation, 1976.
Bailey, S. K., and E. U. Mosher, eds. *ESEA: The Office of Education Administers a Law*. Syracuse, NY: Syracuse University Press, 1976.

Works about Stephen K. Bailey

Binkley, W. E. *The Making of Law*. Washington, DC: Westbury, 1952.
Lyford, J. P. *The Agreeable Autocracies: A Series of Conversations on American Institutions with Stephen K. Bailey* . . . New York: Oceana Publications, 1961.
Quay, R. H. *On Politics and Education: A Bibliography of Stephen Kemp Bailey*. Monticello, IL: Vance Bibliographies, 1981.

BARNARD, CHESTER I. (b. November 1886, Malden, MA; d. 1961, New York), board member; company president; USO president

Barnard attended Mount Hermon High School and received a scholarship to Harvard University. He left in 1909 without having been graduated. His first job was clerical at the American Telephone and Telegraph (AT&T) Company, and later he left for Europe to study the telephone and telegraph systems there. After his return, he improved the commercial practices of AT&T in order to make it more efficient. During World War I, he served on the board of the U.S. Telephone Administration, and in 1926, he became the president of the New Jersey Bell Telephone Company. Later, Barnard joined the United Service Organizations (USO) during a period of major development and became its president (1942–1945). USO was a recreational facility for the wartime personnel to deal with their immediate recreational needs. After the war, the agency continued to be useful to postwar veterans to deal with war-related problems.

At the request of the governor of Massachusetts, Morgan F. Larson, Barnard became the organizer of the Emergency Relief Administration Organization. In that capacity, he developed a case study for Lawrence J. Henderson's course in sociology at Harvard University. Through this interaction, he was able to become acquainted with some of the contributors to organizational theory, including Elton Mayo and Lawrence Lowell. His major concern was the study of employee behavior in the workplace. Barnard used his own experience as a public administrator as well as new theories of organizational behavior that he developed after the Hawthorne experiment to write his major book *Functions of the Executive* in 1938. He was the first to suggest that organizations are sets of cooperative systems and defined the organization at the group level as "a system of consciously coordinated activities or forces of two or more persons." Therefore, to understand organizations, one has to reflect upon individuals' motives in order to secure the contribution of individual members. His theories of organization were based on human motivation and behavior. They reject the orthodox theories of classical schools that were pioneered by Frederick Taylor, Luther Gulick, and Henry Fayol. He contends that managers should realize that employees cannot be motivated through economic means alone: Social needs are also important. He also paid close attention to the problem of leadership in organizations and concepts such as authority, responsibility, and decision making. He argued that in order for organizations to be successful, they should develop a cooperative system between employees and managers.

Barnard argues that the exercise of authority is mostly dependent on the person who receives the order, as opposed to the person who issues it. He developed the concept of the "zone of indifference," by which an employee obeys the order only if it falls within this zone. Outside the zone, employees are not willing to accept authority. According to Barnard, this zone is created through an interaction of individual values, expectations, goals, and organizational values. In sum, employees cannot be motivated beyond their zone of indifference. As a result, a proper communication system is vital to the survival of the organization, and by the same token, communication channels through the "line of authority" as well as communicating messages should be clear. According to Barnard, to facilitate employee cooperation, managers should instill moral norms that are understood by all members. In other words, creating new values that are compatible with the goals of the organization is vital to the success of each organization. In his judgment, a skilled leader is able to communicate order properly and make subordinates obey it. Authority can be exercised if the employee has a cooperative attitude. If the order is not understood, it probably will not be followed. In addition, orders have to fall within certain parameters to be effective. For example, they should be compatible with the overall organizational purpose and should be realistic in terms of physical and mental demands on the individual.

He also emphasized the importance of the role of communication between the executive and his or her subordinates. He argues that organizational purpose and authority can only be legitimized through the cooperation of different members. He perceives the organization as a system of cooperation and exchange among employees. He calls this "satisfactory exchange" in the organization. In his judgment, organizational goals are as important as the individuals who work there. Herbert Simon used Barnard's "satisfactory exchange" concept and called it "organizational equality."

According to Barnard, the overall function of an executive is to oversee the maintenance of the whole operation of the organization and its survival. In addition, he argues that managers possess three different skills: technical, social, and cooperative. He explains that technical skills deal with the utilization of management techniques and technology in the organization. Social skills relate to the ability to bring a balance between the organizational and personal needs of employees. Finally, he emphasizes the significance of cooperation of its members that should be realized through the efforts of managers.

Barnard also paid close attention to the idea of the informal organization that exists side-by-side with the formal. In his judgment, informal organization is the main channel of communication among different positions on the organizational chart. He also pays attention to the significance of the environment outside the organization and how it affects the life of the organization.

BIBLIOGRAPHY

Works by Chester I. Barnard

Barnard, C. *Functions of the Executive*. Cambridge: Harvard University Press, 1938.
———. "Functions and Pathology of Status Systems." In *Organization Management*. Cambridge: Harvard University, Press, 1962. 207–244.

Works about Chester I. Barnard

Crainer, S. *The Ultimate Book of Business Gurus: 110 Thinkers Who Really Made a Difference.* New York: AMACOM, 1998.

Fry, B. R. *Mastering Public Administration: From Max Weber to Dwight Waldo.* Chatham, NJ: Chatham House, 1989.

Grint, K., ed. *Leadership: Classical, Contemporary, and Critical Approaches.* New York: Oxford University Press, 1997.

Scott, W. G. "Barnard on the Nature of Elitist Responsibility." *Public Administrative Review*, 42, 1982, 197–201.

———. *Chester Barnard and the Guardians of the Managerial State.* Lawrence: University Press of Kansas, 1992.

Williamson, O. *Chester Barnard and the Incipient Science of Organization.* Center for Research in Management, University of California, Berkeley Business School, 1989.

———, ed. *Organization Theory: From Chester Barnard to the Present and Beyond.* New York: Oxford University Press, 1990.

BENNIS, WARREN GAMELIEL (b. 1925, New York City), business administrator; professor; university president; consultant

Warren Bennis is recognized for his "humanist" and "democratic" revision of bureaucratic institutions. His concept of a horizontal chain of command turns on the idea that the workplace is a network of "equals" and that vertical hierarchies of leadership cannot accommodate the changing work environment. Bennis conceives the "organic" model of the organization as "temporary systems" in which managers link a network of "task forces" organized in response to specific problems. In this "organic" model, teams of experts replace the traditional pecking order of organizational leaders and subordinates because, realistically, workplaces of the future are diversely populated by individuals of varying competence.

Experience in the field of psychology grounds Bennis's prediction of a "post bureaucratic" future. Prior to publishing in the area of organizational development, Bennis acted as assistant professor of psychology at the Massachusetts Institute of Technology (MIT) from 1953 to 1956. From 1956 to 1959, Bennis was assistant professor of psychology and business at Boston University. He returned to MIT in 1959 and assumed full professorship until 1967 in psychology. In addition to other positions of professional leadership, Bennis was president of the University of Cincinnati from 1971 to 1977; he published *The Leaning Ivory Tower* in 1973 with Patricia Biederman. His education includes a B.A. from Antioch College, completed in 1951, and a Ph.D., completed at MIT in 1955. Co-edited with Kenneth D. Benne and Robert Chine, *The Planning of Change: Readings in the Applied Behavioral Sciences* was published in 1961.

Through the series of major publications, Bennis continued his contributions to the field of organization development, an area involving the social dimension of organizational change. Bennis begins the landmark *Changing Organizations* (1966) with his prediction of "dying bureaucracy." He attributes the changing conventions of organizational leadership to developments in the behavioral sciences and draws upon this field to outline methods of transition for future-oriented institutions: from a workforce of employees to members of professions, from customary operations to rapid technological change, from bureaucratic systems to democratic ones. Social democracy as inevitable is the central thesis for *The Temporary Society* as well, published in 1968 with Philip E. Slater. In 1969, Bennis published *Organization Development*, volume one of a joint-authored, six-volume study dedicated to developing trends in organization development. His volume, which maps the beginning and evolution of the field, posits the idea of "organization development" as "educational strategy" and organizational infrastructures as an adaptive "culture." In this context, "change agents" implement the "new culture" of the organization.

BIBLIOGRAPHY

Works by Warren Gameliel Bennis

Bennis, W. G. *Changing Organizations.* New York: McGraw-Hill, 1966.
———. *Organization Development: Its Nature, Origins, and Prospects.* Reading, MA: Addison-Wesley, 1969.
———. *On Becoming a Leader.* Reading, MA: Addison-Wesley, 1989.
———. *Why Leaders Can't Lead: The Unconscious Conspiracy Continues.* San Francisco: Jossey-Bass, 1989.
———. *Beyond Bureaucracy: Essays on the Development and Evolution of Human Organization.* San Francisco: Jossey-Bass, 1993.
———. *An Invented Life: Reflections on Leadership and Change.* Reading, MA: Addison-Wesley, 1993.
Bennis, W. G., ed. *Interpersonal Dynamics: Essays and Readings on Human Interaction.* Homewood, IL: Dorsey Press, 1964.
———. *American Bureaucracy.* Chicago: Aldine Publishing Company, 1970.
Bennis, W. G., K. D. Benne, and R. Chine, eds. *The Planning of Change: Readings in the Applied Behavior Sciences.* New York: Holt, Rinehart and Winston, 1961.
Bennis, W. G., and P. W. Biederman. *The Leaning Ivory Tower.* San Francisco: Jossey-Bass, 1973.
———. *Organizing Genius: The Secrets of Creative Collaboration.* Reading, MA: Addison-Wesley, 1997.
Bennis, W. G., and J. Goldsmith, eds. *Learning to Lead: A Workbook on Becoming a Leader.* Reading, MA: Addison-Wesley, 1994.
Bennis, W. G., and B. Nanus. *Leaders: The Strategies for Taking Charge.* New York: Harper and Row, 1985.
Bennis, W. G., J. Parikh, and R. Lessem. *Beyond Leadership: Balancing Economics, Ethics, and Ecology.* Cambridge: Blackwell Business, 1994.

Bennis, W. G., and E. H. Schein. *Leadership and Motivation: Essays.* Cambridge, MA: MIT Press, 1966.

Bennis, W. G., and P. E. Slater. *The Temporary Society.* New York: Harper and Row, 1968.

Bennis, W. G., and R. Townsend. *Reinventing Leadership: Strategies to Empower the Organization.* New York: Morrow, 1995.

BLAU, PETER (b. February 7, 1918, Vienna, Austria), sociologist; university professor

Born in Austria to Theodore and Bertha Blau, Peter Blau came to the United States in 1939. Having received B.A. and Ph.D. degrees at Elmhurst College and Columbia University in 1942 and 1952, respectively, Blau held professorships at the University of Chicago, Columbia University, State University of New York, and Cambridge University.

"Dyadic exchange," "heterogeneity," "occupational structure," and "exchange-dependence" are a few of the numerous key concepts Peter Blau has popularized for public administration theory. For example, in *Structural Contexts of Opportunities*, Blau has suggested that social relations are impacted by social structure—which Blau defines as "the distribution of a population among positions in a multidimensional space"—and individuality by social "heterogeneity." Attention to "heterogeneity" nuances his theory of social relations. According to Blau, when there is "a complex web of group affiliations, and individuals find themselves at the intersection of numerous groups . . . this creates cross pressures, which are stressful, but which also weaken the power of a given group to enforce restrictions on individuals, thereby expanding freedom of choice." From Blau's vantage, consequently, the social instability (caused by inequalities, social differences, and disrupted homogeneity) is a significant source of increased freedom of choice on the individual level. In later scholarship, Blau applies his "macrosociological" strategies of the 1960s to "dyadic association" (social practices like friendship and marriage) between individuals from different social positions.

Blau's contemporary scholarship, much like his research published over thirty years ago, privileges demographic and economic considerations over group, cultural, and historical determinants. From the outset, Blau insists that theoretical analysis starts with systems and population structures, not actors. Although some public administrators criticize Blau's formalist approach, others see it as beneficial for interrogating "differentiation" (the vertical hierarchies within social structures) and examining how individual actions either reproduce social structure or subvert normative homogeneity.

In general, Blau is known as a macrosociologist; moreover, as the preface to *Structural Contexts* (1994) reflects, he represents himself as a professionally self-reflective sociologist with regard to how his oeuvre coheres. His work on organizational characteristics and efficiency circulates widely; for his continual consideration of the relationship between hierarchy and equality, Blau's analyses are invested with interdisciplinary value.

Blau, a member of the American Civil Liberties Union, has been University of North Carolina at Chapel Hill's Robert Broughton Distinguished Research Professor of Sociology for over ten years. He has received a variety of honors including a Bronze Star for his wartime service in the U.S. Army Intelligence division from 1943 to 1945, the Fulbright Distinguished Visitor Award for 1965, and the 1968 Sorokin Award for *The American Occupational Structure* (1967). From 1975 to 1976, Blau was a Netherlands Institute for Advanced Study fellow. From 1978 to 1981, Blau served as Distinguished Professor at the State University of New York at Albany.

BIBLIOGRAPHY

Works by Peter Blau

Blau, P. *The Dynamics of a Bureaucracy: A Study of Interpersonal Relations in Two Government Agencies.* Chicago: University of Chicago Press, 1955.
————. *Exchange and Power in Social Life.* New York: John Wiley, 1964.
————. *On the Nature of Organizations.* New York: John Wiley, 1974.
————. *Inequality and Heterogeneity: A Primitive Theory of Social Structure.* New York: Free Press, 1977.
————. "The Cost of Inequality: Metropolitan Structure and Violent Crime." *American Sociological Review,* 47, Fall 1982, 114–129.
————. *Structural Contexts of Opportunities.* Chicago: University of Chicago Press, 1994.
————, ed. *Approaches to the Study of Social Structure.* New York: Free Press, 1975.
Blau, P., and O. Duncan. *The American Occupational Structure.* New York: John Wiley, 1967.
Blau, P., and R. K. Merton, eds. *Continuities in Structural Inquiry.* Beverly Hills, CA: Sage Publications, 1981.
Blau, P., and M. W. Meyer. *Bureaucracy in Modern Society.* New York: Random House, 1956.
Blau, P., and R. Schoeherr. *The Structure of Organizations.* New York: Basic Books, 1971.
Blau, P., and J. Schwartz. *Cross-cutting Social Circles: Testing a Macrostructural Theory of Intergroup Relations.* Orlando, FL: Academic Press, 1984.
Blau, P., and W. R. Scott. *Formal Organizations: A Comparative Approach.* San Francisco: Chandler Publishing, 1962.

Work about Peter Blau

Barry, A., and E. W. Mills. "Occupational Size, Structure, and Efficiency: A Test of a Blau-Hage Model." *American Journal of Economics and Sociology,* 40, 1, January 1982, 43–60.

CROZIER, MICHEL J. (b. November 6, 1922, Sainte Menehould, France), sociologist; consultant; professor; research director

Michel Crozier was born to Joanny A. and Jeanne Crozier in 1922. He received a B.A. from the University of Paris in 1943 and an L.L.D. from the University of Lille in 1949. In 1964 he received the D. State from the Sorbonne, University of Paris. Once a self-described independent Marxist, Crozier is typically known as a French sociologist who has spent considerable time in the United States; his work reflects the comparative vantage he brings to the study of U.S. and French politics.

Crozier's research experience includes several appointments at the Centre Nationale de la Recherche Scientifique in Paris: research attaché from 1952 to 1954, research associate from 1954 to 1964, and research professor in 1964. In 1961 he founded the Centre de Sociologie des Organisations in Paris and became its research director.

Crozier has served in a number of academic positions. From 1967 to 1968 he was professor of sociology at the University of Nanterre. At the Institut d'Etudes Politiques of Paris, he was director of the Post Graduate School of Sociology. He also served on the faculty of two American universities—as a visiting professor at Harvard University from 1966 to 1970 and the University of California at Irvine. From 1959 to 1960 he was a fellow at the Center for Advanced Studies in the Behavioral Sciences at Palo Alto, California. Crozier also served as a consultant to the Rand Corporation, the European Economic Community, and the U.S. Trilateral Commission.

Crozier is best known for his advancement of the concept of bureaucratic pathology. Centering on the impact of culture on organizations' internal culture and behavior, his research explains that every national culture has an impact on its organizations, unlike any other influencing factor. He suggests that cultural impact opens the organization to a pathological myopia, called "bon plaisir" when applied to French organizations.

To test his thesis, Crozier conducted an empirical study of two French bureaucracies—one a clerical agency; the second, a state monopoly. The findings and conclusions of his study are presented in *The Bureaucratic Phenomenon*, published in English in 1964. Crozier found that the bureaucratic nature of the clerical agency reinforced the impersonal environment of the employees, allowing them to avoid direct contact with others in the organization. Inversely, group competition for power in the bureaucratic monopoly supported the highly structured character of the bureaucracy. Crozier posits that four elements should be present to maintain bureaucratic character: impersonal rules, centralization of decision making, isolation of employees at appropriate bureaucratic levels, and the structure of parallel power relationships in areas outside the certainty of the formal bureaucracy. Ironically, Crozier argues in *The Bu-*

reaucratic Phenomenon, subordinates are less dependent on superiors when bureaucratic rules take priority.

Crozier argues that the elements, when present, are so embedded in the organizational bureaucracy that only in a crisis can fundamental changes occur. He further asserts that French organizations are more inclined to resist changes. Explaining that the French bureaucrat, operating out of a shared desire to have a "rational place" in the organization, reinforces the rigidity in the bureaucratic organization because of this belief. Change, when it does happen, Crozier argues, will be revolutionary and comprehensive in French organizations due to the organizational resistance to nonfundamental, innovative changes and to the delay in the changes.

Crozier's interest in revising French political malaise evolved into *Strategies for Change: The Future of French Society* (1982), originally published as *On ne change pas la societe par d'ecrit* (France, 1979). His purpose in both works is criticism of his country's administrative elite, followed by communication of specific strategies for improvement, including political decentralization, starting at the level of local political representation; reconfiguration of the governing class, beginning at the educational level; and creation and utilization of a knowledge-based praxis. Crozier's next work, *Le mal americain* (France, 1980) was published in the United States as *The Trouble with America* (1984). Focusing on an American sense of futility (initiated by satisfaction with short-term goals and worsened with lost innocence during Vietnam), Crozier's analysis of America includes chastisement of impotent bureaucracy manipulated by interest groups.

Crozier's case studies shed new light on the cultural influences on organizations that lead to their pathological nature. That his case studies isolate qualities of French organizations—their applicability to organizations that take on "closed model" characteristics, particularly in resisting environmental influences—on the one hand, and of American structures on the other, is what is valuable to organization behavior research.

BIBLIOGRAPHY

Works by Michel J. Crozier

Crozier, Michel J. *The Bureaucratic Phenomenon*. Chicago: University of Chicago Press, 1964.

————. *Strategies for Change: The Future of French Society*. Trans. W. Beer. Cambridge, MA: MIT Press, 1982.

————. *The Trouble with America*. Trans. P. Heinegg. Berkeley: University of California Press, 1984.

Crozier, M. J., and E. Friedberg. *Actors and Systems: The Politics of Collective Action*. Trans. A. Goldhammer. Chicago: University of Chicago Press, 1980.

Crozier, M. J., S. Huntington, and J. Watanki. *The Crisis of Democracy: Report on the Governability of Democracies to the Trilateral Commission.* New York: New York University Press, 1975.

DAHL, ROBERT A. (b. 1915, Inwood, IA), founder of pluralist theory; university professor; public servant

Dahl received his doctorate in political science in 1940 from Yale University and also received a J.D. from the University of Michigan. In 1940 he worked as management analyst for the U.S. Department of Agriculture and later as an economist in the Office of Production Management. Since 1948 he taught at Yale University and was the chair of the Department of Political Science from 1957 to 1962. He also taught at the University of Chicago in 1957 and was a fellow at the Center for the Advanced Study of the Behavioral Sciences. He received several awards including the Talcott Parsons Prize for Social Sciences from the Academy of Arts and Science and the Woodrow Wilson Prize from the American Political Science Association in 1961. Currently he is an emeritus professor of political science at Yale University.

Dahl advocates a rational approach to decision making, sharing the views of Herbert Simon. He also believes in a positivist approach to social science in that acquisition of knowledge and social inquiry should be based on the examination of facts and "value free." He believes that in order for public administration to be a science, it must adopt the positivist approach in its discipline by separating facts from social values and environmental and cultural influences. Dahl perceives public administration as a profession and believes that a science of public administration can be developed. In his judgment, the scientific public administration is not supposed to get involved with values; public administration should not attempt to determine what the final results should be but deal only with the means of reaching the ends. Therefore, he suggests separation of politics and administration by which the ends are set by political actors, and the bureaucracy is to administer the achievement of goals through scientific means. He contends that in order for the public administration discipline to develop into a science, it also has to concern itself with the study of human behavior. This inquiry is necessary for public administration to deliver the best services to the public.

Dahl also argues that the study of public administration has to take into consideration the various soiological, historical, and economic conditions of its environment. Therefore, he suggests a comparative approach in the study of public administration to discover commonalities that exist exclusive of individual or national experience. Yet as for the question of facts versus values, Dahl advocates a scientific approach to public administration; nevertheless, in 1947 he was first to claim that public administration is not value free and is dominated by the value of "efficiency." Therefore, he challenges Simon's value-free paradigm of scientific approach, by arguing that efficiency by itself is a value that competes with other values in society.

Dahl has contributed a great deal to the study of democratic pluralism, power politics, and social inequality. He relates power to the democratic theory and explains democracy as an ideal type of political system. In his study of power, he approaches the question of power from a practical point of view and the way it operates in political institutions and investigates its main source. In other words, he does not deal with the perception of power but with what really happens in the decison-making process, and he identifies the real decison makers. He relates his pluralist theory with the actual working of urban governments. He conducted a study in New Haven, Connecticut, and used different research techniques including surveys, historical analysis, and case studies to study the decision-making processes at the local government. He concluded that political decisions in New Haven were influenced by a coalition building process and rivalries between different groups. Therefore, based on this study he rejected the "elitist theory" of power and advocates a "pluralist theory" in its place. He argued that democracy is the precondition for proper workings of a political system and referred to pluralism as the existence of many primarily independent organizations actually function under the auspices of the state. In his judgment, the existence of democratic organizations will ensure the survival of democracy by mutual control that is exercised by different organizations on each other.

He also relates the study of power with the study of economic inequality and tries to relate these two concepts. In his view, democracy can only flourish if it corresponds with the democratization of the economic aspect of life. Therefore, one can recognize Dahl's concern for social and economic justice as well as democratic political values. He argues that a republic can exist only if the citizen body continues neither rich nor poor. Therefore, he believes that citizens must enjoy similar circumstances, both socially and economically.

BIBLIOGRAPHY

Works by Robert A. Dahl

Dahl, R. A. *Who Governs? Democracy and Power in an American City.* New Haven, CT: Yale University Press, 1961.
———. *Pluralist Democracy in the United States.* Chicago: Rand McNally & Company, 1967.
———. *After the Revolution?: Authority in a Good Society.* New Haven, CT: Yale University Press, 1970.

———. *Polarchy: Participation and Opposition.* New Haven, CT: Yale University Press, 1971.

———. *A Preface to Democratic Theory.* Chicago: University of Chicago Press, 1976.

———. "Liberal Democracy in the United States." In *A Prospect for Liberal Democracy,* ed. William Livingston. Austin: University of Texas Press, 1979.

———. *Power and Democracy in America.* Westport, CT: Greenwood Press, 1980.

———. *Dilemmas of Pluralist Democracy.* New Haven, CT: Yale University Press, 1982.

———. *Dilemmas of Pluralistic Democracy: Autonomy vs. Control.* New Haven, CT: Yale University Press, 1982.

———. *Modern Political Analysis.* Englewood Cliffs, NJ: Prentice-Hall, 1984.

———. *Democracy, Liberty, and Equality.* New York: Oxford University Press, 1986.

———. *Democracy and Its Critics.* New Haven, CT: Yale University Press, 1989.

Works about Robert A. Dahl

The Constitutional Court and the Draft Russian Constitution: A Briefing Book for the Moscow Seminar with Robert Dahl and Charles Fried. Cambridge, MA: Strengthening Democratic Institutions Project, John F. Kennedy School of Government, Harvard University, 1992.

Lukes, S., ed. *Power.* New York: New York University Press, 1986.

Roosevelt F., and D. Belkin, eds. *Why Market Socialism?: Voices from Dissent.* Armonk, NY: M. E. Sharpe, 1995.

Weinstein, M. A., comp. *Identity, Power, and Change; Selected Readings in Political Theory.* Glenview, IL: Scott, Foresman, 1971.

Zirakzadeh, C. E. "Theorizing about Workplace Democracy: Robert Dahl and the Cooperatives of Mondragon." *Journal of Theoretical Politics,* 2, 1, January 1990.

DENHARDT, ROBERT B. (b. July 1942, USA), ASPA president; university administrator; professor; department chair

Denhardt is the past president of the American Society of Public Administration (ASPA) and vice-provost at the University of Missouri at Columbia. He served for six years as chair of the Governor's Advisory Council on Productivity for the State of Missouri. He has taught at the University of Kansas, Missouri, and New Orleans, Central Florida University, and is presently teaching at the College of Urban Affairs and Public Policy at the University of Delaware. He has written several books and articles on public administration in which he closes the gap between administrative experience and theory. Thus, Denhardt's writings have the general theme of practicality. In his opinion, public administration suffers from overemphasizing rationality and also the politics–administration dichotomy. He argues that this approach has limited the wide spectrum of alternatives available for resolving the social problems and is counterproductive because it makes public organizations obsolete in current realities.

In his view, the job of public administration scholars is to bring public organizations' reality closer to the theoretical world. Denhardt advocates a balanced view, emphasizing efficiency and effectiveness versus democratic accountability and responsibility. He agrees with Paul Appleby and others who deemphasize the role of the public sector in favor of the private sector and holds the private sector as a model for public administration. Denhardt contends that public organizations should be run with democratic values with less emphasis on hierarchical structures. He does not expect democratic output from undemocratic systems. He also agrees with Chris Argyris and other scholars who advocate individual growth and development in organizations by paying more attention to the needs of employees and bringing their needs closer to the goals of the organization. He emphasizes the role of leadership in public organizations and argues that leadership provides organizations with general guidance in order to resolve complex organizational problems.

According to Denhardt, the main function of an effective organizational leader is the integration of organizational values with individual values. Therefore, an effective integration of those two values is indicative of organizational success and a major source for employee motivation. He perceives leadership as a process of social development as opposed to an exercise of power. He contends that the exercise of power is destructive to an organization's harmonioperation. Denhardt argues that this is due to the fact that the main instrument of power is control, which is usually exercised by one individual in favor of his or her own established goals. Denhardt contends that a successful leader facilitates social and individual development of the employees in the organization by creating an environment that is conducive to individual growth. He believes that individual growth can be achieved through self-awareness and self-realization on the part of everyone in the organization. In this process, employees realize their own potential and set their own goals, which are also compatible with the goals of the organization. Therefore, leaders try to fulfill employees' needs by fusing them with the goals of the organization. In his judgment, leadership in public organizations is more complex because democracy, responsibility, responsiveness, freedom, and justice are considered as valuable as efficiency by the leaders.

Denhardt believes that public organizations are suffering from stagnation, and they should be willing to adapt to new circumstances. He develops a three-part administrative model in order to demonstrate three distinctive ways organizational processes can be viewed: rational, interpretive, and critical. The critical model is considered as ideal. This model advocates a paradigmatic change in viewing organizations. In its approach to "knowing," this model follows the critical social theory with its ultimate goal of emancipating individuals from social barriers in order for them to realize their full potential. With respect to decision making, the critical model is "value-critical"; it helps us seek, establish, and reach significant human ideals, including the value of freedom. Finally, this model provides a practical application and exercise of knowledge. It helps individuals to make a connection between personal learning and a connection between theory and practice.

Denhardt advocates an alternative method of management that focuses on individual growth rather than control in order to manage organizations. In addition, he suggests that faulty organizational communicational patterns contribute to malfunctioning of organizations and should be adjusted. In Denhardt's ideal organization, personal development and growth will be realized through adaptation of the critical model and with a commitment to values rather than an emphasis on organizational structure.

BIBLIOGRAPHY

Works by Robert B. Denhardt

Denhardt, R. *In the Shadow of Organization.* Lawrence: Regents Press of Kansas, 1980.
———. "Council-Manager System." *Public Management,* 67, 7, July 1985.
———. "Images of Life and Slavery in Organizational Life." *Journal of Management,* Fall 1987, 174–179.
———. *The Pursuit of Significance.* Belmont, CA: Wadsworth, 1993.
———. *Theories of Public Organizations.* Belmont, CA: Wadsworth, 1993.
Denhardt, R., and S. H. Williams. *Executive Leadership in the Public Service.* Tuscaloosa: University of Alabama Press, 1992.

Work about Robert B. Denhardt

Lynn, N. B., and A. Wildavsky, eds. *Public Administration: The State of the Discipline.* Chatham, NJ: Chatham House, 1990.

DOWNS, ANTHONY (b. November 21, 1930, Evanston, IL), urban economist; political economist; real estate consultant; U.S. naval reservist; National Association for the Advancement of Colored People (NAACP) board director

Anthony Downs was the first and foremost thinker of the 1960s public choice school to forge an understanding of public organizations. Downs is a prolific writer on the bureaucracy and economics of urban affairs, as indicated by the prominence of some of his most well-known publications: *Who Are the Urban Poor?* (1968), *Achieving Effective Desegregation* (1973), *Federal Housing Subsidies: How Are They Working?* (1973), *Opening Up the Suburbs: An Urban Strategy for America* (1973), and *Urban Decline and the Future of American Cities* (1982) with Katherine Bradbury and Kenneth A. Small. Among scholars of public administration, two of Downs's earliest works are frequently referenced: *An Economic Theory of Democracy* (1957) and *Inside Bureaucracy* (1967).

An Economic Theory of Democracy accounts for the rationality of democratic polities and voters. Downs argues that these polities "are analogous to entrepreneurs in a profit-seeking economy." Like entrepreneurs who market products they think gain the most profits, polities formulate the policies they think gain the most votes, and voters support the policies they think reap the most benefits. Coupled with the social science corollary of "uncertainty," Downs's model of economic rationality provides a compelling explanation for voting behavior and the motives of those involved in government.

Downs outlines the two steps involved in goal-oriented economic analysis. The first step involves locating the decision maker's goals. The second step is more detailed and requires analyzing the means by which the goals are met. The action (and even the goal) of a rational decision maker is determined by circumstances like time, effort, and money. Moreover, the steps that a decision maker takes are not divorced from his or her personal qualities. For example, the "rational man" may harbor prejudices but follow the steps and, therefore, still be considered a rational being. Downs's reconciliation of the rational man's disparate qualities parallels his combination of disparate components in organizational theory, such as structure, behavior, and environment.

The behavior of bureaucrats in organizational environments is the focus of Downs's analysis in *Inside Bureaucracy*. For Downs, an organization is a carefully coordinated system consciously created to achieve specific goals; as a large but semiexclusive body, the organization basically meets certain Weberian characteristics and competitively recruits, employs, and objectively evaluates its full-time workers. Downs claims that the five types of bureaucrats within organizations (identified in *Inside Bureaucracy*) share a common denominator of self-interest. The five organizational personalities are (1) climbers, who seek the path of least resistance toward maximizing their personal power, income, and prestige; (2) conservers, who seek to maximize their security and convenience; (3) zealots, who equate public interests and promotion of specific goals; (4) advocates, who are optimistic, energetic, and easily swayed by superiors, equals, and subordinates; and (5) statesmen, whose broad general loyalties encourage them to resolve contentious matters through compromise. According to Downs's model, newer organizations are overrun with climbers, old organizations are dominated by conservers, and statesmen achieve personal satisfaction when "general welfare" is promoted.

Yet rationality does not eliminate organizational problems like increasing rigidity, which Downs refers to as the Law of Hierarchy. As an organization's "sovereign officials" continue to identify and institute more efficient means of control, their reliance on rules and hierarchy usually increases. The consequences of the cycle include reduced employee productivity and increased need for control. When subordinates begin taking measures to circumvent and subvert control measures, the problem intensifies into what Downs calls the Law of Counter Control. *Inside Bureaucracy* is seminal not only because it outlines these laws of organizing but because its calculations of the economics of official behavior are unprecedented. However, Downs does not conclude that bureaucracies obstruct individual freedom. Instead, he credits bureaucratic society with increasing "freedom of choice."

BIBLIOGRAPHY

Works by Anthony Downs

Bradbury, K., A. Downs, and K. Small. *Futures for a Declining City: Simulations for the Cleveland Area*. New York: Academic Press, 1981.
Bradbury, K., A. Downs, and K. Small. *Urban Decline and the Future of American Cities*. Washington, DC: Brookings Institution, 1982.
Downs, A. *An Economic Theory of Democracy*. New York: Harper & Row, 1957.
———. *Inside Bureaucracy*. Boston: Little, Brown, 1967.
———. *Urban Problems and Prospects*. Chicago: Markham Publishing, 1970.
———. *Opening Up the Suburbs: An Urban Strategy for America*. New Haven, CT: Yale University Press, 1973.
———. *Public Policy and the Rising Cost of Housing*. Washington, DC: Brookings Institution, 1978.
———. *Neighborhoods and Urban Development*. Washington, DC: Brookings Institution, 1981.
———. *New Visions for Metropolitan America*. Washington, DC: Brookings Institution, 1994.
———. *Political Theory and Public Choice*. Northampton, MA: E. Elgar, 1998.
Downs, A., and K. Bradbury, eds. *Energy Costs, Urban Development and Housing*. Washington, DC: Brookings Institution, 1984.
Smith, A., A. Downs, and M. L. Lachman. *Achieving Effective Desegregation*. Lexington, MA: Lexington Books, 1973.

Works about Anthony Downs

Boyd, R. W., P. R. Mencher, P. J. Paseltiner, E. Paul, and A. S. Vajda. "The 1984 Election as Anthony Downs and Stanley Kelley Might Interpret It." *Political Behavior*, 10, 3, Fall 1988, 197–213.
Eubank, W. L. "Voter Rationality: A Retest of the Downsian Model." *Social Science Journal*, 23, 3, Fall 1986, 253–266.
Grofman, B. *Information, Participation, and Choice: An Economic Theory of Democracy in Perspective*. Ann Arbor: University of Michigan Press, 1993.   '
Kornberg, A., W. Mishler, and J. Smith. "Political Elite and Mass Perceptions of Party Locations in Issue Space: Some Tests of Two Positions." *Cambridge British Journal of Political Science*, 5, 2, April 1975, 161–185.
Lehner, F. "Cognitive Structure, Uncertainty, and the Rationality of Political Action: A Synthesis of Economic and Psychological Perspectives." *European Journal of Political Research*, 3, 3, September 1975, 275–291.

Lind, N. S. "Anthony Downs' Life Cycle Theory of Organizations: An Empirical
    Test." *Southeastern Political Review*, 14, 2, Fall 1991, 228–247.
Mavrogordatos, G. T. "Downs Revisited: Spatial Models of Party Competition
    and Left-Right Measurements." *International Political Science Review*, 8, 4,
    October 1987, 333–342.
McCurdy, H. E. "Organizational Decline: NASA and the Life Cycle of Bureaus."
    Public Administration Review, 51, 4, July–August 1991, 308–315.
Reisman, D. *Theories of Collective Action: Downs, Olson, and Hirsch.* New York: St.
    Martin's Press, 1990.
Simmons, J. "Economic Theory of Democracy: Revised and Revisited." *New Po-
    litical Science*, 23, Fall 1992, 29–50.

DROR, YEHEZKEL (b. 1928, Vienna, Austria), university professor; policy
consultant, department head

Yehezkel Dror strove to integrate administration and policy for better
policy making. Taking a curative approach to fragmentation and specialization, Dror's "policy science" developed models that challenged the
modern dispersion of the social sciences. He believed that by nurturing
the "organized dreaming" of its members, organizations would develop
new research designs, could broadly contextualize discrete policy issues,
and thereby solve current and future social problems. Dror's version of
policy science capitalizes on the epistemological development of politicians; changes in political, cultural, and educational spheres; and intergenerational participation of the public in public policy making. For all
of these contributions, Dror advanced studies of public administration.
His acclaim in America, however, is eclipsed by his recognition in Israel,
where he received the Rosolio Award in 1965.

Dror was educated in Jerusalem at the Hebrew University and Howard University. In 1957 he joined the faculty of Hebrew University in the
Political Science Department. In addition to his service as senior policy
and planning consultant in the Israeli government, Dror consulted for
European, Asian, and American educational and government institutions
as well. Dror worked in New York and California for the Rand Corporation from 1968 to 1970.

In 1968, Dror made his mark in public administration, publishing *Public Policymaking Reexamined*. This book launches a call for rational public
policy formation but has become a statement of Dror's refusal to acknowledge that incrementalism is justified when knowledge is scanty.
Dror includes an ideal model for policy making in his study, suggesting
its replacement of normative models that help evaluate policy making
for flaws but fail to meet required challenges. The study includes three
central ideas (net output, meta–policy making, and policy science) and
attentively outlines meta–policy making's three elements: identifying
problems and resources, evaluating and revising policy production sys-

tems, and determining policy-making strategies. Overall, Dror fore-grounds the "gap between the ways individuals and institutions make policy and the available knowledge on how policies can best be made" in this theoretically constructed project, the revised version of which appears as *Policymaking under Adversity* (1986).

BIBLIOGRAPHY

Works by Yehezkel Dror

Dror, Y. *Public Policymaking Reexamined.* Seranton, PA: Chandler, 1968.
———. *Design for Policy Sciences.* New York: American Elsevier, 1971.
———. *Ventures in Policy Sciences: Concepts and Applications.* New York: American Elsevier, 1971.
———. "Features of a Meta-Model for Policy Studies." *Policy Studies Journal,* 3, 3, Spring 1975, 247–255.
———. "On Becoming More of a Policy Scientist." *Policy Studies Review,* 4, 1, August 1984, 13–21.
———. *Policymaking under Adversity.* New Brunswick, NJ: Transaction Books, 1986.

DYE, THOMAS R. (b. December 1935, Pittsburgh, PA), public servant; university professor; policy analyst

Dye received a B.A. and M.A. from Pennsylvania State University (1957) and a Ph.D. from the University of Pennsylvania (1961). He taught at the University of Wisconsin at Madison from 1960 through 1963. Later he moved to Georgia and became an associate professor and chair of the Department of Political Science at the University of Georgia at Athens (1963–1968). In 1968, he moved to Florida and has been professor and chair of the Department of Government at Florida State University at Tallahassee to the present. He also served in the U.S. Air Force (1961–1962). Dye's major contribution is in the area of public policy making and the analysis of its nature.

Dye defines *public policy* as "whatever governments choose to do or not to do" and deals with the question of public policy making, using a scientific approach that analyzes the causes and consequences of policy formulation. His emphasis is on the public policy-making process, and he argues that the "process" plays an important role in determining the success and failure of policies. In his judgment, understanding the process of policy making will have many advantages in developing satisfactory results, including identification of different forces that shape the public policy process and providing understandable explanations about political outcome and events.

He argues that public policy making is identical to a decision-making process and has to be approached properly by recognizing and using proper models of decision making. He suggests several models of public policy making based on different theories. They include systems theory, elite theory, group theory, rational comprehensive theory, incremental theory, and the institutional model. He contends that different policies can be explained through different models. For example, the budgeting process is more compatible with the incremental model, and civil rights policies are a manifestation of the elite model. He applies those models to several different policies to demonstrate their practicality. While he does not make any value judgment concerning the preferability of those models, he believes that the American political system is more identifiable with the elite model of decision making. He defines *elites* as those who are formally in charge of the decision making in different sectors in the United States. Therefore, the elites are those who occupy the highest decision-making positions and who usually do not like to acknowledge their power. He summarizes his elites model as follows:

1. Society is divided into the few who have power and the many who do not. Only a small number of persons allocate values for society; the masses do not decide public policy.
2. The few who govern are not typical of the masses who are governed. Elites are drawn disproportionately from the upper socioeconomic strata of society.
3. The movement of non-elites to elite positions must be slow and continuous if stability is to be maintained and revolution avoided. Only non-elites who have accepted the basic elite consensus are admitted to governing circles.
4. Elites share a consensus on the basic values of the social system and the preservation of the system. They disagree only on the narrow range of issues.
5. Public policy does not reflect demands of masses but rather the prevailing values of the elite. Changes in public policy will be incremental rather than revolutionary.
6. Active elites are subject to relatively little direct influence from the apathetic masses. Elites influence masses more than masses influence elites. (Dye and Ziegler 1984, 6)

He contends that although the Constitution promotes the equality of men and equality of rights, the way it is designed, elites influence the policy-making process, not the masses. In his judgment, the founders of the Republic did not intend to bring equality to society and have accepted inequality as a natural phenomenon. In fact, the Constitution itself was written by a small number of elites, not the masses. He concentrates on the civil rights movement and its aftermath and believes that what came out of the movement was due to the response of the elites to the demands of a minority. In other words, it was not the response by the masses to the needs of the minority but only the elites' response to the demand of a minority group. He believes there is a gap between the attitude of the majority of ordinary whites toward the condition of blacks and the white elites in America. According to him, most white Americans do support equality with blacks, but they are opposed to integration and approve of "separate but equal." However, white elites are more sympathetic to the concerns of racial integration.

He analyzed the root causes of the urban riots and argues that they are a form of political activity by African Americans who live in the ghettos. They simply demonstrate their frustration with the conditions in society. He argues that in order to understand policies, one needs to ask questions concerning top decision makers, their background, the nature of their competition, their values, the process of making important decisions, and finally, if there are any major changes in the composition of the decision makers. He believes that there are twelve major sectors in the United States that provide the basis of institutional power: industrial corporations, utilities and communication, banking, insurance, investment, mass media, law, education, foundations, civic and cultural organizations, government, and military. He argues that those who are capable of making major decisions in those sectors are the real decision makers and those who make policies in the United States.

His analysis of the government elite in the Unites States indicates that they are more concentrated than the other elites and are composed of both elected and nonelected officials (the bureaucrats). According to Dye, government elites have not been born into their positions but have reached them through their personal efforts. He argues that although other elites affect the public policy process and are part of the environment that effects policy making, political elites are the major players in the making of public policy decisions.

BIBLIOGRAPHY

Works by Thomas R. Dye

Dye, T. R. *Understanding Public Policy*. Englewood Cliffs, NJ: Prentice-Hall, 1972.
———. *A Florida Income Tax: Fueling Government, Stalling the Economy*. Tallahassee: Florida State University, Policy Sciences Program, 1991.
———. *Who's Running America? The Clinton Years*. 6th ed. Englewood Cliffs, NJ: Prentice-Hall, 1995.
———, ed. *The Political Legitimacy of Markets and Governments*. Greenwich, CT: JAI Press, 1990.
Dye, T. R., and L. Andrade. *Study Guide [to accompany] Politics in America*, 3d ed. Upper Saddle River, NJ: Prentice-Hall, 1999.
Dye, T. R., and L. H. Zeigler. *The Irony of Democracy: An Uncommon Introduction to American Politics*. 6th ed. Monterey, CA: Brooks/Cole, 1984.

Works about Thomas R. Dye

Elowitz, L. *Instructor's Manual for Power and Society: An Introduction to the Social Sciences, Third Edition, Thomas R. Dye*. Monterey, CA: Brooks/Cole, 1983.
Himmelberg, R. F., ed. *Regulatory Issues Since 1964: The Rise of the Deregulation Movement*. New York: Garland, 1994.
Pickering, J. W., and R. J. Leonard. *Manual for Instructors, the Irony of Democracy:*

An Uncommon Introduction to American Politics, Third Edition: Thomas R. Dye, L. Harmon Zeigler. Belmont, CA: Duxbury Press, 1975.

Reinighaus, R. D., and K. E. Weiss. *Participation Manual for American Government: Theory, Structure, and Process, Thomas R. Dye, Lee S. Greene, George S. Parthemos.* Belmont, CA: Duxbury Press, 1972.

EASTON, DAVID (b. June 1917, Toronto, Canada), political scientist; consultant; university professor; APSA president

Easton attended the University of Toronto where he received a B.A. in 1939 and an M.A. in 1943. In 1947, he was awarded a Ph.D. from Harvard University and taught there for three years (1944–1947). He taught at the University of Chicago from 1947 to 1955. He also taught at many other prestigious universities including Queens University (Kingston, Canada), and from 1981 to the present, he has taught at the University of California at Irvine, where he chairs the International Committee for the Study of the Development of Political Science. He also worked at the Center for Advanced Studies in the Behavioral Sciences at Stanford University (1957–1958) and received a Ford Research Professorship in Governmental Affairs (1960–1961). He was a consultant to the Brookings Institution in 1953 and president of the American Political Science Association from 1968 to 1969.

His major work concerns the development of a general theory of political science and the different categories that support its theoretical structure. Easton argues that to understand political theory, one has to understand several stages of its development. He identifies four stages including formal, traditional, behavioral, and postbehavioral. The formal stage that dominated the field during the nineteenth century supports the importance of political institutions and the laws that govern public organizations. Therefore, to understand organizations, one looks at the laws and constitutions to find out how they operate. The second stage (traditional) is the discovery of the informal structure and behavior that influence the decision-making process. This movement was dominant during the early 1900s. After World War II began the behavioral movement, which emphasizes the importance of scientific analysis in determining the behavior of organizations and individuals. Postbehavioralism began in the 1960s and continues to the present. It rejects many of the tenets and assumptions of previous stages and argues that the scientific approach cannot be value free. It also questions the fundamental assumptions of positivism in behavioral science. Easton favors the development of a new theoretical framework in order to understand the workings of political institutions.

Easton views political life from a systems perspective that he developed in 1957. He offers a theory that supports a coherent relationship between the state and its environment. According to this theory, a political system is surrounded and affected by the many different variables in its environment. Therefore, he perceives political life as part of an open system exposed to many influences, including biological, social, psychological, and physical. These influences provide input to the system in the form of demand from the government. Demand is influenced by the individuals, processes, and procedures of the political system that is called "the government." The end result is the promulgation of rules and regulations that are the output of the system and the decisions of the authorities. He distinguishes between the constitutional order, which is more of a reflection of what the political norms should be, and the reality of the political system, which deals with what really is taking place.

The output by itself influences the environment and generates reaction from it. Therefore, the aggregate reaction toward the output becomes new input to the system. He argues that the survival of any system depends heavily on the degree of its adaptability and responsiveness to its environment. He explains the feedback process and believes that through feedback the system copes with stress and regulates disturbances that might hurt the system as a whole. He criticized the political system for being overly concerned with "equilibrium" analysis, which emphasizes the importance of warding off anything that might cause any displacement and disturbance. His emphasis is on "adaptation," which implies bringing change and modification to either the environment or the system or both. He believes that the political system is different from other systems in that it deals with authoritative allocation of values and has the task of introducing those values to their citizens as binding.

Easton argues that a political system has both intrasocietal and extrasocietal environments. The intrasocietal is composed of the system itself, including its organization, whereas the extrasocietal is composed of social structure, culture, economy, attitude, behavior, and ideas outside the organizational structure. In addition, the extrasocietal environment also influences the system through the international society. In his judgment, the only danger to the stability of the system occurs when the critical elements that compose the system in its totality are stretched beyond their "critical range."

BIBLIOGRAPHY

Works by David Easton

Easton, D. *A System Analysis of Political Life.* New York: John Wiley & Sons, 1965.
————. *The Political System: An Inquiry into the State of Political Science.* New York: Alfred A. Knopf, 1967.
————, ed. *Varieties of Political Theory.* Englewood Cliffs, NJ: Prentice-Hall, 1966.
Easton, D., J. G. Gunnell, and L. Graziano, eds. *The Development of Political Science: A Comparative Survey.* London, New York: Routledge, 1991.

Easton, D., J. G. Gunnet, and M. B. Stein, eds. *Regime and Discipline: Democracy and the Development of Political Science*. Ann Arbor: University of Michigan Press, 1995.

Easton, D., and C. S. Schelling, eds. *Divided Knowledge: Across Disciplines, across Cultures*. Newbury Park, CA: Sage, 1991.

Works about David Easton

Baruah, A. K. *Systems Analysis in Political Science: A Marxist Critique of David Easton*. New Delhi: Uppal Publishing House, 1987.

Farr, J., and R. Seidelman, eds. *Discipline and History: Political Science in the United States*. Ann Arbor: University of Michigan Press, 1993.

Kennedy, K. D. *Cybernetics in Political Theory: The Work of David Easton and Karl Deutsch*. 1966.

Monroe, K. R., ed. *Contemporary Empirical Political Theory*. Berkeley: University of California Press, 1997.

Sorzano, J. S. *The Conceptual Requirements of Systems Analysis: An Examination of Adam Smith, Talcott Parsons and David Easton*. 1972.

Weinstein, M. A., comp. *Identity, Power, and Change: Selected Readings in Political Theory*. Glenview, IL: Scott, Foresman, 1971.

ELAZAR, DANIEL JUDAH (b. August 25, 1934, Minneapolis, MN), writer; consultant; "farmer–laborer"; university professor; director

Elazar has widely published in the area of American federalism, which he regards as an inventive construction. He delineates Constitution, administration, and policy, the three interworking planes of government. He fashions the term "noncentralized" to describe how the U.S. political system is neither centralized nor decentralized; rather, general governments of particular authority coexist. Elazar earned critical acclaim following his 1966 publication of *American Federalism: A View from the States*. He focuses on intergovernmental relations in this study and analyzes state political culture and state response to intergovernmental partnership. This text also encouraged the fame of the Center for the Study of Federalism (directed by Elazar since 1967) at Temple University, where Elazar has taught on the political science faculty since 1964. Elazar's additional collaborative and independent publications include *The American Partnership: Intergovernmental Cooperation in the Nineteenth-Century United States* (1962) and *The Politics of American Federalism* (1968).

American political "culture types" is also a primary concern of Elazar's. Geographically determined, culture types reveal the beliefs regarding government shared by groups of people and their expectations for the ways to act toward government. In this area, Elazar has published *Land, Space and Civil Society in America* (1970) and *Cities of the Prairie: The Metropolitan Frontier and American Politics* (1970), which analyzes how ten medium-sized midwestern cities responded to rural to urban migration in the 1940s and 1950s. With the assistance of Rozann Rothman, Elazar published an update to *Cities of the Prairie* in 1986: *Cities of the Prairie*

Revisited: The Closing of the Metropolitan Frontier, which recounts "what happened since the migration stopped and the metropolitan frontier closed." This study is appreciated for its attention to federalism, and interdisciplinary use of theory, cultural history, empirical data, and political material.

Elazar's contributions to academia in the form of comparative analyses and as an academic who fulfills many pedagogical roles cannot be overstated. In "Sidelights," an interview with *Contemporary Authors* (Gale Literary Databases, The Gale Group, 1999), Elazar describes himself as a social scientist who uses qualitative and quantitative research methods, as a scholar who "writes to teach," and as a writer "who has a commitment to the art and craft of writing as well as to the discovery and dissemination of knowledge." The son of an educator, Elazar sees himself as a worker on behalf of students, with whom he shares facts and analyses "that will lead people to build better understanding of the world in which they live, particularly in its political dimensions." Several of Elazar's major publications reflect both the cultural appreciation and the cross-cultural vantages he brings to his scholarship.

Moving Up: Ethnic Succession in America: With a Case History from the Philadelphia School System (1976) is one example of the cultural interest Elazar pursues in the domestic context. Internationally, Elazar has taken up Jewry in Israel and the diaspora as subject matter. *Israel* (1986) outlines a number of Elazar's observations on the relationship between the frontier and new societies. *The Other Jews: The Sephardim Today* (1988) is a less localized but equally provocative study, the result of participant observation research in global Sephardim. Considered the first full-scale (if possibly polemical) study of its kind, *The Other Jews* provides a current survey of major communities worldwide, including those within Zaire, Zambia, and Zimbabwe, in which Sephardic communities are considered obscure. Additionally, a book on political planning in Minneapolis, St. Paul, and Jerusalem is currently forthcoming.

Much of Elazar's knowledge of the Middle East has come firsthand during his previous tenure at Hebrew University of Jerusalem from 1968 to 1971 and current service as professor of political science and head of Institute of Local Government at Bar Ilan University, Israel, for over twenty years. Prior to his international lifestyle, Elazar pursued formal education in the United States, beginning with his B.A. from Wayne State University in 1954 and continuing at the University of Chicago, where he completed an M.A.–Ph.D. in 1959. While finishing his secondary education, Elazar worked as a consultant and teacher in the Institute of Government and Public Affairs at the University of Illinois. From 1963 to 1964, he served as Huntington Library Fellow and on the faculty of the University of Minnesota; from 1964 to 1965, he was a Guggenheim fellow. The following year, Elazar was a lecturer of the U.S. Civil Service

Commission executive training program (a service he continues to provide), and in 1967, he joined the Advanced Commission of Education Commission of the States, in which he currently participates. Since 1970, Elazar has presided over the Jerusalem Center for Public Affairs based in Jerusalem and Philadelphia.

BIBLIOGRAPHY

Works by Daniel Judah Elazar

Elazar, D. J. *The American Partnership: Intergovernmental Cooperation in the Nineteenth-Century United States*. Chicago: University of Chicago Press, 1962.

————. *Cities of the Prairie: The Metropolitan Frontier and American Politics*. New York: Basic Books, 1970.

————. *Land, Space and Civil Society in America*. Philadelphia: Temple University Press, 1970.

————. *The Politics of Belleville: A Profile of the Civil Community*. Philadelphia: Temple University Press, 1971.

————. *The Ends of Federalism: Notes toward a Theory of Federal Political Arrangements*. Philadelphia: Center for the Study of Federalism, Temple University, 1976.

————. *The Generational Rhythm of American Politics*. Philadelphia: Center for the Study of Federalism, Temple University, 1976.

————. *Covenant as the Basis of the Jewish Political Tradition*. Ramat-Gan, Israel: Bar-Ilan University, Department of Political Studies, 5737, 1977.

————. *The Camp David Framework for Peace: A Shift toward Shared Rule*. Washington, DC: American Enterprise Institute for Public Policy Research, 1979.

————. *Federalism and Political Integration*. Ramat Gan, Israel: Turtledove Publishing, 1979.

————. "The Federal Government and Local Government Reform." *National Civic Review*, 72, April 1983, 190–198.

————. *American Federalism: A View from the States*. New York: Thomas J. Crowell, 1966, 1972; New York: Harper and Row, 1984.

————. *Building Cities in America: Urbanization and Suburbanization in a Frontier Society*. Cleveland, OH: Hamilton Press, 1987.

————. *Exploring Federalism*. Tuscaloosa: University of Alabama Press, 1987.

————. *The American Constitutional Tradition*. Lincoln: University of Nebraska Press, 1988.

————. *People and Polity: The Organizational Dynamics of World Jewry*. Detroit: Wayne State University Press, 1989.

————. *Constitutional Design and Power-Sharing in the Post-Modern Epoch*. Lanham, MD: University Press of America, 1991.

————. *Building toward Civil War: Generational Rhythms in American Politics*. Lanham, MD: Madison Books, 1992.

————. *The American Mosaic: The Impact of Space, Time, and Culture on American Politics*. Boulder, CO: Westview Press, 1994.

————. *Covenant in the Nineteenth Century: The Decline of an American Political Tradition*. Lanham, MD: Rowman and Littlefield Publishers, 1994.

------. *Federalism and the Way to Peace*. Kingston, Ontario: Institute of Intergovernmental Relations, Queen's University, 1994.

------. *Community and Polity: The Organizational Dynamics of American Jewry*. 1976. Philadelphia: Jewish Publication Society, 1995.

------. *Covenant and Polity in Biblical Israel: Biblical Foundations and Jewish Expressions*. New Brunswick, NJ: Transaction Publishers, 1995.

------. *The Covenant Tradition in Politics*. New Brunswick, NJ: Transaction Publishers, 1995.

------. *Covenant and Commonwealth: From Christian Separation through the Protestant Reformation*. New Brunswick, NJ: Transaction Publishers, 1996.

------. *Constitutionalizing Globalization: The Postmodern Revival of Confederal Arrangements*. Lanham, MD: Rowman and Littlefield Publishers, 1998.

------, ed. *Cooperation and Conflict: Readings in American Federalism*. Itasca, IL: F. E. Peacock, 1968.

------. *The Politics of American Federalism*. Lexington, MA: Heath, 1968.

------. *The Federal Polity*. New Brunswick, NJ: Transaction Books, 1974.

------. *Republicanism, Representation, and Consent: Views of the Founding Era*. New Brunswick, NJ: Transaction Books, 1979.

------. *Self Rule/Shared Rule: Federal Solutions to the Middle East Conflict*. Ramat Gan, Israel: Turtledove Publishing, 1979.

------. *Governing Peoples and Territories*. Philadelphia: Institute for the Study of Human Issues, 1982.

------. *Constitutionalism: The Israeli and American Experiences*. Lanham, MD: University Press of America, 1990.

------. *Authority, Power, and Leadership in the Jewish Polity: Cases and Issues*. Lanham, MD: University Press of America, 1991.

Elazar, D. J., and S. Cohen. *The Jewish Polity: Jewish Political Organization from Biblical Times to the Present*. Bloomington: Indiana University Press, 1985.

Elazar, D. J., and M. Friedman. *Moving Up: Ethnic Succession in America: With a Case History from the Philadelphia School System*. New York: Institute on Pluralism and Group Identity, 1976.

Elazar, D. J., and E. Katz, eds. *American Model of Revolutionary Leadership: George Washington and Other Founders*. Philadelphia: Center for the Study of Federalism, 1992.

Elazar, D. J., and J. Kincaid. *Covenant, Polity, and Constitutionalism*. Lanham, MD: University Press of America, 1983.

Elazar, D. J., and R. Rothman. *Cities of the Prairie Revisited: The Closing of the Metropolitan Frontier*. Lincoln: University of Nebraska Press, 1986.

Elazar, D. J., and the Staff of the Jerusalem Center for Public Affairs. *Federal Systems of the World: A Handbook of Federal, Confederal and Autonomy Arrangements*. London: Longman, 1994.

Elazar, D. J., and J. Zikmund. *The Ecology of American Political Culture: Readings*. New York: Crowell, 1975.

ETZIONI, AMITAI (b. January 4, 1929, Cologne, Germany), sociologist; university professor; director

Amitai Etzioni was born to Wili Falk and Gertrude Etzioni in 1929

Germany. Amitai was raised in Germany until 1935 when his family fled to Palestine to escape Nazism. Like passionate politics, the spirit of community continued to be important to Amitai, whose parents worked humble jobs in a Jewish cooperative outside of Tel Aviv. Of this aspect of his past, Etzioni recalls "the right mixture of togetherness and individuality." Also during his formative years, Etzioni joined the Israeli underground; in 1948 he fought in the Arab-Israeli war. Soon after, he immigrated to the United States.

In America, Etzioni received his education. He earned his B.A. in 1954 from Hebrew University and his Ph.D. from the University of California at Berkeley in 1958. He began to teach almost immediately.

From 1958 to 1959, Etzioni was an instructor at Columbia University. He ascended to assistant professor in 1959, serving the term for three years before becoming associate professor in 1961. In 1967, Etzioni became a full professor of sociology. During this time, he also served as director for the Center for Policy Research until 1980 when he joined the faculty at George Washington University as university professor and worked briefly under the Carter administration.

Inspired perhaps by his early communal experience, Etzioni's pedagogy was imbued with ethics. While teaching at George Washington, he brought to campus scholars who addressed the morality of American society and politics. The consensus among the visitors was that the American families and communities were weakening; the effects of crime increasing. All involved called for America's moral rebirth and, in 1991, named their platform "communitarianism." As spokesperson, Etzioni was nicknamed its father. He insisted that Americans locate a way to bring their entitlement in concert with their responsibility to the good of the community. Communitarianism is significant not only due to its founders and proponents but because of its historical sources as well. The philosophy (and the movement that was its application) developed between 1965 and 1990, reaching its height as America shifted from the Carter administration to the Reagan era—when materialism, self-entitlement, and individual interest ruled the land.

Although Etzioni is popularly known for the development of significant terms for the comparative approach of control factors in organization theory (coercive, utilitarian, normative-social), his fairly extensive oeuvre documents the conceptual variation he brought to writing public administration theory. Etzioni published a number of key texts in addition to *Social Change: Sources, Patterns, and Consequences*, edited in 1964 with his first wife, Eva (Horowitz) Etzioni. In 1961, *A Comparative Analysis of Complex Organizations* and *Complex Organizations: A Sociological Reader* were published, followed by a sequence of analyses, including the noted *Modern Organizations* in 1964. Written as an introduction to the theory of organizations, *Modern Organizations* covers Etzioni's structuralist theories as well as classic ideas, including scientific management, human relations, and Weber's theory of bureaucracy.

Two years later, *Studies in Social Change* was published; he edited *International Political Communities* the same year. In 1968 and 1969, respectively, Etzioni published *The Active Society: A Theory of Societal and Political Processes* and edited *Readings on Modern Organizations*. One of Etzioni's most recent works, *Public Policy in a New Key*, was published in 1993. Etzioni's later works such as *The Spirit of Community Rights, Responsibilities and the Communitarian Agenda*, also published in 1993, offer communitarian praxis.

BIBLIOGRAPHY

Works by Amitai Etzioni

Atkinson, C., A. Etzioni, and I. Tinker. *Post-secondary Education and the Disadvantaged: A Policy Study*. New York: Center for Policy Research, 1969.

Diprete, T., and A. Etzioni. "The Decline in Confidence in America: The Prime Factor—A Research Note." *Journal of Applied Behavioral Science*, 15, 4, October–November–December 1979, 520–526.

Etzioni, A. *Complex Organizations: A Sociological Reader*. New York: Holt, Rinehart and Winston, 1961.

———. *The Hard Way to Peace: A New Strategy*. New York: Collier Books, 1962.

———. *Modern Organizations: A Sociological Reader*. Englewood Cliffs, NJ: Prentice-Hall, 1964.

———. *Winning without War*. Garden City, NY: Doubleday, 1964.

———. *Political Unification: A Comparative Study of Leaders and Forces*. New York: Holt, Rinehart and Winston, 1965.

———. *Studies in Social Change*. New York: Holt, Rinehart and Winston, 1966.

———. *The Active Society: A Theory of Societal and Political Processes*. New York: Free Press, 1968.

———. *A Sociological Reader on Complex Organizations*. New York: Holt, Rinehart and Winston, 1969.

———. *Demonstration Democracy*. New York: Gordon and Breach, 1970.

———. *A Comparative Analysis of Complex Organizations: On Power, Involvement, and Their Correlates*. 1961. New York: Free Press, 1975.

———. *Social Problems*. Englewood Cliffs, NJ: Prentice-Hall, 1976.

———. "Beware: Economic Theories." *National Journal*, 13, 5, January 13, 1981, 207–209.

———. *An Immodest Agenda: Rebuilding America before the Twenty-first Century*. New York: New Press, 1983.

———. *Capital Corruption: The New Attack on American Democracy*. San Diego: Harcourt Brace Jovanovich, 1984.

———. "Do Defense Contractors Map Our Military Strategy?" *Business and Society Review*, Fall 1984, 29–34.

———. *The Moral Dimension: Toward a New Economics*. New York: Free Press, 1988.

———. *A Responsive Society: Collected Essays on Guiding Deliberate Social Change*. San Francisco: Jossey-Bass, 1991.

———. *Public Policy in a New Key*. New Brunswick, NJ: Transaction Publishers, 1993.

———. *The Spirit of Community Rights, Responsibilities and the Communitarian Agenda*. New York: Crown Publishers, 1993.

———. *The Spirit of Community: The Reinvention of American Society*. New York: Simon and Schuster, 1993.

———. *Rights and the Common Good: The Communitarian Perspective*. New York: St. Martin's Press, 1995.

———. *The New Golden Rule: Community and Morality in a Democratic Society*. New York: Basic Books, 1996.

———, ed. *International Political Communities*. New York: Anchor Books, 1966.

———. *Readings on Modern Organizations*. Englewood Cliffs, NJ: Prentice-Hall, 1969.

———. *New Communitarian Thinking: Persons, Virtues, Institutions, and Communities*. Charlottesville: University Press of Virginia, 1995.

———. *The Essential Communitarian Reader*. Lanham, MD: Rowman and Littlefield, 1998.

Etzioni, A. and F. DuBow, eds. *Comparative Perspectives: Theories and Methods*. Boston: Little, Brown, 1969.

Etzioni, A., and E. Etzioni, eds. *Social Change: Sources, Patterns, and Consequences*. New York: Basic Books, 1964.

Etzioni, A., and P. Lawrence, eds. *Socio-economics: Toward a New Synthesis*. Armonk, NY: M. E. Sharpe, 1991.

Etzioni, A., and R. Remp. *Technological Shortcuts to Social Change*. New York: Russell Sage Foundation, 1973.

Works about Amitai Etzioni

Antonides, Gerrit, W. Arts, and W. F. van Raaij, eds. *The Consumption of Time and the Timing of Consumption: Toward a New Behavioral and Socio-economics: Contributions in Honor of Amitai Etzioni*. New York: North-Holland, 1991.

Shields, P. "A New Paradigm for Military Policy: Socioeconomic." *Armed Forces and Society*, 19, 4, Summer 1993, 511–532.

FAYOL, HENRY (b. 1841, France; d. 1925), engineer; executive; pioneer of administrative management school

Fayol studied engineering and started his work as an engineer. In 1888 he became the managing director of S.A. Commentary Fourchambaut. He held the position until 1918. He developed most of his ideas in management and administration during this period. His thinking was heavily influenced by Adam Smith and Cartesian philosophy. Fayol's emphasis on organizational structure and functions forms a direct link to Adam Smith's division of labor.

His main approach is in line with classical organization theory; therefore, he tries to develop several scientific principles to organizations. He believes in a generic set of management principles that can be applied in any organization regardless of its nature (public or private). He draws his principles from the actual workings of organizations. By applying those principles, organizations can be run more efficiently and effectively. His contribution to public administration was in line with the philosophy that "management is management," a slogan he used to promote reform in public institutions. Therefore, he disagrees with the distinction between public administration and business administration. He summarizes his principles of management into planning, organization, command, coordination, and control.

Fayol believes that organizations are constructed to carry out certain activities. In order to be successful, they are supposed to follow certain principles that are universal in nature. Fayol suggests organizations perform the following six major types of activities: technical (production of goods); financial (acquisition and usage of capital); commercial (buying and selling); security (internal and external protection of organizational units and employees); accounting; and managerial (planning, organization, command, coordination, and control). Fayol explains that managerial activity is the most sensitive and important activity. Therefore, he develops fourteen different principles to explain the best ways to handle it: division of work; commensurating authority and responsibility; discipline; unity of command; unity of direction; subordination of individual interest to general interest; remuneration of personnel; centralization; scalar principle; order; equity; stability of tenure of personnel; taking an initiative; and esprit de corps. Since those principles can be taught, Fayol reasons management training should be emphasized. He believes everyone who works in organizations should be familiar with principles of management, not only the managers. In his judgment, the higher an employee is in organizational hierarchy, the more this person needs to be educated in managerial skills. He also believes that training should not stop at any time in the organization and puts a lot of responsibility on the shoulders of high-ranking administrators. Thus, in every organization high officials are the ones who should initiate change and teach others the principles of management, according to Fayol.

He contends management is essential to the functioning of all organizations independent of scope or application. He argues that management principles (functions) should be taught at schools as well as in other settings because those principles are universal and applicable in any setting. If those principles are violated or are not adapted, Fayol believes those organizations will have major problems. For example, regarding "unity of command," Fayol believes that a shop cannot be run in flagrant violation of "unity of command." Like all other pioneers of the administrative management school, his focus of attention in developing his principles of management was on the upper hierarchical part of the organization. Therefore, he does not put much attention on the needs of employees and those who work on the lower parts of organizational hierarchy.

BIBLIOGRAPHY

Works by Henry Fayol

Fayol, H. "The Administrative Theory in the State." In *Papers in the Science of Administration*, ed. L. Gulick and L. Urwick. New York: Columbia University Press, 1937.

———. *General and Industrial Management*. Trans. Constance Storrs. London: Pitman, 1949.

Works about Henry Fayol

Gager, H. "Management throughout History." In *Top Management Handbook*, ed. H. B. Mayward. New York: McGraw-Hill, 1960.

Gulick, L., and L. Urwick, eds. *Papers on the Science of Administration, by Luther Gulick and Others*. Clifton, NJ: A.M. Kelley, 1973.

Owen, R., et al. *Classics of Modern Management Theory*. London: Routledge/Thoemmes, 1993.

FOLLETT, MARY PARKER (b. September 3, 1868, Quincy, MA; d. 1933, Boston, MA), social worker; organizer; lecturer; pioneer in industrial management

Follett, the elder of two children, had responsibility at an early age to her younger brother and to her invalid mother who could not always care for him following the death of Mary's father, a shoe factory machinist. Obligated to her family's needs, Mary consistently sacrificed academic time. Nonetheless, from an early age, she was a thriving academician, completing Thayer Academy in Braintree, Massachusetts, at the age of fifteen in 1884. By 1898, when awarded her A.B. from the institution now known as Radcliffe, Follett's altruism and intellect combined to form a career in social work and authorship. Her philosophically idealistic work introduced behavior or "group dynamics" as a new and necessary aspect of administration. This "humanistic school" would replace the classical and neoclassical "systems" of public administration—the "scientific management" methodologies that dominated the 1920s.

Prior to writing about American government, Follett worked as a school and recreation agency organizer and wage board member. Following work with boys' clubs, Follett accepted the position of chairman of the Committee for Extended Use of School Buildings within the Women's Municipal League of Boston. The year was 1908; the following year, she served as chairman of the School House Sub-Committee of the Boston Women's Municipal League. Three years later, she shifted to management and joined the Placement Bureau Committee of Boston. During this time. Follett stressed to educators that young people's participation in a group activity like sports was a cooperative experience readying them for democratic citizenship. Follett's work during these years was a testament to her ability to wed community service and the study of human interaction. An unprecedented theory of interaction and group process was the result. Follett's intellectual legacy can best be gleaned through the work that survives her, both changes in the management and network of citywide bureaus and her published works.

Follett was also an industrial management lecturer. Although it was not until 1925 that Follett's lecture circuit reached professional status, she presented papers at industrial administration conferences from 1915 to 1933 and delivered her first paper, on the U.S. House of Representatives, in 1891 in England, while enrolled at Cambridge University. Her first book, *The Speaker of the House of Representatives*, was published while she was still at Radcliffe. In 1929, she moved to England to continue lecturing on and studying human behavior as an industrial issue. Until death, she maintained cultural and social interests in England.

Follett published widely on the humanistic dimension of political science. In her life's scholarship and work, she searched for the fundamental principle that coordinates human interaction. In fact, this is widely recognized as her longest-lasting contribution to studies of industry. Coincidentally, during her lifetime, Follett rarely received credit for the unprecedented interventions she developed that flourished decades later (Fox 1968; Prasad, Prasad, and Satyanarayana 1980). Follett attributed a symbiotic relationship to humanity and society: One influences and is influenced by the other. According to Follett, the significance of this is that the collective, during "group work," benefits from a synthesis necessitated by human interaction, that is, "interpenetration." Likewise, the aspect of compromise characterizing group work requires "reciprocal abandonments," on which every member of the group is reliant. In the contexts Follett developed of group motivation and "group work," her principle of the "law of the situation" is among her most famous. The law basically stipulates that orders are dictated per situation; they are not the inherent emanations of superiors—that is, "one person should not give orders to another person, but both should agree to take orders from the situation."

Follett believed, however, that conflict is inevitable and requires either domination, compromise, or integration for social resolution. Of these three methods she considered integration the most effective for reconciling most differences. With the combined effects of domination and compromise, integration resolves conflicts by equalizing the concerns and contributions of group members. In this context, disruption is viewed as a new spark of "integration," not a problem per se because confrontation does not have to mean opposition. Many businessmen located in these principles convincing and current methods for handling professional problems because compromise determined by a specific "situation" lends productive relations between workers at each level of management. "Circular response" is the means through which reciprocity is achieved.

The New State (1918), Follett's second book, began as a publication of her findings from working at community centers. But more important for public administrators, this book critiques American political science and theory while introducing group dynamics, the theme she would follow throughout her career. *Creative Experience* (1924) also focuses on group experience and develops ideas introduced in *The New State.*

BIBLIOGRAPHY

Works by Mary Parker Follett

Follett, M. P. *Henry Clay as Speaker of the United States House of Representatives.* Washington, DC: American Historical Association, 1892.
———. *Creative Experience.* London: Longmans Green, 1924.
———. *The New State: Group Organization the Solution of Popular Government.* New York: Longmans, Green, 1918; Gloucester, MA: Peter Smith, 1965.
———. *The Speaker of the House of Representatives.* 1891. New York: Longmans, Green and Company, 1986.

Works about Mary Parker Follett

Fox, E. M. "Mary Parker Follett: The Enduring Contribution." *Public Administration Review*, November–December 1968, 520–529.
Graham, P., ed. *Mary Parker Follett—Prophet of Management: A Celebration of Writings from the 1920s.* Boston: Harvard Business School Press, 1996.
Metcalf, H. C., and L. Urwick. *Dynamic Administration: The Collected Papers of Mary Parker Follett.* New York: Harper and Row, 1940.
Prasad, D. R., V. S. Prasad, P. Satyanarayana, eds. *Administrative Thinkers*, 1st ed. New Delhi: Light & Life, 1980.

FREDERICKSON, H. GEORGE (b. July 17, 1937, Twin Falls, ID), political scientist; public administrator; director; dean

H. George Frederickson was born to John C. Frederickson and Zelpha Richins. He earned his B.A. in 1959 from Brigham Young University. In 1961 he completed his M.P.A. from the University of California at Los Angeles, followed by his Ph.D. in 1967 from the University of Southern California. He holds an honorary L.L.D. from Dongguk University, Korea, and the Dwight Waldo Award. He has served as a research assistant, lecturer, director, fellow, and dean in various universities, including University of Maryland, Syracuse University, the University of North Carolina, Indiana University, and the University of Kansas. He served as president of Eastern Washington University, Cheney, from 1974 to 1987.

Public, for Frederickson, is a crucial but neglected concept in public administration studies. He explains that government is merely a "manifestation" of the public but that, on the whole, "public" and "government" are independent entities. Frederickson has delineated five vantages on the idea of public: as interest group, as consumer, as represented, as client, and as citizen. He concludes that theories of the public should be embedded with a spirit of collectivity, ethical commitment, citizenship, and responsiveness as well as the Constitution of the United States.

Frederickson has invested considerable research effort into exploring new trends, often referred to as "the new public administration." The new public administration was born from 1960s political emphases on "relevance," as Frederickson explains in "Comparing the Reinventing Government Movement with the New Public Administration" (1996). This article offers a detailed analysis of the differences between reinventing government and the new public administration; Frederickson's argument gains momentum as he concludes that reinventing government is "old wine in new bottles." Like the new public administration, reinventing government was instigated by the need for change, although the latter bestows upon government significant immediate improvements, despite "considerable cost in the long-range capacity of public institutions." In fleshing out the terms of his observations, Frederickson builds his project around key concepts—rationality and relevance, responsiveness and empowerment, for example—and begins with a chart comparing the characteristics of both trends.

Frederickson's "research-based" *Ethics and Public Administration* (1993) and *The Spirit of Public Administration* (1997) are two later works that are heralded as thought-provoking and challenging, if less comprehensive than their contemporary rivals. Ever dedicated to production of usefully applicable theory for practitioners, Frederickson in these works is more prescriptive than investigative.

The Spirit of Public Administration finds Frederickson assailing "new public management theory" and defending the public administration field against skepticism in the form of the "anti-bureaucratic, probusiness ethos" circulating among economists and business managers. Privileging a "Hamiltonian approach," Frederickson assures readers that "bureaucracy works" and that its failure is due solely to the inherent complexity of public problems or unchecked corruption at the public service level.

Historically, *The Spirit of Public Administration* represents Frederickson's direct response to questions he raised during the 1968 Minnowbrook Conference at Syracuse University. The collected papers from this conference of emerging public administration scholars were published as *Toward a New Public Administration* (1971), thus inaugurating the new public administration movement. During the conference, Frederickson suggested that the new public administrationists were "second-generation behaviorists," a comparison predicated on generational continuity, much like Frederickson's 1996 correlation of new public administration and reinventing government.

BIBLIOGRAPHY

Works by H. George Frederickson

Cho, Y., and H. G. Frederickson. *The White House and the Blue House: Government Reform in the United States and Korea*. Lanham, MD: University Press of America, 1997.

Frederickson, H. G. "The Lineage of New Public Administration." *Administration and Society*, 8, 2, August 1976, 149–174.

———. *The New Public Administration*. Birmingham: University of Alabama Press, 1980.

———. "The Recovery of Civism in Public Administration." *Parameters*, 42, 6, November 1982, 501–508.

———. "Citizenship and Public Administration: Proceedings of the National Conference on Citizenship and Public Service, April 14–16, 1983, New York City." *Public Administration Review*, 44, March 1984, 99–206.

———. "Public Administration and Social Equity." *Public Administration Review*, 50, 2, March–April 1990, 228–237.

———. "Government Regulating Itself: A Canadian–American Comparison." *Administration and Society*, 22, 4, February 1991, 418–423.

———. "Toward a Theory of the Public for Public Administration." *Administration and Society*, 22, 4, February 1991, 395–417.

———. "Comparing the Reinventing Government Movement with the New Public Administration." *Public Administration Review*, 56, 3, May–June 1996, 263–270.

———. *The Spirit of Public Administration*. San Francisco: Jossey-Bass, 1997.

———, ed. *Ethics and Public Administration*. Armonk, NY: M. E. Sharpe, 1993.

———. *Public Policy and the Two States of Kansas*. Lawrence: University Press of Kansas, 1994.

Frederickson, H. G., and D. G. Frederickson. "Public Perceptions of Ethics in Government." *Annals of the American Academy of Political and Social Science*, 537, January 1995, 163–172.

Frederickson, H. G., and R. Mayer, eds. "Minnowbrook II: Changing Epochs of Public Administration." *Public Administration Review*, 49, March–April 1989, 95–227.

Frederickson, H. G., and C. Wise, eds. *Public Administration and Public Policy*. Lexington, MA: Lexington Books, 1977.

Wise, C., and H. G. Frederickson, eds. "Symposium on Administering Public Policy." *Policy Studies Journal*, 5, Autumn 1976, 4–113.

FREUD, SIGMUND (b. May 6, 1856, Moravia; d. September 23, 1939, London), organizational psychologist; clinical director; lecturer; therapist

Freud lived in an average size family of two brothers and was the child of his father's second marriage. He was home schooled by his father until the age of seven, when he went to a private school. A book collector from an early age, he was nine years old when he took an examination to allow him to enter high school (Sperl Gymnasium, Vienna). During his high school years he was one of the best recognized students in his class. He graduated from high school at seventeen, entering the University of Vienna in 1873 to study medicine. Subjects such as psychological neuroses and the physiology of human sexuality attracted him. He married in 1886 and had six children.

Freud graduated from the University of Vienna in 1881 and accepted a research job at Brücke Institute and Physiology Laboratory. Later he became a clinical director at Nothangel's Division of Internal Medicine where he was appointed lecturer in neuropathology. He continued his medical practice concurrently with his research in neuroscience. In 1884 Freud discovered the therapeutic effects of cocaine and presented his findings at a conference on the topic titled "A Therapeutic Project and a Hope." He discovered that the cocaine could elevate mood in humans. In addition, cocaine increases the capacity to endure physical pain and suffering. He believed that depression is a neurotic malfunction that lowers the energy level. According to Freud, such afflictions can be reversed by injecting cocaine into the patient's blood. Freud developed his psychoanalytic ideas through an evolutionary path. They include his experience with the therapy of hysteric patients that led him to construct his theory of human thought and behavior. He eventually perfected his psychoanalytic ideas, and by 1895 he wrote a document titled "The Project for Scientific Psychology," which explained his belief that neurological events were determinants of human behavior.

Freud was famous as a lecturer by 1904 and visited many universities including Yale, Harvard, and others in many countries to speak. He served as the president of many medical and psychiatric organizations and wrote many books and articles concerning his findings. His major work in psychology was in dream interpretation and the theory of personality development. He invented such concepts as "ego," "superego," and "id" in order to explain ideas concerning the unconscious mind and repressive thought.

From childhood he was interested in the role of dreams and recorded his dreams on a regular basis. He published his first work on analyzing dreams in 1895. He argued that dreams are the manifestation of hidden wishes. He believed that dreams can be used to identify the sources of illness and unsatisfied human needs. He argued that when individuals cannot satisfy their wishes, they are suppressed into the unconscious mind and can influence behavior and growth. He is the first therapist to use the "couch theory," by which a therapist establishes a trusting relationship with the patient who then reveals his or her unconscious mind to the therapist. He argued that id represents the psychic energy that exists within each individual, whereas the superego represents social values and societal ideals that control and regulate human impulses. Those impulses, according to Freud, have the capability of causing social damage. These two forces are usually in conflict and compete for control of an individual's behavior. According to him, ego serves as a mediator between human needs and the objective society, and individuals generally compromise between those two forces. He contends that the distribution of energy within different parts of the human mind will determine the dynamic of individual personality. For example, if energy is controlled by superego, the individual's conduct will be moralistic; if it is controlled by ego, his or her behavior is realistic; and if it is controlled by id, it will be impulsive.

By early 1900, Freud was recognized as the most influential authority on the interpretation of dreams and had published his famous work on the subject titled *The Interpretation of Dreams*. This work was published eight times during his lifetime and brought him worldwide acclaim. He is also popular for his theories concerning human sexuality. He argued that children develop sexual feelings from a young age. He believed that the ages between one and three are the prehistoric age and the source of unconscious and the major cause of psychoneurosis. He believed that at age three, children develop sexual orientations and that some manifestation of their feelings can be observed in the erotic and sometimes hostile relationship between the child and his or her parents. He called this phenomenon the "Oedipus Complex."

His analysis of the human mind and suppression of individuals' needs and wishes bring individuals into the organizational life. He argues that when people's wishes are suppressed, they cannot be productive and therefore exhibit abnormal behavior. His discoveries relating to the human mind and needs led the organizational behavioralists to look further into the mind in order to remedy abnormal behaviors. His understanding of individual behavior made a great contribution to the subject of organizational behavior and helped improve working conditions within organizations. His work sets the stage for behavioral theorists in management. He contends that organizations, by nature, are oppressive and inhibit individuals from exhibiting their true needs. His view of organizations is therefore negative.

BIBLIOGRAPHY

Works by Sigmund Freud

Freud, Sigmund. *Modern Sexual Morality and Modern Nervousness*. New York: Critic and Guide Co., 1915.

———. *Psychopathology of Everyday Life*. Special Edition. New York: The Classics of Medicine Library, 1998.

Works about Sigmund Freud

Cavell, M. *The Psychoanalytic Mind*. Cambridge: Harvard University Press, 1993.

Deutsch, K. *How People Decide Their Fate*. Boston: Houghton Mifflin, 1970.

Freud, E. *Letters of Sigmund Freud and Arnold Zweing*. New York: Basic Books, 1970.

Fromm, E. *Sigmund Freud's Mission*. New York: Harper & Brothers Publishers, 1959.

Hall, C. *A Primer of Freudian Psychology*. New York: New American Library, 1954.

Hubback, C.J.M., trans. *Beyond the Pleasure Principle, by Sigmund Freud*. New York: Boni and Liveright Publishers, 1924.

Jones, E. *The Life and Work of Sigmund Freud*. New York: Basic Books, 1961.

Ricoer, P. *Freud and Philosophy*. New Haven, CT: Yale University Press, 1970.

Riviere, J. *A General Introduction of Psychoanalysis by Sigmund Freud*. New York: Pocket Books, 1953.

Strachey, J., ed. and trans. *New Introductory Lectures on Psychoanalyses: Sigmund Freud*. New York: Norton, 1965.

———. *The Interpretation of Dreams: Sigmund Freud*. 3d. ed. New York: Avon, 1998.

GALBRAITH, JOHN KENNETH (b. October 15, 1908, Iona Station, Ontario), government official; economist; ambassador; presidential advisor

John Galbraith is a public administration and governmental reformer. His economically informed models provide the philosophical groundwork for social and environmental programs instituted during the 1960s and 1970s. Signs of social consciousness and sources of social and environmental development motivate Galbraith's work in public administration reform. Greatly impressed by the powerful leadership and New Deal programs of Franklin Roosevelt's presidency, Galbraith desired to serve in the administration upon earning his Ph.D. The goal was realized during the 1940s when Galbraith worked with the Office of Price Administration. At the University of California at Berkeley, Galbraith completed his Ph.D. in Agricultural Economics in 1934, after completing a B.A. in the same area at Ontario Agricultural College in 1930.

During his service to the U.S. government, Galbraith also worked in the U.S. Department of Agriculture, as U.S. ambassador to India, and as a member of the Council of Economic Advisors for the Kennedy administration. In 1973, Galbraith published *Economics and the Public Purpose*. During the 1950s and 1960s as well as the 1970s, Galbraith published influential texts that explore government spending issues and suggest that the American public maintain a high level of involvement in this process.

Published in 1958, *The Affluent Society* calls for progressive change in the quality of public education, health, environment, and the lives of the poor. Galbraith critiques businessmen for encouraging a "myth of scarcity," which dupes the public into excessive consumption of private goods. His economic analysis parts company with the approach of traditional economists whose foci (production, efficiency, and the redistribution of wealth) are outdated concerns for affluent societies in which most people have transcended subsistence lifestyles.

Galbraith deconstructs free enterprise theories of neoclassical economists in *The New Industrial State*, published in 1967. He dedicates this project to a transitional moment in government and entrepreneuralship: the beginning of the age of "technostructure." This new system values profit over stability; its managers control modern corporations. Furthermore, "planned demand" replaces the priority once held by the consumer and the market system. Public and corporate sectors merge due to governmental effort to maintain demand and to stabilize the economy. Overall, Galbraith was centrally preoccupied with public interest. For over four decades, he remains a leading critic of public policy drafted to protect the interests of elite Americans and overlook the needs of other Americans.

BIBLIOGRAPHY

Works by John Kenneth Galbraith

Galbraith, J. K. *The New Industrial State.* Boston: Houghton Mifflin, 1967.
————. *Ambassador's Journal: A Personal Account of the Kennedy Years.* Boston: Houghton Mifflin, 1969.
————. *Money: Whence It Came, Where It Went.* Boston: Houghton Mifflin, 1975.
————. *The Affluent Society.* 1958. Boston: Houghton Mifflin, 1976.
————. *The Age of Uncertainty.* Boston: Houghton Mifflin, 1977.
————. "The Defense of the Multinational Company." *Harvard Business Review*, 56, March–April 1978, 83–93.
————. "The Government vs. Small Business." *Washington Monthly*, 10, Spring 1978, 42–44.
————. "Market Power, Inflation, and Unemployment: Monetarism versus Price Controls." *Wage Price Law and Economics Review*, 3, 1, 1978, 67–82.
————. *A Life in Our Times: Memoirs.* Boston: Houghton Mifflin, 1979.
————. "Asean Today: Feeling the Heat." *Asian Affairs*, 8, 1, September–October 1980, 31–40.
————. "The Role of the Preservationists—Reaping What They Sow." *Current*, 227, November 1980, 15–19.
————. "The Conservative Onslaught." *New York Review of Books*, 27, 21–22, January 22, 1981, 30–36.
————. "The Market and Mr. Reagan." *The New Republic*, 185, 12, September 23, 1981, 15–18.
————. "The Budget and the Bust." *The New Republic*, 186, 11, March 17, 1982, 9–13.
————. "The Social Consensus and the Conservative Onslaught." *Millennium*, 11, Spring 1982, 1–13.
————. "The Way Up from Reagan Economics: Out of the Rubble of This Administration's Monetary Policy and Supply-Side Economics, a Workable Plan Can Be Devised." *Harvard Business Review*, 60, July–August 1982, 6–8.
————. *The Anatomy of Power.* Boston: Houghton Mifflin, 1983.
————. "Galbraith and the Theory of the Corporation." *Journal of Post Keynesian Economics*, 7, 1, Fall 1984, 43–60.

————. "The American Economy Now and When the Returns Come In." *Business Forum*, 12, Summer 1987, 8–11.

————. *Economics in Perspective: A Critical History*. Boston: Houghton Mifflin, 1987.

————. "The Congress: Fifty Years Back, Fifty Years On." *CRS Review*, 11, 1–2, January–February 1990, 5–6.

————. "The Power of Beliefs: The Dynamics of Change." *Current*, 319, January 1990, 35–39.

————. *The Culture of Contentment*. Boston: Houghton Mifflin, 1992.

————. "Reading the Fed." *Nation*, 263, 10, October 7, 1996, 6–7.

————. "The Clinton Administration's Vision." *Challenge*, 40, 4, July–August 1997, 45–57.

————. "Fixing the Fed." *Nation*, 264, 21, June 2, 1997, 5.

Galbraith, J. K., and S. Menshikov. *Capitalism, Communism and Coexistence: From the Bitter Past to a Better Prospect*. Boston: Houghton, 1988.

Galbraith, J. K., and A. Williams, eds. *Annals of an Abiding Liberal*. Boston: Houghton Mifflin, 1979.

Works about John Kenneth Galbraith

Gambs, J. S. *John Kenneth Galbraith*. Old Tappan, NJ: Twayne Publishers/Macmillan Publishing, 1975.

Hession, C. H. *John Kenneth Galbraith and His Critics*. New York: New American Library, 1971.

Lamson, P. *Speaking of Galbraith: A Personal Portrait*. New York: Ticknor and Fields, 1991.

Okroi, L. J. *Galbraith, Harrington, Heilbroner: Economics and Dissent in an Age of Optimism*. Princeton, NJ: Princeton University Press, 1988.

Pratson, F. J. *Perspectives on Galbraith: Conversations and Opinions*. Princeton, NJ: CBI Publishing, 1978.

GAWTHROP, LOUIS (b. October 27, 1930, Baltimore, MD), university professor; editor

The editor in chief of the *Public Administration Review* from 1978 to 1984, Louis Gawthrop is a professor of government and public administration at the University of Baltimore. He has taught previously at Erasmus University in The Netherlands, Indiana University at Bloomington, the State University of New York at Binghamton, and the University of Pennsylvania. Gawthrop has been a visiting researcher at the Netherlands Institute for Advanced Study in the Humanities and Social Sciences, the Harvard Divinity School, and the Weston School of Theology, from which he holds a Master's of Divinity. Gawthrop studied political science at Johns Hopkins University, from which he holds a B.A.

Gawthrop has contributed research and writing on the moral and ethical dimensions of public policy and on administrative implementation. His consideration of the "reality" that lies outside of one's environment reflects the diversity of his research experiences domestically and abroad.

This is precisely the vantage he casts upon the new public administration—a movement that culminated at the Minnowbrook Conference of the 1970s.

Gawthrop's earliest work, *Bureaucratic Behavior in the Executive Branch* (1969), applies concepts from organization theory to problems of decision making and conflict resolution in the federal government. Gawthrop makes brief comparison to general characteristics of private organizations and reviews existing theories of how executive agencies resolve internal conflict, seek rational decisions, and pursue loyalty. The study also includes an overview of administrative response to environmental change. Gawthrop analyzes the forces favoring the strategy of either "consolidation" (withdrawal to routine tasks) or "innovation." Gawthrop takes examples from major issues in federal policy making.

BIBLIOGRAPHY

Works by Louis Gawthrop

Gawthrop, L. C. "Changing Membership Patterns in House Committees." *American Political Science Review*, 60, June 1966, 366.
————. *Bureaucratic Behavior in the Executive Branch: An Analysis of Organizational Change*. New York: Free Press, 1969.
————. *Administrative Politics and Social Change*. New York: St. Martin's Press, 1971.
————. "Organizing for Change." *Annals of the American Academy of Political and Social Science*, 466, March 1983, 119.
————. *Public Sector Management, Systems, and Ethics*. Bloomington: Indiana University Press, 1984.
————. "Ethics and Democracy: The Moral Dimension." *Journal of State Government*, 62, 5, September–October 1989, 180–184.
————. "Minnowbrook: The Search for a New Reality." *Public Administration Review*. 49, 1989, 2.
————. "The Ethical Foundations of American Public Administration." *International Journal of Public Administration*, 16, 2, 1992, 139–164.
————. "In the Search for Democracy." *International Journal of Public Administration*, 17, 12, 1994, 2195–2230.
————. "Democracy, Bureaucracy, and Hypocrisy Redux: A Search for Sympathy and Compassion." *Public Administrative Review*, 57, 3, May–June 1997, 201–210.

Work about Louis Gawthrop

Luke, J. S. "A Response to Louis C. Gawthrop: Looking Outward More, Inward Less: Expanding Our Attention in the Search." *International Journal of Public Administration*, April–May 1997, 857–860.

GILBRETH, FRANK B. (b. July 7, 1868, Fairfield, ME; d. June 14, 1924, near Montclair, NJ), contracting engineer; efficiency expert; originator of the science and motion study; consultant

Frank Gilbreth was born in Maine of Scottish ancestry. Gilbreth's career reflects the hard work and discipline it took to grow up fatherless at an early age in a farming family in New England. After attending Andover Academy and Boston Grammar School, at seventeen Gilbreth started an apprenticeship in building contracting, although he was accepted at the Massachusetts Institute of Technology. In this area he developed a number of innovative tools in the field.

With the publication of *Field System* and *Concrete System* in 1908, Frank Gilbreth's entry into the general management literature began. His most significant contribution was the development of a methodology for revealing unnecessary movement in production. He theorized that there was "one best way" to perform each movement of work.

Gilbreth's original time and motion study sought to increase efficiency of work by breaking down steps involved in bricklaying into simple movements. His experience as a building contractor allowed him to test time and motion theory in its development stage. Much of Gilbreth's work parallels that of Frederick Taylor, who pioneered scientific management. While both Gilbreth and Taylor held the position that a united effort of labor and management was critical in establishing the linkage between scientific management's success and an increase in profits, they differed in the level of labor's involvement in the implementation of the principles.

Frank Gilbreth's focus on the social sciences, specifically in acknowledging the worker's higher-order needs on the job, reflects his wife Lillian's influence as a psychologist. Their study in 1916 established linkages between the organization's success in drawing and maintaining the best workers and the consideration of the needs of organizational members.

Gilbreth's application of motion study went beyond labor use. He served as major of engineers in the U.S. Army from 1917 to 1918. His association with the military afforded him the opportunity to use his methodology in this area. Inefficiency in production and laws of motion economy also have roots in Gilbreth's science of motion study.

In recognition of their contributions to the science of time and motion and to general management, Gilbreth, along with Lillian Gilbreth, received the Gantt Medal from the American Society of Mechanical Engineers and the Institute of Management.

Frank Gilbreth died at age fifty-six while preparing to attend the Prague International Management Congress. Lillian Gilbreth presented his paper at the conference.

BIBLIOGRAPHY

Works by Frank B. Gilbreth

Gilbreth, F. *Concrete System*. New York: Engineering News Publishing Company, 1908.

————. *Field System*. New York and Chicago: Myron C. Clark Publishing Company, 1908.

————. *Motion Study: A Method for Increasing the Efficiency of the Workman*. New York: D. van Nostrand Company, 1911.

————. *Primer of Scientific Management*. New York: D. van Nostrand Company, 1912.

————. *Applied Motion Study*. New York: Sturgis and Walton Company, 1917.

————. *Fatigue Study: The Elimination of Humanity's Greatest Unnecessary Waste: A First Step in Motion*. London: Routledge, 1919.

Work about Frank B. Gilbreth

Spriegel, W. R., and C. Myers, eds. *The Writings of the Gilbreths*. Homewood, IL: Richard D. Irwin, 1953.

GOLEMBIEWSKY, ROBERT T. (b. 1932, Trenton, NJ), political scientist; university professor; editor; consultant

Golembiewsky attended Princeton University and received an A.B. in 1954. Later, he joined Yale University for graduate work and received an M.A. in 1956 and a Ph.D. in instructional politics in 1958. After graduation he joined the University of Illinois to teach management from 1960 to 1964 and, later, the University of Georgia to teach political science and management (1964–1967). He consulted at several private institutions, including James A. Hamilton Hospital, AT&T (American Telephone and Telegraph), and UNIDO (United Nations Industrial Development Organization) on sensitivity training. He received many prestigious awards, including the Administrator's Book Award, 1967; the Douglas McGregor Award in 1975; and the Chester Barnard Memorial Award in 1980. He also received the Ford Summer Fellowship in mathematical applications in business (1961–1962).

Golembiewsky's major work is in organizational development (OD), and he is called an organizational humanist in favor of building a public organization theory from several miniparadigms. According to Golembiewsky, it is unlikely that general consensus will emerge in a single paradigm. In his approach to organizations, he tries to bring individuals and organizations together. He argues against the traditional organizational theories with their emphasis on hierarchy, rules, structure, and control. In his judgment, the traditional approach inhibits individual growth and development. He believes that the most important aspects of an organization are the dominant values that ultimately shape the relationships among members of the organization. Those values influence the character and quality of individual employees. He believes in continual organizational change and constant diagnosis of organizational processes to bring about harmony and equilibrium in an organization. He argues that this process can be facilitated by using an interventionist, who also plays a role as teacher, and brings about necessary change in the organization. He believes that public organizations are most in need of change because of their political nature.

Golembiewsky argues that public organizational change has to deal with structural as well as policy matters. In addition, he emphasizes that because the public is different from the private sector, different methods should be utilized to bring about change. He introduces a new direction into organizational life by emphasizing the importance of values and ethics. He believes that in order to operationalize an ethical environment, certain values (Mets-values) should dominate, including:

(1) Work must be psychologically acceptable to the individual. . . . (2) Work must allow men to develop his own faculties . . . (3) The work task must allow the individual considerable room for self-determination . . . (4) The worker must have the possibility of controlling, in a meaningful way, the environment within which the task is to be prepared. . . . (5) The organization should not be the sole and final arbiter of behavior; both the organization and the individual must be subject to an external moral order. (1967a, 65)

In his judgment, these values create an organizational culture that brings employees together. He contends that the major problem with most organizations is that their cultures are created by top organizational authorities and reflect their values, which are usually at odds with those of individual employees. He also talks about organizational structure and favors decentralization. He argues that a decentralized structure provides the opportunity for employees to grow and develop themselves and benefits the organization.

Golembiewsky also studied small group structure and behavior and created several categories concerning group properties, including group structure, group style, and member characteristics. He relied on his studies on the dynamics of small group behavior using a laboratory approach to bring about organizational change and development. He sets out certain criteria for conducting laboratory research in order to ensure its success. For example, he emphasizes that interpersonal relations between the subjects and experimenters must be based on open communication, recognition of choice, collaboration, cooperation, and authenticity.

He believes that small groups usually develop their own structure, style, and norms of behavior that are unique to them and based on common values. He has also contributed to the knowledge of individual behavior in an organizational setting. He puts great emphasis on individual members and believes that individual freedom has to be achieved within the organizational context. He believes several goals are essential for the civil service movement. They include guarantee of equal treatment among all employees, the application of the theories of management, and development of a public career service.

BIBLIOGRAPHY

Works by Robert T. Golembiewsky

Golembiewsky, R. T. *Behavior and Organization*. Skokie, IL: Rand McNally, 1962.
————. *The Small Group: An Analysis of Research Concepts and Operations*. Chicago,
   IL: University of Chicago, 1962.
————. *Managerial Behavior and Organization Demands: Management as a Linking of
   Levels of Interaction*. Chicago: Rand McNally, 1967a.
————. *Men, Management and Morality: Toward a New Organizational Ethic*. New
   York: McGraw-Hill, 1967b.
————. *Approaches to Organizing*. New York: Marcel Dekker, 1979.
————. *Approaches to Planned Change*. New Brunswick, NJ: Transaction Publish-
   ers, 1984.
————. *Humanizing Public Organizations*. Mount Airy, MD: Lomond Publications,
   1985.
————. *Ironies in Organizational Development*. New Brunswick, NJ: Transaction
   Publishers, 1990.
————. *Ironies in Organizational Development Transaction*. New York: Marcel Dek-
   ker, 1991.
————, ed. *Handbook of Organizational Consultation*. New York: Marcel Dekker,
   1992.
————. *Handbook of Organizational Behavior*. New York: Marcel Dekker, 1993.
Golembiewsky, R. T., and R. Munzenrider. *Phases of Burnout*. New York: Praeger,
   1988.
Golembiewsky, R. T., R. Munzenrider, and J. Stevenson. *Stress in Organizations*.
   New York: Praeger, 1986.
Golembiewsky, R. T., et al., eds. *Public Administration: Readings in Institutions,
   Processes, Behavior*. Chicago: Rand McNally, 1966.

GOODNOW, FRANK J. (b. 1859, Brooklyn, New York; d. November 1939,
Brooklyn, NY), administrator; university professor

Goodnow is an early scholar in public administration who wrote the
first textbook on public administration (*Politics and Administration*) in
1900. He is an advocate of separation of administration and politics and
argues in favor of studying the real functioning of government. He believes that politics deal with the "expression of the will of the state in
policies, and administration is concerned with the execution of that will."
In other words, separation of powers between the legislative, executive,
and judicial branch is emphasized in the Constitution. However, in reality politics and administration are mixed together. For example, although executive and legislative power are supposed to be separated,
the executive branch has considerable legislative power contrary to the
constitutional idea of political control over administration. In his judgment, politics and administration could be separated in some areas.
Therefore, his ideas correspond with the reform movement after the Pen-
dleton Act of 1883. Goodnow argues that bureaucracy has to implement

the will of the legislative body impartially without the interference of government. However, he argued that the separation of powers has been diluted through the implementation process.

Goodnow contends that government has two functions: One "has to do with policies of expression of the state will"; the other is the administration that is involved with the "execution of those policies." Therefore, administration and bureaucracy are the tools of political masters to implement the will of the state. This will is manifested in the policy-making function of the legislative and judicial branches of government. The hallmark of Goodnow's idea is the dichotomy between administration and politics, with politics ranked superior to administration. In addition, he contends that bureaucracy should be apolitical and neutral.

Goodnow believes that a large part of administration can be operated without the interference of politics. Therefore, it falls in the realm of scientific and quasi-business activity. In this area, the interference of politics is counterproductive. However, he also realizes that there are aspects of administration and politics that merge and cannot be separated. At times Goodnow gives the impression that he is advocating nonseparability of politics and administration. It can be argued that his writings influenced the scientific management movement and acceptance of the politics–administration dichotomy during the early 1900s. Eventually the idea of separation of politics and administration manifested itself in the practice of the council–manager form of city government in which the council makes policy decisions and the manger implements them. In addition, the establishment of a special-purpose district to depoliticize the administration of schools is another alternative to separate politics and administration.

Goodnow also emphasizes the importance of political control over bureaucracy to ensure political accountability. Therefore, several civil service commissions were created to ensure the neutrality and nonpartisan function of public organizations in carrying out their employment practices. His ideas were instrumental in the establishment of regulatory commissions to control businesses.

In his analysis of the relationship between central and local government, he clearly traces the ways in which local needs undermine the will of the state. He concludes this is due to the tendency of legislative bodies to centralize while administrative bodies decentralize. Therefore, the will of the state is practically altered by bureaucracy to fit the needs of the local constituency. As a result, he advocates greater administrative centralization and more autonomy for local legislative bodies. In his analysis, a centralized administrative system will inevitably make it more responsive to the will of the legislative body. In addition, it makes government more efficient by relieving itself from engaging in politics, which usually slows down its proper functioning.

BIBLIOGRAPHY

Works by Frank J. Goodnow

Goodnow, F. J. *Municipal Home Rule: A Study in Administration.* New York: Columbia University Press, 1895. Reprint. Buffalo, NY: W. S. Hein, 1997.
————. *Politics and Administration.* New York: Macmillan, 1900.
————. *Comparative Administrative Law: An Analysis of the Administrative Systems, National and Local, of the United States, England, France, and Germany.* New York: Burt Franklin, 1903, 1970.
————. *City Government in the United States.* New York: Century, 1904, 1910. Reprint. New York: Arno Press, 1974.
————. *The Principles of the Administrative Law of the United States.* New York, London: G.P. Putnam's Sons, 1905.
————. *Municipal Government.* New York: Century, 1909.
————. *Municipal Problems.* New York: Columbia University Press, 1911.
————. *Principles of Constitutional Government.* New York: Harper, 1916.
————. *China, an Analysis.* New York: Arno Press, 1926, 1979.
————. *Politics and Administration: A Study in Government.* New York: Russell & Russell, 1967.

Works about Frank J. Goodnow

Haines, C. G., and M. E. Dimock, eds. *Essays on the Law and Practice of Governmental Administration.* New York: Greenwood Press, 1968.
Montjoy, R. S., and D. J. Watson. "A Case for Reinterpreted Dichotomy of Politics and Administration as a Professional Standard in Council–Manager Government." *Public Administration Review,* 55, 1995, 231–239.
Richardson, I. L., and S. Baldwin. *Public Administration: Government in Action.* Columbus, OH: Charles E. Merrill, 1976.
Rosenbloom, D. H. *Public Administration: Understanding Management, Politics, and Law in the Public Sector.* New York: Random House, 1986.

GULICK, LUTHER (b. January 1892, Osaka, Japan; d. 1993, St. Lawrence, NY), public city administrator; administrative consultant; political scientist; university professor

Gulick received most of his education at home through tutoring or from his parents during his childhood in Japan. Later his parents moved to Germany, where he received some formal education. They relocated to the United States, where he was graduated from Hotchkiss Preparatory School and received a B.A. from Oberlin College in 1914. He obtained a master's degree in political science in 1915 and went to Columbia University to obtain his Ph.D. (1920). He joined the New York Bureau of Municipal Research for training in public service and was the city administrator for New York City from 1954 to 1956. He also worked at the Council of National Defense during World War I and became a captain responsible for statistical analysis. After graduation he joined Columbia University to teach courses in public administration and to continue his work at the New York Bureau of Municipal Research. He also held several posts in the field of tax administration and was a consultant in administration for several countries.

Gulick contributed a great deal to the theories of public administration due to his theoretical and practical experience in the public sector. He was an advocate of separating politics and administration. He argued that there should be two distinct areas of governmental function: administration and policy making. In 1933, he became the director of the Commission of Inquiry on Public Service Personnel. He embarked on a study investigating the conditions of public service and produced a report that reflected his findings. In that report, he criticized the conditions that surround public service and the quality of public servants. He made several recommendations to remedy conditions, including merit-based recruitment and promotion. His recommendations received considerable attention and were used to bring change into civil service employment. He also worked with the President's Commission on Administrative Management from 1936 to 1938.

He believed in a generic approach to management and argued that there is a body of knowledge that can be attributed to the advancement of the science of management. Therefore, his writing deals with the theory of administration rather than that of public organization. However, his main concern was making organizations (public and private) work more efficiently and effectively. His ideas were influenced by his experiences at public agencies and by the works of Frederick W. Taylor and Henry Ford. They developed the classical theory of organization or "administrative management theory." His first major work with Lyndell Urwick was a collection of edited work titled *Papers on the Science of Administration*, which was published in 1937. His work is the reflection of the influence of the classical approach to administration with emphasis on organizational structure and function. Although he developed several theories on administration, he totally ignored the role of employees and considered the main function of management the proper design of the organizational structure. Among a number of principles that were introduced by the classical theorists, Gulick paid special attention to the "division of labor" and considered it the most important base for organizations. He believes that "because men differ in nature, capacity and skill, and gain greatly in dexterity by specialization," their tasks should be divided to take advantage of the most talented and experienced employees. His second emphasis is on the "coordination of work," or the process of bringing together what was divided to serve the ultimate goal of the organization. He suggests two primary ways to co-ordinate:

1. By organization, that is, by interrelating the subdivisions of work by allotting them to men who are placed in a structure of authority, so that the work may be coordinated by orders of supervisors to subordinates, reaching from the top to the bottom of the entire enterprise.
2. By dominance of an idea—that is, the development of intelligent singleness of purpose in the minds and wills of those who are working together as a group, so that each worker will, of his own accord, fit his task into the whole with skill and enthusiasm. (Gulick and Urwick 1937, 5–6)

Finally, he emphasizes the significance of organizational patterns to deal with the overall view of an organization and fix the emphasis to deal with everyday organizational problems. He argues that "in any practical situation, the problem of organization must be approached from both the top and bottom." However, he places a great deal of emphasis on the role of the executive branch in organizations. His emphasis on the role of the chief executive is derived from the principle of "unity of command." He believes that there must be a concentration of power in the chief executive. He contends that "in periods of change, government must strengthen those agencies which deal with administrative management, that is, with coordination, with planning, with personnel, with fiscal control, and with research. These services constitute the brain and will of any enterprise." The job of the chief executive is summarized in his acronym POSDCORB: Planning, Organizing, Staffing, Directing, Co-ordinating, Reporting, and Budgeting. The major goal of developing these functions was to increase the efficiency of organizations.

In his analysis of organizational structure, he believes that organizations should be established and structured based on their main functions. His theory of departmentalization suggests four main parts that can be used to divide work and create different departments: purpose (function), process, place, and clientele (person).

BIBLIOGRAPHY

Works by Luther Gulick

Gulick, L., F. Biddle, L. Wolman, et al. *Wharton Assembly Addresses, 1936*. Philadelphia: University of Pennsylvania Press, 1936.

Gulick, L., and L. Fitch. *Making Democracy Work*. Berkeley: Institute of Governmental Studies, University of California at Berkeley, 1991.

Gulick, L., and L. Urwick. "Notes on the Theory of Organization." In *Papers on the Science of Administration*, ed. L. Gulick and L. Urwick. New York: Institute of Public Administration, 1937.

———, eds. *Papers on the Science of Administration*. New York: Institute of Public Administration, 1937.

Lowden, F. O., and L. Gulick. *Liquor Control: Principles, Model Law. A Report of the Committee on Liquor Legislation of the National Municipal League.* New York: National Municipal League, 1934.

Works about Luther Gulick

Body, Mind, and Spirit. Sound recording. Crofton, MD: Recorded Resources Corp., 1985.
Etzioni, A. *Modern Organizations.* New Delhi, India: New Delhi Press, 1965.
Gathrop, L. C. *Bureaucratic Behavior in the Executive Branch.* New York: Free Press, 1969.
Gulick, C. V. *The Luther Gulick Camps on Lake Sebago.* Boston, MA: C. V. Gulick, 1921.
Gvishiani, D. *Organizations and Management.* Moscow: Progress Publishers, 1972.
Jarrett, H., ed. *Perspectives on Conservation: Essays on America's Natural Resources, by John Kenneth Galbraith [and others].* Baltimore: Johns Hopkins Press, 1958.
Luther Gulick: Wharton Assembly Addresses, 1936–38. Philadelphia: University of Pennsylvania Press, 1936–1938.
The Luther Gulick Camps, South Casco, Maine. Andover, NH: The Luther Gulick Camps, 1949–1951.
Public Authorities: A Background Compilation of Articles, Position Papers, and Data on Public Authorities as a Governance Mechanism and Their Application in the City of Jacksonville, Florida. Jacksonville, FL: Jacksonville Council on Citizen Involvement, 1978.
Schorr, P., ed. *Critical Cornerstones of Public Administration.* Boston, MA: Oelgeschlager, Gunn & Hain, 1985.
Shafritz, J. M., and A. C. Hyde, eds. *Classics of Public Administration.* Pacific Grove, CA: Brooks/Cole Pub. Co., 1992.
Subramanian, V. "The Classical Organization Theory and Its Critics." *Public Administration Review*, Winter 1966, 435–442.
Wren, D. *The Evolution of Management Thought.* New York: Roland Press, 1972.

HERZBERG, FREDERICK (b. 1923, Lynn, MA), clinical psychologist; professor of management

Falling under the category of content theories, Herzberg's research is considered some of the most academically and practically useful in the literature. Known for their emphasis on organizational environments that lend themselves to the satisfaction of employee needs, content models have universal appeal. Overlapping the humanist school of organization theory, content theories suggest that intrinsic or internal dimensions are primary motivators in satisfying organizational members.

The humanistic model posits two arguments: that organizations have the responsibility of meeting the needs of their members and that when worker needs are met, production will increase. Humanists attempt to determine the linkage between worker satisfaction and production. In other words, they suggest that organizations that satisfy human needs create work situations of high productivity.

The humanistic model's assumptions—that work was central to the life of workers; that work could meet the intrinsic needs of workers; and that workers seek to satisfy both on-the-job and off-the-job needs—are reflected in other theories, such as Theory Y, System 4, Self-actualization, and Intrinsic Motivation Theory, all of which link the satisfaction of human needs with the satisfaction of organizational needs.

Based on respondents' recollections of situations resulting in job satisfaction and dissatisfaction in his study of the subject in a Pittsburgh company, Herzberg found that distinct factors account for satisfaction and dissatisfaction on the job. Dichotomizing organizational needs into two types—"motivators" and "hygienic"—his two-factor model of job satisfaction suggests that while the former are foremost predictors of job satisfaction and high work performance, the latter are correlated with job dissatisfaction. In a study of both American and Korean workers, the two-factor theory of motivation was found to have equal applicability.

According to Herzberg, hygiene factors, also called "extrinsic" factors or "dissatisfiers," include factors such as pay, working conditions, peer relations, security, and company policies. Motivators, or the "intrinsic" dimensions of the model, are exemplified by personal advancement, growth and development, recognition, and the opportunities to participate in organizational decision making and to self-actualize.

Before Herzberg's research, motivation theory, as well as the practice of organizational motivation, emphasized extrinsic factors. Herzberg offers managers an opportunity to differentiate among organizational dimensions. However, his research is not without criticism. Among them is the claim that his methodology lacks empirical rigor and consistency of results when replicated. For example, in some situations while pay resulted in satisfaction, it generated feelings of dissatisfaction in other situations. Another reported fault is that the underlying theory does not consider individual differences.

Herzberg's two-factor theory of motivation carries several implications. The theory directs managers to focus on intrinsic factors, such as participatory decision making and recognition, to raise motivation and subsequently job satisfaction. On the other hand, extrinsic or hygiene factors, such as status, organization policies and procedures, and pay, should be deemphasized in order to avoid dissatisfaction. In spite of some disconfirming evidence, Herzberg's impact on the notion of job design remains significant.

BIBLIOGRAPHY

Works by Frederick Herzberg

Herzberg, F. *Work and the Nature of Man*. Cleveland, OH: Thomas Crowell, 1966; Cleveland, OH: World Publishing, 1967.

————. *The Managerial Choice: To Be Efficient and to Be Human*. Homewood, IL: Dow Jones–Irwin, 1976.

Herzberg, F., B. Mausner, and B. Snyderman. *The Motivation to Work*. New York: John Wiley and Sons, 1959.

Work about Frederick Herzberg

Ewen, R. B., P. C. Smith, C. L. Hulin, and E. A. Locke. "An Empirical Test of the Herzberg Two-Factor Theory." *Journal of Applied Psychology*, 50, 1966, 544–550.

JANIS, IRVING L. (b. 1918, Buffalo, NY; d. 1990, Santa Rosa, CA), psychologist; public servant; theorist; fellow

Janis received a B.S. from the University of Chicago in 1939 and an M.A. in 1940. He later attended Columbia University and obtained a Ph.D. in 1948. He then attended New York Psychoanalytic Institute for his postdoctoral study and was graduated in 1953. His major area of concentration was in experimental methods and psychological research. He became a research assistant at the Library of Congress in 1941 and a senior social science analyst at the U.S. Department of Justice from 1941 to 1943. Later he served on the U.S. Army Research Board from 1943 to 1945. He joined the faculty of Yale University in 1947 to teach psychology, and in 1985, he became professor emeritus there. He also taught at the University of California at Berkeley in 1985. He received several awards for educational achievements, including the American Academy of Arts and Sciences Award, the Hofheimer Prize of the American Psychiatric Association, and the Fulbright Award.

Janis's major contribution has been in the area of group dynamics, group decision making, and the concept of "groupthink." In order to develop his theory of groupthink, he studied several cases of governmental decisions that were either very successful or absolute failures. He uses the term "groupthink" to explain an atmosphere that is created by the members of a group to assure a great deal of conformity and obedience. It controls all aspects of the member's life, including the thinking process. The group develops a closed system by separating itself from its environment, which is considered detrimental to the needs and goals of the group. In the decision-making process, the group usually makes irrational decisions because of the fear of nonconformity among the members.

According to Janis, the decision makers who are influenced by groupthink do not evaluate alternatives in reaching decisions. Therefore, he used the groupthink theory to indicate that most of the decisions that are made by public officials who act as groups can lead to irrational actions. In any group decision making, decisions made under pressure are going to cause many faulty outcomes. In other words, groupthink is detrimental to the decision-making process. He observes that there are some signs that signal the existence of groupthink during the decision-making process. One is the avoidance of any disagreement with leadership or among group members. Harmony and complete agreement are essential on important issues. Members of the decision-making group simply lose their ability to think critically and independently. In an atmosphere of irrationality and submission, leaders are able to abuse their power and create an inhumane atmosphere. Other symptoms that can be used to identify the existence of groupthink include invulnerability, irrationality, stereotypes, pressure, self-censorship, and mind-guards. Members simply develop a naive image of reality and ignore external factors that might affect their decisions. Therefore, whenever groups make decisions, there is always the danger of the effect of groupthink and hence the possibility of faulty decisions.

Janis's work on group behavior extends to many other areas, including the development of theories of group identification problems in organizations. He studies how groups rally together and how group cohesiveness increases due to external factors and threats. He indicates that group values, which usually emanate from the leader, socialize group members and give them a point of identification. He notes that a form of "postponed obedience" occurs after the loss of the leader, and the members often develop unconscious and even stronger adherence to the ideals of their lost leader. He extends his studies on society and holds that the role of television is a major contributor to personal decision making in one's life. He argues that when people face personal problems in lifestyle, marriage, career, and so on, they identify with television events and make decisions accordingly.

BIBLIOGRAPHY

Works by Irving L. Janis

Janis, I. L. *Group Dynamics: Research and Theory*. New York: Harper and Row, 1968.

———. *Adaptive Personality Changes Resulting from Stressful Episodes*. New York: Harcourt, Brace, and World, 1969.

———. *The Influence of Television on Personal Decision-Making*. Hillsdale, NJ: Erlbaum, 1980.

———. *Stress, Attitude, and Decisions: Selected Papers*. New York: Praeger, 1982.

———. *Short-Term Counseling: Guidelines Based on Recent Research*. New Haven, CT: Yale University Press, 1983.

Janis, I. L., and D. Wheeler. *A Practical Guide for Making Decisions*. New York: Free Press, 1980.

Work about Irving L. Janis

Neck, C., and G. Moorhead. "Groupthink Remodeled: The Importance of Leadership, Time Pressure, and Methodical Decision-Making Procedure." *Human Relations*, 85, 1995, 537–567.

KAHN, ROBERT L. (March 1918, Detroit, MI), public servant; professor; high school teacher

Kahn attended the University of Michigan and received a B.A. in English (1939) and one year later received a Master of Arts in the same field. He continued his graduate work at the University of Michigan in social psychology and received a Ph.D. in 1952. His main area of study was organizational psychology, including factors affecting organizational life such as conflict and stress in the workplace. He was active in many organizations, including the American Psychological Association (1954–1956); Society for the Psychological Study of Social Issues (1955–1958), serving as president from 1970 to 1971; American Statistical Association; Michigan Psychological Association; and National Training Laboratories. He also received many awards and grants for his contributions to the science of social psychology, including the American College of Hospital Administrators Award in 1968.

Kahn taught high school while he was attending the University of Michigan and working on his graduate studies. He joined the U.S. Bureau of the Census as the state supervisor and later became the acting chief of the division (1942–1948). He accepted a teaching position at the University of Michigan (Survey Research Center) in 1948. In this capacity, he worked with Daniel Katz, with whom he wrote many books and articles. While working at the University of Michigan in the area of social psychology, he also took visiting professorships at the Massachusetts Institute of Technology (1965–1966) and Cambridge University (1969–1970).

Kahn's major work in "systems theory" was accomplished in cooperation with Daniel Katz. They wrote extensively on the "open system theory," which originated with Floyd H. Allport's "general theory of event-system." As a social psychologist, Kahn tries to understand human organizations and predict future behavior in relation to their functions and norms. He believes that an organization is a social system that has certain characteristics and is a manifestation of the goals of its founders, and individuals who work in that system have their own values and personal goals that might be different from the goals of the organization. In addition, he notes that organizations are involved with exchange of information with their environment for their own survival. Therefore, he contends that in order to determine an organization's functions the researcher has to study the link between the organization and its environment. This is an exchange function that is composed of input, output, and feedback. Therefore, the systems theory's main concern is the relationship between the different subsystems (organs) that compose the system. It assumes a dynamic cycle of the giving and receiving of energy between a system and its environment.

Most of Kahn's writing is based on applied research studies, surveys, and interviews. He developed certain characteristics to describe open systems. An open system (1) receives energy from its environment, (2) transforms the received energy, (3) exports the transformed energy to the external environment as a form of output, (4) exchanges energy continuous in a cyclical pattern, (5) measures the uncertainty of events via negative entropy (the higher the entropy, the higher the uncertainty), (6) contains a feedback mechanism to inform the system of its overall performance, (7) maintains a state of equilibrium, due to constant exchange of energy (dynamic homeostasis), (8) moves toward more specialized functions as opposed to diffused functions (differentiation), and (9) reaches the same final condition through different paths (equifinality).

Through his writings, Kahn investigates findings on organizational behavior and incorporates them into his open system theory. A field study of six large industrial plants demonstrated the effects of environment on the mental health of employees. According to Kahn, the results indicate that there are two main sources of organizational stress that affect employees. One he calls "role conflict" and the other "role ambiguity." He explains how stressful environments influence organizational productivity and the behavior of individuals. According to him, individuals respond to stressful situations differently. In 1953, he conducted a study with Daniel Katz at the University of Chicago to study the relationship between organizational productivity and managerial supervision. This study was conducted in four different industries including railroading, tractor, manufacturing, and insurance. They found that there is a direct correlation between the time that managers spend on supervising employees and organizational productivity. Therefore, they became advocates for effective management to ensure the success of organizations as well as the building of employee morale.

BIBLIOGRAPHY

Works by Robert L. Kahn

Kahn, R. L. *The Dynamics of Interviewing: Theory, Technique, and Cases.* New York: John Wiley and Sons, 1957.
————. *Organizational Stress: Studies in Role Conflict and Ambiguity.* New York: John Wiley and Sons, 1965.
————. "Violent Man: Who Buys Bloodshed and Why." *Psychology Today*, 6, June 1972, 82–84.
————. "Organizational Development: Some Problems and Proposals." *Journal of Applied Behavioral Science*, 10, 1974, 485–502.
————. *Work and Health.* New York: Wiley and Sons, 1981.
————. "Leading Indicators and the Law." *Detroit College of Law Review*, December 1983, 1311–1315.
————. "Productive Behavior: Assessment, Determinants, and Effects." *Journal of the American Geriatrics Society*, December 1983, 750–757.

————. "Productive Behavior through the Life Course: An Essay on the Quality of Life." *Human Resource Management*, 23, March 1984, 5–22.

————. "Alternatives to Current Work and Leisure Styles Require Innovating, Experimenting." *Business and Health*, 1, September 1984, 59–60.

Kahn, R. L., and C. F. Cannell. *The Dynamics of Interviewing*. New York: Academic Press, 1957.

Kahn, R. L., and D. Katz. "Leadership Practices in Relation to Productivity and Morale." In *Group Dynamics*, ed. D. Cartwright and A. Zander. Evanston, IL: Row, Peterson, 1953.

————. *The Social Psychology of Organizations*. New York: John Wiley and Sons, 1966.

Works about Robert L. Kahn

Boulding, E., and R. L. Kahn. *Power and Conflict in Organizations*. New York: Basic Books, 1964.

Katz, D., R. L. Kahn, and J. S. Adams, eds. *The Study of Organizations*. San Francisco, CA: Jossey-Bass, 1980.

KATZ, DANIEL (b. July 1903, Trenton, NJ; d. February 28, 1994, Ann Arbor, MI), sociologist; social psychologist; university professor

Katz received a B.A. in sociology from the State University of New York at Buffalo in 1925. He attended Syracuse University to study social psychology and received a Master of Arts in 1926 and a Ph.D. in 1928. He was a member of the Fulbright Committee on International Exchange of Scholars and also the American Council for Behavioral Sciences. He served as the president of the Society for the Psychological Study of Social Issues during 1949 and 1950 and was a member of the board of directors of the American Psychological Association from 1960 to 1963. He was recognized for his outstanding work in social psychology and received many awards including the Kurt Lewin Memorial Award for his contribution to social research in 1965. He also received the Gold Medal Award of the American Psychological Foundation in 1973. He has contributed editorially to several journals, including the *Journal of Abnormal Psychology* (1962–1964) and the *Journal of Personality and Social Psychology* (1964–1967).

In his research methodology, he utilizes survey research to clarify many social problems including nationalism and varying forms of prejudice. He taught psychology at Princeton University from 1928 to 1943. He conducted several famous studies including a study with Kenneth Barely in 1935 that dealt with social prejudices; he later published a book with Richard L. Schank, *Social Psychology*, that dealt with a similar concept. In 1943 he moved to Brooklyn College of the City University of New York (Brooklyn College) where he became the chair of the Department of Psychology. He joined a research organization at Brooklyn College that was affiliated with the Department of Agriculture and headed by Renis Likert. He later joined the Office of War Information where he studied the morale of wartime soldiers and conducted a survey of the psychological effects of bombing on the civilian population for the United States of Strategic Bombing Survey (1945).

He joined the University of Michigan to teach psychology in 1947 and chaired the Survey Research Center from 1945 to 1950. He helped establish "organizational psychology" as a doctoral field in the Department of Psychology. He taught at the University of Michigan from 1947 to 1973 as a professor of psychology and became professor emeritus in 1973. He was also a visiting professor at the University of Aarhus, Denmark, in 1971–1972.

Through his association and work with Robert Kahn, he constructed a comprehensive theory of organizations. Their emphasis was on people working in organizations and their states of mind. They put great emphasis on employees and argued that their needs should be critical if organizations are to be productive. They also studied organizations from a systems theory perspective. Systems theory views organizations as complex compositions of subsystems; each subsystem contributes to the working of the whole. They introduced the concept of "open system theory," which emphasizes the relationship between organizations and their environment as a constant interaction. They argue that if organizations are to survive and avoid "entropy," they have to be responsive to their environment. They attempt to apply this theory to different issues that arise within organizations as well. They explain the role of people in organizations and how they try to adjust to environmental change by generating "throughputs."

Katz also tackles major organizational issues including decision making, motivation, leadership, and more important, communication. He believes that communication, which is the exchange of information through a social process, is key to the functioning of any social system or organization. Communication is thus a social process of the broadest relevance in the functioning of any group, organization, and society. He also emphasizes the importance of the organizational roles that are assigned to everyone in an organization. He argues that organizations maintain their stability and predictability by using "patterned recurrences" of certain acts with organizationally assigned roles to members. In his judgment, those roles become more important than individual members in relation to an organization's operation.

In 1953, Katz and Kahn conducted a study at the University of Michigan to study the supervisors and managers of several industries including railroading, manufacturing, and insurance. The main task of this study was to understand the effect of managerial functions on the productivity of those industries. They measured the relationship between the productivity and the time that those managers spent on their jobs. The results indicated that management and supervision have a positive effect on the productivity of those industries. In other words, the more time supervisors spend with their employees, the more productive the organization will be. Using this study, they developed several theories on leadership and morale building in organizations.

BIBLIOGRAPHY

Works by Daniel Katz

Katz, D. "Employee Groups: What Motivates Them and How They Perform." *Advanced Management*, September 1949, 1–6.

———. "Introduction to the Issue: Human Relations Research in Large Organizations." *Journal of Social Issues*, 7, 1951, 4–7.

———. "Satisfaction and Deprivation in Industrial Life." In *Industrial Conflict*, ed. A. Kornhauser. New York: McGraw-Hill, 1954.

———. "Nationalism and Strategies of International Conflict Resolution." In *International Behavior: A Social-Psychological Analysis*, ed. H. C. Kelman. New York: Holt, Rinehart and Winston, 1965.

———. *Bureaucratic Encounters: A Pilot Study in the Evaluation of Government Services*. Ann Arbor: Survey Research Center, University of Michigan, 1975.

Katz, D., and R. L. Kahn. *The Social Psychology of Organizational Change*. New York: John Wiley and Sons, 1966.

Katz, D., R. L. Kahn, and J. S. Adams, eds. *The Study of Organizations*. San Francisco, CA: Jossey-Bass, 1980.

Katz, D., and R. L. Schank. *Social Psychology*. New York: John Wiley and Sons, 1938.

Works about Daniel Katz

Allport, F. H., and D. Katz. *Student's Attitude*. Syracuse, NY: Craftsman Press, 1931.

Becker, T. L., ed. *Political Trials*. Indianapolis; Bobbs-Merrill, 1971.

Childs, H. L., and J. B. Whitton, eds. *Propaganda by Short Wave*. Princeton, NJ: Princeton University Press, 1942.

Executive Personality and Job Success. Microform. New York: American Management Association, 1948.

Gottfried, D. *Essays on the American Constitution: A Commemorative Volume in Honor of Alpheus T. Mason*. Englewood Cliffs, NJ: Prentice-Hall, 1964.

Guetzkow, H., ed. *Groups, Leadership and Men: Research in Human Relations*. Pittsburgh: Carnegie Press, 1951.

Kahn, R. L., and D. Katz. "Leadership Practices in Relation to Productivity and Morale." In *Group Dynamics*, ed. D. Cartwright and A. Zander. Evanston, IL: Row, Peterson, 1953.

Knutson, J. N., ed. *Handbook of Political Psychology*. San Francisco: Jossey-Bass, 1973.

Pratkanis, A. R., S. J. Breckler, and A. G. Greenwald, eds. *Attitude Structure and Function*. Hillsdale, NJ: L. Erlbaum Associates, 1989.

Research on Human Relations in Administration. Conference of the American Society for Public Administration, n.p., 1949.

Ross, A. M., and H. Hill, eds. *Employment, Race, and Poverty*. New York: Harcourt, Brace & World, 1967.

Shafritz, J. M., and A. C. Hyde, eds. *Classics of Public Administration*. Pacific Grove, CA: Brooks/Cole, 1992.

KAUFMAN, HERBERT (b. 1922, New York, NY), political scientist; research associate; university professor; consultant; board member

Born to Benjamin Harry and Gertrude Kaufman, Herbert Kaufman's academic training centered in New York City. As current head of the Brookings Institution, he was trained in the field of political science. He received a B.S. from City College of the City University in New York in 1942. In 1946 Kaufman received an M.A. from Columbia University and in 1950 a Ph.D. from the same university.

Kaufman's research career began in 1948 as a research associate at the Institute of Public Administration in New York City. He served as a lecturer in government for New York City from 1951 to 1953. He began an assistant professorship at Yale University in 1953 and became associate professor and then professor of political science in 1963. He became chair of the department in 1964. He served as lecturer at the University of Alabama in 1970. Other academic appointments included a visiting scholar's position at the Russell Sage Foundation and the Brookings Institution and professor of American politics at Boston College. Kaufman has also served on a number of commissions and boards, as well as in several consultant roles, such as the U.S. Bureau of the Budget and the New York State Health Department. He served in the U.S. Army from 1942 to 1946.

During the 1960s and 1970s, Kaufman's publications on administrative reorganization made groundbreaking contributions to classical organization theory. Concern for the role of government response to social problems informs his analyses of federal bureaucracy. Kaufman's models also consider related issues, such as the "bureaucratic fear" of political constituents and the accountability of power structures.

Kaufman outlined principles of administrative reorganization, four of which regard centralization of authority, for example, the 1965 creation of the Office of Civil Rights under the Department of Health, Education, and Welfare, and three that regard its decentralization, for example, the 1978 bifurcation of the Department of Health, Education, and Welfare. These principles include the following: grouping related functions under one command; granting extensive reorganizational powers to elected or appointed officials; insulating career public servants from political changes; and expanding opportunities for public participation. Kaufman's scholarship reflects consciousness of American social changes in the areas of war, racial conflict, and environmental concerns.

In *Time, Chance, and Organizations*, Kaufman proposes that the relationship between an organization and its environment can be likened to prebiological evolution. Kaufman hypothesizes that the success of organizations to effectively respond and survive does not depend on leadership ability, adaptability, or intelligence and other learned behaviors but rather on a probability function. Rejecting the idea that rationality drives organization survival in an environment, Kaufman argues that while environmental change is "volatile," comparable organization change is impossible. Survival in the organization, he explains, is most likely due to chance. Kaufman's assertion that randomness plays a greater role in survival success than does rationality is a departure from the traditional leadership theories.

Using an ecological analogy to underscore the benefits of natural selection, Kaufman argues for organizational diversity, which can occur only if organizational deaths are allowed to happen, that is, allowed to be tested by a natural selection of organizational survival.

Kaufman explains that the death of an organization is a part of an organizational evolution. The longevity rate among organizations is low, he notes, especially among younger organizations. He cites that beginning in the 1920s organizational deaths numbered twenty-seven over a fifty-year period in the federal government alone.

According to Kaufman, short of complete organizational dissolution, reorganization can take several forms. Kaufman offers seven prescriptions on reorganization in the executive branch: reducing the span of control in program management; functional grouping; enlargement of the executive staff; empowerment of elected and appointed executives with reorganization discretion; ensuring that career bureaucracts can carry out their responsibilities in an apolitical fashion; administrative decentralization; and a widening of public participation in administrative decisions. Although his model has drawn criticism regarding its empirical validity, his analysis of organization ecology based on resource exchanges between organization and environment continues to find support.

Following the completition of his field study of the U.S. Forest Service, Kaufman published *The Forest Ranger: A Study in Administrative Behavior* in 1960. It remains a seminal public administration study of administrative behavior. Kaufman examines problems of formal procedures faced by the U.S. Forest Service. He concludes that punishment, rather than professionalism, prohibits the integration of policies—for example, rules, clearance procedures, and budgeting. When this is the case, the practices of a decentralized field management fragment administration and discourage conformity among forest rangers. The work is primarily a descriptive analysis of a government organization's fight to overcome the constraints of massive organizations.

In *Administrative Feedback*, coauthored in 1973 with Michael Couzens, Kaufman diagnoses and addresses a number of bureaucratic problems within nine federal agencies. The study examines the effects of subordinate noncompliance in the workplace. It outlines formal and informal sources top-level officials have for evaluating organizational fragmentation, signs of management crisis, and the behavior of subordinates.

Kaufman provides a framework for analyzing principal, though conflicting, goals in public personnel administration. He argues that in the continuing evolution of public administration there is a pattern of cylical values that continually resurface—each taking a turn in dominating administrative thinking. According to Kaufman, the values—representativeness, neutral competence, and executive leadership—are reflected in different time periods in the development of public personnel administration.

The early search for representativeness is rooted in colonialism. Emphasis during the period was on accountability of public administrators to public policies formulated by elected representatives. The quest for administrative representativeness is also reflective of practices in the 1970s. During much of this decade, bureaucracts played the role of policy advocates—a role that removed them from executive control. Administrative emphasis, therefore, was shared with the search for neutral competence. Having roots in the 1800s in which the spoils system contributed to the undermining of objective administrative decisions, the search for neutral competence was an effort to address the corrupt personnel and legislative practices in the 1800s by implementing an apolitical system of administration.

In the late 1970s and early 1980s, a challenge to neutral competence was asserted by conservative think tanks in an effort to reestablish executive control as a driving force of policy initiatives. These groups called for bureaucratic support of presidential policy positions, and not neutral competence—in their interpretation, a blind execution of the law that does not recognize the executive control of personnel practices. Indeed, Kaufman's interpretation of neutral competence is based on similar thinking. According to Kaufman, neutral competence involves the implementation of programs legitimated by elected individuals.

The search for executive leadership grew out of the concern that personnel theory should consider issues such as budgeting and reorganization.

BIBLIOGRAPHY

Works by Herbert Kaufman

Kaufman, H. *The New York City Health Centers.* New York: Inter-University Case
     Program, 1952.
———. "Emerging Conflicts in the Doctrines of Public Administration." *American
     Political Science Review,* 50, 4, December 1956, 1057–1073.
———. *The Forest Ranger: A Study in Administrative Behavior.* Baltimore: Johns
     Hopkins University Press, 1960.

———. *Politics and Policies in State and Local Governments*. Englewood Cliffs, NJ: Prentice-Hall, 1963.

———. *The Limits of Organizational Change*. Tuscaloosa: University of Alabama Press, 1971.

———. *The Natural History of Human Organizations*. Washington, DC: Brookings Institution, 1975.

———. *Are Government Organizations Immortal?* Washington, DC: Brookings Institution, 1976.

———. *Red Tape, Its Origins, Uses and Abuses*. Washington, DC: Brookings Institution, 1977.

———. *The Administrative Behavior of Federal Bureau Chiefs*. Washington, DC: Brookings Institution, 1981.

———. "Fear of Bureaucracy: A Raging Pandemic." *Public Administration Review*, 41, 1, January–February 1981, 1–9.

———. *Time, Chance, and Organizations: Natural Selection in a Perilous Environment*. Chatham, NJ: Chatham House, 1985.

Kaufman, H., and M. Couzens. *Administrative Feedback: Monitoring Subordinates' Behavior*. Washington, DC: Brookings Institution, 1973.

Sayre, W., and H. Kaufman. *Governing New York City: Politics in the Metropolis*. New York: Russell Sage Foundation, 1960.

KEY, VALDIMER ORLANDO (b. March 13, 1908, Austin, TX; d. 1963), political scientist; university professor

The boy born Valdimer Orlando in Austin spent his youth in Lamesa, West Texas. From his youth, V. O. Key was analytical and sharply intuitive. Following his father's lead, Key's interest in political science stemmed from his father's interest in local politics. Key attended McMary College in Abilene from 1925 to 1927 and completed his B.A. at the University of Texas in 1929. In 1934, Key completed his Ph.D. at the University of Chicago. His doctoral dissertation, "The Techniques of Political Graft in the United States," examined politics as a form of social influence. His later works, particularly *Southern Politics* (1949), which won the 1949 Woodrow Wilson Foundation Award of American Political Science, and the textbook *Politics, Parties and Pressure Groups* (1942), are widely used in the classroom.

Key readily earned acknowledgment in academic circles as the leading student of American politics in his generation. He is the recipient of the Rockefeller Foundation grant for the study on electoral process in the South. *Southern Politics*, during the year of its distribution, earned high praise for both depth and readibility. The study, which examined the prevailing practices of the American South at midcentury, capitalized on the significance of African Americans in the South and the undemocratic, one-party politics beholden to each former Confederate state. Critics were willing to overlook Key's omission of solutions to the problem and settled on his major conclusion that "in the final analysis the peculiarities of southern white politics come from the impact of the black race."

Overall, Key's approach to issues of democratic government is an empirical one. His research is known to examine three areas of political science: party politics, public administration, and public opinion. Key's contributions have led to the increased specialization of political scientific descriptions.

BIBLIOGRAPHY

Works by Valdimer Orlando Key

Key, V. O. *Politics, Parties and Pressure Groups*. New York: Crowell, 1942.
———. *Southern Politics in State and Nation*. New York: Alfred A. Knopf, 1949.
———. *A Primer of Statistics for Political Scientists*. New York: Crowell, 1954.
———. *American State Politics: An Introduction*. New York: Alfred A. Knopf, 1956.
———. *Public Opinion and American Democracy*. New York: Alfred A. Knopf, 1962.
Key, V. O., with W. M. Crouch. *The Initiative and the Referendum in California*. Berkeley: University of California Press, 1939.

Works about Valdimer Orlando Key

Rabin, J., ed. "Symposium on Budgeting." *New Directions in Public Administration Research*, 2, April 1989, 15–95.
Straussman, J. D. "V. O. Key's 'The Lack of a Budgetary Theory: Where Are We Now?' " *International Journal of Public Administration*, 7, 4, 1985, 345–374.

KRISLOV, SAMUEL (b. October 1929, Cleveland, OH), political scientist; editor; university professor; fellow

Krislov attended Western Reserve University (1947) before transferring to New York University and there received a B.A. (1951) and M.A. (1952). He later moved to Princeton University, where he obtained a Ph.D. in 1955. After graduation from Princeton University, he began his teaching career at the University of Vermont at Burlington (1955), and shortly after, he moved to New York City to teach at Hunter College (1955–1956) and the University of Oklahoma at Norman (1956–1959). In 1959 he transferred to East Lansing, Michigan, where he started a new teaching career at Michigan State University (1959–1964). His last move was to Minneapolis, where he began to teach in the Department of Political Science at the University of Minnesota in 1965 as a full professor.

He is the recipient of several grants and fellowships, including social science research grants, 1958, 1961; Ford Foundation International Relations grants, 1969; a Ford Faculty Fellowship, 1972–1973; a Guggenhein fellowship, 1979–1980; a Fulbright Research Award to the Netherlands, 1982–1983; and a Bush Fellowship, 1982–1983. He was the editor of *Law and Society* from 1963 to 1973 and has written frequently on forecasting the impact of legislation on courts.

His writing touches on many social issues of his time and underscores major deficiencies in our society. He believes that there are still institutionalized prejudices based on race in society and that this prejudice can only be eradicated through organizational commitment to change, which ensures equal treatment. He argues that public bureaucracy should spearhead the fight against racial prejudice. In other words, he suggests that government build a service that helps women and minorities gain access to jobs and promotions. Krislov argues that the passage of the Civil Service Act of 1883 was the major force in bringing the black population of the United States into the workforce. However, he argues that institutionalized prejudice did not allow for full realization of the merit system, because bringing about major organizational change is extremely difficult.

He believes that there is still a long way to the realization of substantive social equality. He reviews the history of the Office of Equal Employment Opportunity (EEO) and argues that in order for such agencies to be effective they should stand for and promote their ideals and goals vigorously. He analyzes the structure of EEO and believes that the decentralization scheme did not work well because it was based on the previous ineffective and faulty organization of the Civil Service Commission. He uses available data from studies done at state and local levels and argues that a structure that holds a chief executive responsible for the operation of an agency works best. He believes that EEO's policies are the result of two opposing forces: those who believe in the merit system and those who are in favor of "compensating policies" to "make up for" unfair practices of the past.

He deals with the question of bureaucratic image and argues that the public sector's image has been distorted and that there should be more emphasis on the positive aspect of it. He also believes that bureaucracy is a powerful tool in policy making, almost as powerful as the legislative branch of government. He contends that policy making is bureaucracy's everyday task. He also emphasizes the importance of using bureaucracy as a vehicle for social change and for gaining power by minority groups. Therefore, he suggests a representative bureaucracy, similar to the legislative body. In his judgment, a representative bureaucracy is a less elitist and less class-biased civil service. This is because bureaucracy by nature is the very essence of political power. Krislov argues that the EEO should not only promote minority employment but also pay attention to their position in the organizational hierarchy so that they have more effect on social policies. He distinguishes between equal opportunity and compensatory opportunity. In his judgment, equal opportunity implies that everyone be treated the same, whereas compensatory opportunity addresses historical injustices and attempts to make up for them. He holds that equal opportunity is politically more appealing to the majority of citizens than compensatory opportunity. He also addresses personnel issues and believes that job analysis can be utilized to compensate jobs fairly. However, according to Krislov, some concepts such as merit, reward, and equality (which are the determinants of compensatory policies) are politicized and become the source of conflict.

Krislov argues that representative bureaucracy stands for valuable ideals and implies that (1) everyone has equal representation in the political system and is able to influence it; (2) representation of minorities in the system makes them more loyal and willing to cooperate in the implementation of policies; (3) representation creates a sense of unity and increases the efficiency and effectiveness of the system; (4) public policies will be the reflection of the needs of all groups and therefore benefit everyone in society; and (5) it compensates for the lack of representation of minorities in other branches of government that are dominated by the majority.

He believes that our academic institutions are not responsive enough to the needs of political institutions and that the quality of our system of education is declining. For example, he emphasizes the importance of teaching regulatory process and administrative procedures. He argues that curricula have not given enough importance to the subject of administrative law. He has also conducted studies on American public opinion regarding the question of civil liberty. He believes that most Americans are in favor of civil liberties in general but on specific issues are more cautious and antilibertarian.

BIBLIOGRAPHY

Works by Samuel Krislov

Burkhart, J. A., S. Krislov, and L. Raymond. *The Clash of Issues: Reading and Problems in American Government*. Englewood Cliffs, NJ: Prentice-Hall, 1981.

Krislov, S. *The Politics of Regulation: A Reader*. Boston, MA: Houghton Mifflin, 1964.

———. *The Supreme Court in the Political System*. New York: Macmillan, 1965.

———. *The Negro in Federal Employment*. Minneapolis: University of Minnesota Press, 1967.

———. *Representative Bureaucracy*. Englewood Cliffs, NJ: Prentice-Hall, 1974.

———. *Projecting Legislative Impact on the Courts*. Washington, DC: National Academy of Science, 1980.

———. *Constitutional Law*. New York: Little, Brown, 1985.

Krislov, S., and D. H. Rosenbloom. *Representative Bureaucracy and the American Political System*. New York: Praeger, 1981.

Muslof, L. D., and S. Krislov. *The Politics of Regulation*. Boston, MA: Houghton Mifflin, 1964.

Works about Samuel Krislov

Gibbs, J. P., ed. *Social Control: Views from the Social Sciences*. Beverly Hills, CA: Sage, 1982.

International Political Science Association. Interim Meeting of the Research Committee on Comparative Judicial Studies. Microform (December 14, 1986). Center for the Study of Law and Society, University of California, Berkeley. Ottawa: IPSA, 1986.

———. IPSA Research Committee on Comparative Judicial Studies, Interim Meeting in Victoria, British Columbia, Canada (May 26–27, 1990). Microform. Ottawa: IPSA, 1990.

Kurland, P. B., ed. *The Supreme Court Review*. Chicago, IL: University of Chicago Press, 1968.

Ranney, A., ed. *Courts and the Political Process: Jack W. Peltason's Contributions to Political Science*. Berkeley: Institute of Governmental Studies Press, University of California, Berkeley, 1996.

Rosenbloom, D. H., and R. D. Schwartz, eds. *Handbook of Regulation and Administrative Law*. New York: Marcel Dekker, 1994.

Shafritz, J. M., and A. C. Hyde, eds. *Classics of Public Administration*. Fort Worth, TX: Harcourt Brace, 1992.

Silbey, J. H., ed. *Encyclopedia of the American Legislative System. Volume III: Studies of the Principal Structures, Processes, and Policies of Congress and the State Legislatures Since the Colonial Era*. New York, Toronto: C. Scribner's Sons, Maxwell Macmillan International, 1994.

Spitzer, S., and R. J. Simon, eds. *Research in Law Deviance and Social Control: A Research Annual, Vol. 4*. Greenwich, CT: JAI Press, 1982.

Swanson, C. R., and S. M. Talarico, eds. *Court Administration: Issues and Responses*. Athens: Carl Vinson Institute of Government, University of Georgia, 1987.

KUHN, THOMAS (b. July 18, 1922, Cincinnati, OH; d. June 19, 1996, Cambridge, MA), philosopher; historian; scientist; university professor

Kuhn taught at Harvard, Berkeley, and Princeton universities and later at the Massachusetts Institute of Technology (MIT), where he became professor emeritus. While he was at Harvard, he taught science and later taught the history of science in order to discover the main force behind scientific change. He primarily taught philosophy and the history of science at MIT. He served as the president of the History of Science Society and the Philosophy of Science Association.

Kuhn's ideas were influenced by Alexander Kyre, who was a science historian. Kuhn argues that progress in science is made through spurts of sometimes seemingly unrelated discovery rather than through an orderly progression. He contends that through construction of new paradigms, scientific breakthroughs have been achieved. In his judgment, a paradigm is a scientific achievement that is accepted by the community and provides a coherent guide and worldview for scientific inquiry.

Kuhn was able to relate social science and hard science to make sense of the reality of the world. He is famous for his concept of "paradigm," which was explained in his book *The Structure of Scientific Revolutions*. He believed that sciences are interrelated and affect each other in many different ways. According to Kuhn, a model of scientific inquiry is a consistent pattern and tradition of experimentation within different disciplines in the scientific community. He believes that development of paradigms does not occur incrementally but that different paradigms compete with each other to be adopted by scientists. The primary reason for the development of new paradigms is the discovery of anomalies in the existing paradigms. This creates the conflict that leads to the emergence of a new paradigm.

Kuhn argues that within every paradigm a set of taxonomic structures exists that pulls together the differing parts. When a paradigm changes, the whole taxonomy (new relationship) develops among the parts. Therefore, the terms of the old paradigm are no longer usable in the new paradigm, which is a holistic doctrine with a holistic structure. He contends that the new paradigm is not necessarily a better reflection of reality but is able to solve problems that are not solvable by the old paradigm. He argues that reality is a relative concept and that only within the context of paradigm can we find answers to our questions.

BIBLIOGRAPHY

Works by Thomas Kuhn

Kuhn, T. S. *The Structure of Scientific Revolutions*. 2nd ed. Chicago: University of Chicago Press, 1970.
———. *The Essential Tension*. Chicago: University of Chicago Press, 1977.

Works about Thomas Kuhn

Horwich, P. *Thomas Kuhn and the Nature of Science*. Cambridge: MIT Press, 1993.
Pollock, J. "Kuhn and Goodman: Revolutionary vs. Conservative Science." *Philosophical Studies*, November 1983, 376–394.

LASSWELL, HAROLD D. (b. February 13, 1902, Donnellson, IL; d. December 18, 1978, New York, NY), political scientist; university professor; fellow; consultant

Harold Lassell's parents were Rev. Linden Downey Lasswell, an Illinois Presbyterian minister, and Anna Prather, a former high school teacher. Following his graduation from Decatur High School in 1918, where he was valedictorian of his class, Lasswell entered the University of Chicago on scholarship. Here he was inducted into Phi Beta Kappa. He received both bachelor and doctorate degrees from the University of Chicago in 1922 and 1926, respectively.

In 1922 Lasswell began a sixteen-year teaching relationship with the University of Chicago: in 1922 as an assistant in the Political Science Department; in 1924 as an instructor; in 1927 as an assistant professor; and in 1932 as an associate professor. He left the University of Chicago in 1938 to teach at the Yale Law School as a visiting lecturer and later become a professor of law. In 1928 Lasswell served as a fellow at the Social Science Research Council of New York. He has held a number of consulting positions, including those in the Department of Agriculture and the Department of State and to Encyclopedia Britannica Films. In the latter position he was responsible for the development of educational films. In 1955 he was elected president of the American Political Science Association.

In his articulation of the "policy orientation" of social science, Lasswell posits that the evolution of the policy sciences is characterized by three dimensions: (1) multidisciplined, (2) contextual, and (3) problem oriented. He also posited his theory linking psychological factors and political behaviors. Having undergone psychoanalysis with an associate of Freud's while in Berlin on a fellowship, Lasswell's commitment to studying the linkages between psychological theory and political behavior was evidenced early in his career.

His interest in determining patterns of bureaucratic decision making and behaviors led him to investigate and typologize, in *Psychopathology and Politics*, the kinds of individuals who are attracted to public bureaucracies. Having reviewed the cases of mentally ill patients who were former decision makers in public bureaucracies, Lasswell discovered that behaviors of bureaucrats were driven more by informal, and often invisible, motives than organizational factors. The revelation that the major source of bureaucratic power is psychological conflicted with the classical school of thought that focuses on external factors, such as formal structure and hierarchy, as explaining bureaucratic behavior.

Lasswell's exploration of the role of psychological fundaments, such as personality traits, in the exercise of power in public organizations contributed to the recognition that nonrational factors are important in explaining bureaucratic decision making.

In *Politics: Who Gets What, When, and How*, Lassell suggests that individual concerns with security via income, respect, and safety form the basis of political behavior. He argues that competition among political actors for attainment of these goals impacts political actions.

BIBLIOGRAPHY

Works by Harold D. Lasswell

Arens, R., and H. D. Lasswell. *In Defense of Public Order: The Emerging Field of Sanction Law*. New York: Columbia University Press, 1961.

Arora, S. K., and H. D. Lasswell. *Political Communication: The Public Language of Political Elites in India and the United States*. New York: Holt, Rinehart and Winston, 1969.

Atkins, W. E., and H. D. Lasswell. *Labor Attitudes and Problems*. New York: Prentice-Hall, 1924.

Chen, L., and H. D. Lasswell. *Formosa, China, and the United Nations: Formosa in the World Community*. New York: St. Martin's Press, 1967.

Lasswell, H. D. *Democracy through Public Opinion*. Menasha, WI: George Banta Publishing, 1941.

————. *The Analysis of Political Behaviour: An Empirical Approach.* New York: Oxford University Press, 1949.

————. *Language of Politics: Studies in Quantitative Semantics.* New York: G. W. Stewart, 1949.

————. *National Security and Individual Freedom.* New York: McGraw-Hill, 1950.

————. *Power and Society: A Framework for Political Inquiry.* New Haven, CT: Yale University Press, 1950.

————. *Political Writings.* Glencoe, IL: Free Press, 1951.

————. *The World Revolution of Our Time: A Framework for Basic Policy and Research.* Stanford, CA: Stanford University Press, 1951.

————. *The Future of Political Science.* New York: Atherton Press, 1963.

————. *Politics: Who Gets What, When, and How.* New York: P. Smith, 1936, 1950; Cleveland, OH: Meridian Books, 1958, 1965.

————. *World Politics and Personal Insecurity.* New York: McGraw-Hill, 1935; Free Press, 1965.

————. *Psychopathology and Politics.* Chicago, IL: University of Chicago Press, 1930; 1977; New York: Viking Press, 1960, 1966.

————. *Essays on the Garrison State.* New Brunswick, NJ: Transaction Publishers, 1977.

————. *Harold D. Lasswell on Political Sociology.* Chicago: University of Chicago Press, 1977.

Lasswell, H. D., and D. Lerner, eds. *World Revolutionary Elites: Studies in Coercive Ideological Movements.* Cambridge, MA: MIT Press, 1965.

Lasswell, H. D., D. Lerner, and I. Pool. *The Comparative Study of Symbols: An Introduction.* Stanford, CA: Stanford University Press, 1952.

Lasswell, H. D., D. Lerner, and C. E. Rothwell. *The Comparative Study of Elites: An Introduction and Bibliography.* Stanford, CA: Stanford University Press, 1952.

Lasswell, H. D., and M. S. McDougal. *Jurisprudence for a Free Society: Studies in Law, Science, and Policy.* New Haven, CT: New Haven Press, 1992.

McDougal, M. S., H. D. Lasswell, and J. C. Miller. *The Interpretation of Agreements and World Public Order: Principles of Content and Procedure.* New Haven, CT: Yale University Press, 1967; Boston: Martinus Nijhoff Publishers, 1994.

Works about Harold D. Lasswell

Bell, W. "H. D. Lasswell and the Futures Field: Facts, Predictions, Values and the Policy Sciences." *Futures,* 25, 7, September 1993, 806–813.

Bozeman, B. " 'The Policy Orientation' Revisited." *The Bureaucrat,* 10, 1, Spring 1981, 51–53.

Czudnowski, M., and H. Eulau. *Elite Recruitment in Democratic Politics.* Beverly Hills: Sage Publishing, 1976.

Dorsey, G. L. "Agora: McDougal-Lasswell Redux." *American Journal of International Law,* 82, 1, January 1988, 41–50.

Eulah, H. *Politics, Self and Society: A Theme and Variations.* Cambridge: Harvard University Press, 1986.

Henry, N. "The Lasswellizer and I." *The Bureaucrat,* 10, 1, Spring 1981, 553–554.

Marvick, D. "The Work of Harold D. Lasswell: His Approach, Concerns, and Influence." *Political Behavior,* 2, 3, 1980, 219–229.

Stanley, J. "Harold Lasswell and the Idea of the Garrison State." *Society*, 33, 6, September–October 1996, 46–52.

Togerson, D. "Origins of the Policy Orientation: The Aesthetic Dimension of Lasswell's Political Division." *History of Political Thought*, 2, Summer 1990, 339–352.

Walker, S. G., and S. Lang. "The 'Garrison State Syndrome' in the Third World: A Research Note." *Journal of Political and Military Sociology*, 16, 1, Spring 1988, 105–116.

LAWLER, EDWARD E., III (b. June 16, 1938, Alexandria, VA), consultant; director; psychologist

Lawler received a B.A. from Brown University in psychology in 1960 and continued his graduate work at the University of California at Berkeley in the same discipline, receiving a Ph.D. in 1964. He joined the University of Southern California in 1978 and became the director of the Center for Effective Organizations in 1979. He also consults both private and public organizations concerning employee development, participation, compensation, and organizational change. He studies different aspects of organizations, including organizational change, compensation, productivity, employee behavior, performance appraisal, and participative management. His main emphasis is on employee involvement in the decision-making process, which ultimately will help the employees make the connection between individual ideas and organizational goals. Therefore, they are able to fuse their own goals with organizational goals and be more productive. According to Lawler, this can be accomplished through a decentralized and participatory system of management. He conducted a comprehensive study on the most successful companies in the United States with two other authors (Mohrman and Ledford, 1995) and found that they mainly rely on employee involvement and the use of Total Quality Management (TQM) in their organizations. He also emphasized the importance of change and adaption to new environmental realities, as well as to structural change and successful internal management for organizations.

In his analysis of organizations, he argues that the most successful organizations are high involvement. He recommends that to develop high-involvement strategies, organizations need to bring about major changes in many aspects including physical layout, managerial roles, staffing and personnel policies, training and development, information systems, and the reward system. His strongest emphasis is on bringing change and adaptation in organizations through flattening organizational structure and developing interpersonal relationships. In his judgment, each one of those areas has to be approached separately and modified. For example, concerning information systems, he believes that everyone in the organization should have access to the most up-to-date information concerning the direction of the organization and organizational objectives. Also, he argues that employee training and development can be achieved through proper job enrichment and by creating a less controlled environment in which employees are in more control of their own destiny and work. This is a form of empowering the employees and providing them with adequate control over their jobs and their schedule by allowing them to plan the completion of their own work. He believes that organizations should do away with organizational hierarchy in order to bring about more of a sense of equality in organizations. He also believes that in a high-involvement organization the reward system is directly related to performance. Therefore, the employee should perceive the reward system as equitable. He argues that employees' perceptions depend on three factors: the abilities and skills that employees have; the requirements of the jobs to be performed; and a sense of fairness in regard to the reward system and as compared to other employees in the organization.

He suggests that organizations adapt themselves to some of those changes, although he is realistic enough to accept that not all of his ideas can be operationalized in their entirety. His attention to organizational behavior and employee motivation led Lawler to the development of the "expectancy theory." In his book *Motivation in Work Organizations*, he explains four principles that underlie his theory.

1. People have preferences among the various outcomes that are potentially available to them.
2. People have expectations about the likelihood that an action (effort) on their part will lead to the intended behavior or performance.
3. People have experiences about the likelihood that certain outcomes will follow their behavior.
4. In any situation, the actions a person chooses to take are determined by the expectancies and the preferences that a person has at that time.

He argues that there are two principles at work in relation to the role of individuals in organizations. First is the internal belief that a person holds concerning the probability that he or she is able to perform the job that is assigned to him or her. The second principle is the belief concerning the occurrence of a certain outcome (reward) after the accomplishment of the job. The first relationship he terms $E \rightarrow P$, the expectancy that effort will result in certain performance. The second relationship he terms $P \rightarrow O$, which is the expectancy that performance will lead to certain outcome. According to him, motivation is the force that represents the sum of those two relationships. Therefore, in his expectancy theory he constructs a relationship between three major components that ultimately determine the job performance (effort, performance, and positive outcome). In his judgment, if the employee is assured that he or she is capable of performing the job and will be rewarded for it, he will be motivated to perform. Here he emphasizes the importance of the pay system and that it should be directly tied to performance. According to Lawler, each organization has to design a pay system that fits its needs, including fringe benefits, cafeteria benefits, merit raises, and so on. He values the individual employee and believes that the most important aspect of the employee-management relationship is close attention to employee needs.

Lawler also emphasizes the fairness of the reward system and its direct relationship to performance. He also indicates that the reward must be worthwhile for the employee to be motivated. In addition, he pays close attention to the organizational structure, pay structure, and job design and believes that they are important factors that have direct effect on employee motivation. He argues that an effective organization must strive for high performance, which will have a positive relationship in terms of employee satisfaction rather than the other way around. This way, organizations achieve their goals and individuals also receive job satisfaction. This is a win situation that leads to more employee satisfaction.

Lawler believes that organizational success depends on creating a balance or right combination (fit) among different factors that influence the operation. Those factors include the reward system, knowledge acquisition, power, and information. They should be balanced at all different levels of the organization. In addition, the organizational design and management system has to fit the strategic needs of the organization.

BIBLIOGRAPHY

Works by Edward E. Lawler III

Lawler, E. E., III. *Motivation in Work Organizations*. Monterey, CA: Brooks/Cole, 1973.

———. *High-Involvement Management: Participative Strategies for Improving Organizational Performances*. San Francisco, CA: Jossey-Bass, 1986.

———. *Strategies Pay: Aligning Organization Strategies and Pay Systems*. San Francisco, CA: Jossey-Bass, 1991.

———. *The Ultimate Advantage: Crafting the High-Involvement Organization*. San Francisco, CA: Jossey-Bass, 1992.

———. *From the Ground Up: Six Principles for Creating the New Logic Organizations*. San Francisco, CA: Jossey-Bass, 1996.

Lawler, E. E., III, S. A. Mohrman, and G. E. Ledford. *Creating High Performance Organizations: Surveyed Practices and Results of Employee Involvement and Total Quality Management in Fortune 1000 Companies*. San Francisco, CA: Jossey-Bass, 1995.

Lawler, E. E., III, and J. G. Rhode. *Information and Control in Organizations*. Pacific Palisades, CA: Goodyear, 1976.

Porter, L. W., and E. E. Lawler III. *Managerial Attitudes and Performance.* Home-
    wood, IL: Irwin-Dorsey, 1968.
Porter, L. W., E. E. Lawler III, and R. Heckman. *Behavior in Organizations.* New
    York: McGraw-Hill, 1975.

Work about Edward E. Lawler III

Respess, T. *Oral History of Edward Lawler: Interview with Mr. Edward Lawler, 18th
    March 1992.* Transcribed by T. Respess and Susan Howarton. Memphis,
    TN: Oral History Research Office, Memphis State University, 1992.

LIKERT, RENSIS (b. August 5, 1903, Cheyenne, WY; d. 1981), sociologist;
psychology professor; director

Rensis Likert's penchant for research has been well established since
he earned his Ph.D. from Columbia University in 1931. From 1935 to
1939, Likert was research director for the Life Insurance Agency Management Association while serving simultaneously as head of the Division of Program Surveys for the U.S. Bureau of Agricultural Economies
and director of the Morale Division of the U.S. Strategic Bombing Survey
until 1946. In 1956, at the University of Michigan, Likert founded the
Survey Research Center, which expanded into the Institute for Social
Research in 1957. Until 1970, he acted as director of the Center for Research on the Utilization of Scientific Knowledge, one of two organizations within the Institute for Social Research. Devoted to the analysis of
management practice in American business and government, the Institute conducted studies of industrial and commercial firms, transportation, and educational and health institutions. Since 1971, Likert has been
chairperson of the board of directors of Rensis Likert Associates, Inc.,
based in Ann Arbor, Michigan. Among Likert's numerous contributions
to public administration are considerable research efforts and methods,
psychological and sociological perspectives, and two extremely significant studies of organization.

Likert published *New Patterns of Management* in 1961 and thus filled a
major gap in the field of organizational development. Drawing on research collected at the University of Michigan's Institute for Social Research, Likert answers a call for empirical evidence substantiating the
efficacy of participatory management. It is important to note that this
volume comprises development trends now referred to as the Michigan
tradition, such as (1) a move toward increased specialization, (2) a move
toward studying executives as well as workers and supervisors, (3) a
move toward studying labor unions and volunteer organizations, and
(4) definite consideration of the first three issues in the context group's
location in the organizational structure.

Overall, Likert attributes managers' reluctant adaptation of participatory management to their focus on short-term financial gain and the
inability to assess human assets. Likert's analysis includes identification

of the forces that increase the pressure for high performance in American businesses.

Likert describes four effective organizational models, of which he determines "participative group" to be most appropriate. This model provides each member of the group with the means to channel personal values, needs, and goals that effectively translate into a specific organizational objective. Cooperative motivation is a central component of this system.

Finally, *New Patterns of Management* introduced the concepts for which Likert is noteworthy in the field of organizational development: the "linking pin" method of organization that he preferred and the "man to man" hierarchy he worked to dissolve. Likert believed that the "linking pin" model would destroy the traditional hurdles in most hierarchical systems and encourage organizational coherence through the multiple organization linkages that develop interaction-influence. Likert continues to develop the ideas in *New Patterns of Management* in a subsequent study aimed at managers: *The Human Organization: Its Management and Value* (1967).

The newer work, while recounting a significant portion of Institute research published in 1961, establishes an alternate model of management organized around four systems called Systems 1, 2, 3, and 4: the exploitive-authoritative, the benevolent-authoritative, the consultative, and the participative-group management. After distributing to managers a questionnaire devised from a table Likert published in *New Patterns of Management*, Likert concludes that while managers appreciate and even prefer the efficacy guaranteed by System 4, they usually rely on a System 1 form of leadership. From the empirical results, Likert attributes the discrepancy to managers' concentration on end results rather than causal and intervening variables. System 1 was found productive in labor contexts with high repetition. Likert's final call in *The Human Organization* is for "estimates of the current value of the human organization in all financial reports of the firm"—that is, organizations need to consistently assess and appreciate the financial value of their human assets.

BIBLIOGRAPHY

Works by Rensis Likert

Likert, R. *New Patterns of Management*. New York: McGraw-Hill, 1961.
———. *The Human Organization: Its Management and Value*. New York: McGraw-Hill, 1967.
Likert, R., and J. G. Likert. *New Ways of Managing Conflict*. New York: McGraw-Hill, 1976.

Work about Rensis Likert

Brody, C. J., and J. Dietz. "On the Dimensionality of the Two-Question Format Likert Attitude Scales." *Social Science Research*, 26, 2, June 1997, 197–204.

LINDBLOM, CHARLES E. (b. 1917, Turlock, CA), political economist; university professor; fellow

Charles Lindblom was born to Charles August and Emma Lindblom. He attended Stanford University, receiving a B.A. in 1937. He received a Ph.D. from the University of Chicago in 1945.

One of Lindblom's first academic positions was an instructorship at the University of Minnesota, from 1939 to 1946. In 1946 he began an assistant professorship at Yale University and later accepted the position of professor of economics and political science at the same university. Lindblom also held the Guggenheim fellowship in 1951 and a fellowship at the Center for Advanced Study in the Behavioral Sciences from 1954 to 1955.

Lindblom offers an alternative to the rational comprehensive decision-making model. Arguing the impracticality of the model, he suggests the approach "incrementalism," which mirrors actual decision making—policy decisions are based on modifications in existing policy. His critique, which appears in his well-known 1959 publication "The Science of Muddling Through," outlines the limited intellectual capabilities of man—the challenge in identifying all values in society, lack of sources of information, as well as time and money—all of which are required in rational decision making. He challenges the approach that fails to consider these limitations. Contrasting the rational-comprehensive approach or, "root method," and the successive limited comparisons model, or "branch" method, he explains that the latter allows the decision maker to "muddle through" the process, considering a smaller number of alternatives. Writing on the advantages of "muddling through" in *The Intelligence of Democracy: Decision Making through Mutual Adjustment* in 1965, Lindblom argues that this approach not only permits the decision maker to consider a reduced number of alternatives and comparisons to be compared but also directs attention to policies that require only small changes in existing policies. He explains that the consideration of incremental changes in policy is more palatable politically and, therefore, allows the decision maker to win more support for the policy decision. In a similar vein, incrementalism's focus on finding solutions to current problems and less on fundamental changes points to its practical usage.

Recognizing the involvement of different interest groups in government decision making, Lindblom notes the feasibility in incrementalism's consideration of mutual consensus building among competing interests. In 1953, in *Politics, Economics, and Welfare*, Lindblom, with Robert Dahl, elaborates on the idea of "partisan mutual adjustment." He suggests that "partisan mutual adjustment" that lends itself to policy evaluation by interest groups, rather than by policy analysts, is more democratic as it takes policy decision making beyond the agency to include positions of various interests. Lindblom believes that policy outcomes resulting from a consensual process are more efficient.

The publication of *Inquiry and Change* (1990) shows Lindblom as dedicated to reaching a democratic ideal as forty years ago, and consistently committed to incrementalism as the proper means for its realization. In this work, Lindblom not only critiques social science but promises nothing less than thorough examination of how "persons [in contemporary industrialized societies] set or define problems, think about and establish goals, find opportunities, cope with complexity, seek or take advantage of information and helpful analysis, inform and misinform each other." Finally, in a move to initiate the reversal of "socially caused incompetence in inquiry," Lindblom seeks to "create answers when they cannot discover them." This contemporary work is uniformly praised for its evaluation of socialization, interrogation of elitist self-entitlement, and circulation of rational, even wholesome ideas.

Nevertheless, incrementalism has not escaped criticism. Just as Theodore Lowi criticizes advocates of administrative pluralism for inhibiting meaningful social change, critics of incrementalism label the approach as conservative and claim that it upholds the status quo in situations that call for broad-based and fundamental changes to ensure social justice. Nevertheless, Lindblom is credited with helping to reframe the debates on modern decision theory and implementation research in public administration.

BIBLIOGRAPHY

Works by Charles E. Lindblom

Lindblom, C. *Unions and Capitalism*. New Haven, CT: Yale University Press, 1949.
———. "The Science of Muddling Through." *Public Administration Review*, 19, Spring 1959, 79–88.
———. *The Intelligence of Democracy: Decision Making through Mutual Adjustment*. New York: Free Press, 1965.
———. *The Policy-making Process*. Englewood Cliffs, NJ: Prentice-Hall, 1968.
———. *Politics and Markets: The World's Political-Economic Systems*. New York: Basic Books, 1977.
———. "The Market as Prison." *Journal of Politics*, 44, 2, May 1982, 324–336.
———. *Democracy and Market System*. Oslo: Norwegian University Press; New York: Oxford University Press, 1988.
———. *Inquiry and Change: The Troubled Attempt to Understand and Shape Society*. New Haven, CT: Yale University Press, 1990.
Lindblom, E., and R. Dahl. *Politics, Economics, and Welfare: Planning and Politico-Economic Systems Resolved into Basic Social Processes*. New York: Harper, 1953; Chicago: University of Chicago Press, 1976.

Work about Charles E. Lindblom

Gregory, R. "Political Rationality or 'Incrementalism'? Charles E. Lindblom's Enduring Contribution to Public Policy Making Theory." *Policy and Politics*, 17, 2, April 1989, 139–154.

LOWI, THEODORE J. (b. July 9, 1931, Gadsden, AL), political scientist; university professor; fellow

Originally from Alabama, Lowi attended Michigan State University and completed a B.A. in 1954, followed by an M.A. the following year. In 1961, he earned a doctoral degree from Yale University. A quintessential educator of public policy and government, Lowi has been researching and teaching for forty years, twenty-six of which he has dedicated to Cornell University. After several years of research in New York government and politics, and through the Ford Foundation, Lowi took up his first teaching position at the University of Chicago, where he taught for eleven years. A steady stream of funded research efforts began in 1963, when he was a Social Science Research Council fellow, and continued through 1968, when his tenure as a Guggenheim Foundation fellow ended. In 1977 Lowi was a National Endowment for Humanities fellow and in 1981, a Fulbright fellow.

In addition to teaching American institutions courses at Cornell University, Lowi is known for research and academic posts abroad. In 1962, Lowi was awarded the French-American Foundation Award; from 1981 to 1982, Lowi chaired the American Civilization Department. An expert on American institutions and civilization, Lowi's elaboration of the presidency culminated in a study of the social contract shared by the American people and the president instigated during the New Deal era: *The Personal President: Power Invested, Promise Unfulfilled* (1985). Lowi argues that since the 1930s, American citizens have operated from the assumption that investing more support and power in the president guarantees them a return of what they most want from government. Lowi established the theoretical pattern of negotiating and trafficking American power and services in *The End of Liberalism* (1969), his legendary project on interest group liberalism.

In this study, Lowi takes up the problem of fledgling democracy in government, an ethical challenge he distinguishes from pluralistic theory, which reaches compromise out of competition. Lowi attributes the monopolizing tendency of interest group liberalism to competition among dominant groups for power and equity. Lowi suggests that unlike a democracy that accounts for debates between all players ("conservative" and "liberal") framed by mutual appreciation for morality, the autonomous agencies (or interest groups) participating in the new "policy marketplace" must merely stake their claim on policy rewards, not compete for them. By the closure of his study, Lowi calls for reinstatement of "juridical democracy" under which the unified authority of Congress would check potentially dubious collaborations between agencies and interest groups. Lowi's recommendations change the direction of new Public Administration, which called for decentralization and maximum citizen participation. Mapping the four "arenas of power"—redistributive, distributive, constituent, and regulative—is a key aspect of *The End of Liberalism*.

BIBLIOGRAPHY

Works by Theodore J. Lowi

Lowi, T. *At the Pleasure of the Mayor: Patronage and Power in New York City, 1898–1958*. New York: Free Press, 1964.

———. *The End of Liberalism: Ideology, Policy, and the Crisis of Public Authority*. New York: Norton, 1969.

———. *Four Systems of Policy: Politics and Choice*. Syracuse, NY: Inter-University Case Program, 1971.

———. *The Politics of Disorder*. New York: Basic Books, 1971.

———. *The End of Liberalism: The Second Republic of the United States*. New York: Norton, 1979.

———. *The Personal President: Power Invested, Promise Unfulfilled*. Ithaca, NY: Cornell University Press, 1985.

———. "Why Is There No Socialism in the United States?" *Society*, 22, January–February 1985, 34–42.

———. "A Review of Herbert Simon's Review of My View of the Discipline." *Political Science and Politics*, 26, 1, March 1993, 51–52.

———. *The End of the Republican Era*. Norman: University of Oklahoma Press, 1995.

———, ed. *Private Life and Public Order: The Context of Modern Public Policy*. New York: Norton, 1968.

Lowi, T., and R. Ripley, eds. *Legislative Politics U.S.A.: Congress and the Forces That Shape It. Readings*. Boston: Little, Brown, 1973.

Lowi, T., and J. Romance. *A Republic of Parties? Debating the Two-Party System*. Lanham, MD: Rowman and Littlefield, 1998.

Lowi, T., and A. Stone, eds. *Nationalizing Government: Public Policies in America*. Beverly Hills, CA: Sage Publications, 1978.

Works about Theodore J. Lowi

Anderson, J. "Governmental Suasion: Refocusing the Lowi Policy Typology." *Policy Studies Journal*, 25, 2, 1997, 266–282.

Calvert, R. L. "Lowi's Critique of Political Science: A Response." *Political Science and Politics*, 26, 2, June 1993, 196–198.

Daynes, B. "Moral Controversies and the Policymaking Process: Lowi's Framework Applied to the Abortion Issue." *Policy Studies Review*, 3, 2, February 1984, 207–222.

Grady, R. "Juridical Democracy and Democratic Values: An Evaluation of Lowi's Alternative to Interest-Group Liberalism." *Polity*, 16, 3, Spring 1984, 404–422.

Sanders, E. "The Contributions of Theodore Lowi to Political Analysis and Democratic Theory." *Political Science and Politics*, 23, 4, December 1990, 574–576.

Schaefer, D. "Theodore J. Lowi and the Administrative State." *Administration and Society*, 19, 4, February 1988, 371–398.

Spitzer, R. "Liberalism and Juridical Democracy, or What's Interesting about Interest Group Liberalism." *Political Science and Politics*, 23, 4, December 1990, 572–574.

Tatlovich, R., and B. Daynes. "The Lowi Paradigm, Moral Conflict, and Coalition-Building: Pro-Choice versus Pro-life." *Women and Politics*, 13, 1, 1993, 39–66.

Wilson, J. Q. "Juridical Democracy versus American Democracy." *Political Science and Politics*, 23, 4, December 1990, 570–572.

MARCH, JAMES G. (b. 1928, Cleveland, OH), educator (political science); poet; public servant; sociologist; political scientist; university professor; dean; fellow

March spent most of his early life in Wisconsin. He served in the army during 1946–1948. He received his B.A. in political science from the University of Wisconsin in 1949. Later he attended Yale University and received an M.A. in political science (1950) and a Ph.D. (1953). After graduation he joined the faculty of Carnegie Mellon to teach industrial administration and psychology. In 1964, he became the dean of the School of Social Sciences at the University of California at Irvine. He joined the faculty of Stanford University in 1970, where he has been teaching management, political science, and sociology to the present. He also has held several professorships and has been a fellow at the Center for Advanced Study in the Behavioral Sciences and Hoover Institute. He became an emeritus at Stanford in 1995 and taught a course on leadership. He received honorary doctorates from the Swedish School of Economics in Helsinki (1979), the University of Wisconsin at Milwaukee (1980), the Copenhagen School of Economics (1978), the Dublin City University (1994), Uppsala University (1987), University of Burgen (1980), and Helsinki School of Economics (1991). He also has won numerous awards and been a member of many national and international academic organizations.

March has written several books and articles primarily on organizations, behavioral theories, leadership, and decision making. He also has written several books on poetry. He argues that decision making is an important aspect of any organizational life and has to be approached with a clear understanding of its unique quality. He indicates that decisions are partly based on values and preferences and are made to optimize outcome. However, he believes that decisions are consequential and depend on many other factors. For example, he argues that the decision-making environment is key to the decision-making process. The decision maker's environment might contain opportunities, clarity, and consistency or inconsistency and confusion. He also argues that organizational decisions have different foundations that determine their outcome. He believes they are either "choice-based" or "rule-based." The first category implies that there is a great deal of discretion for the decision maker. Therefore, he or she could weigh different alternatives and choose the best alternative. On the other hand, the rule-based decision-making approach does not offer much choice to the decision maker, and he or she is bound by organizational rules and regulations. In the same context, he raises another question concerning the nature of organizational decisions. He argues that decisions can reflect the attitude and aspirations of the individuals and are different from decisions that are the result of interactions among other elements in the organization. He believes if decisions are rule-based, a set of procedures exist that help participants interpret conduct during the process of decision making.

March is mostly associated with the "garbage can" model that he originally developed along with Michael D. Cohen and John P. Olsen (1972). It is part of the organizational decision-making theory that rejects the rational comprehensive as well as the incremental models of decision making in organizations. It implies that organizations are collections "of choices looking for problems; issues and feelings looking for decision situations in which they might be aired; solutions looking for issues to which they might be the answer; and decision-makers looking for work." Therefore, he argues that organizations are like garbage cans in which problems and opportunities are dumped, and one person's problem might be another's opportunity. According to this theory, the process is more important than the organizational goal. In his garbage can model, a decision is an outcome or interpretation of different organizational trends.

According to the garbage can model, there are four variables (streams) that make up the process of decision making. They include choice opportunities, participants, problems, and solutions. Based on these variables, decisions are made in organizations. The choice opportunities model refers to the timing and necessity of making certain decisions (something that cannot be avoided in an organization). The "participants" variable deals with those who are involved in the decision-making process. He argues that they are not stable and usually change over time. The third variable is "problems," which are everywhere in an organization and range from small, individual problems to major organizational problems that demand solutions. Finally, the "solution" variable is considered the personal reactions of individuals working in the organizations to problems. According to this model, all those variables set the stage for decision making concerning conditions in the organization.

There are three approaches in making decisions: oversight, flight, and resolution. The "oversight" approach refers to the procedure of ignoring problems and making decisions that require minimum time and energy. The second approach in the decision-making process is "flight or avoidance," which indicates that the decision maker simply passes the buck or postpones the making of decisions. Finally, "resolution" refers "to making decisions in a situation where the previous methods cannot be used and a decision has to be made." It deals with solving minor problems that do not demand a great deal of time and energy to solve. According to this model, decisions usually do not solve problems; they only move the problems around. March also deals with organizational conflict and the process of bargaining, as well as decision making under ambiguity.

BIBLIOGRAPHY

Works by James G. March

Cohen, M. D., J. Olsen, and J. March. "Garbage Can Model of Organizational Choice." *Administrative Science Quarterly*, 17, March 1972, 1–23.
March, J. G. *A Behavioral Theory of the Firm.* Englewood Cliffs, NJ: Prentice-Hall, 1963.
———. *A Primer on Decision-making: How Decisions Happen.* New York: Free Press, 1994.
———. "A Scholar's Quest." *Stanford Business Magazine*, October 1996, 13–25.
———, ed. *Handbook of Organizations.* Chicago: Rand McNally, 1965.
March, J. G., and M. D. Cohen. *Leadership and Ambiguity.* New York: McGraw-Hill, 1974.
March, J. G., and B. R. Gelbaum. *Mathematics for the Social and Behavioral Sciences.* New York: Saunders, 1968.
March, J. G., and H. Simon. *Organizations.* New York: John Wiley, 1958.
———. *Organizations.* 2nd ed. Oxford: Blackwell Publishers, 1993.
March, J. G., and R. Wessinger-Baylon. *Ambiguity and Command: Organization Perspectives on Military Decision-making.* Marshfield, MA: Pitman, 1986.

Works about James G. March

Bell, D. E., H. Raiffa, and A. Tversky, eds. *Decision Making: Descriptive, Normative, and Prescriptive Interactions.* Cambridge, New York: Cambridge University Press, 1988.
Collins, R., ed. *Four Sociological Traditions: Selected Readings.* New York: Oxford University Press, 1994.
Easton, D., ed. *Varieties of Political Theory.* Englewood Cliffs, NJ: Prentice-Hall, 1966.
Elster, J. *Rational Choice.* New York: New York University Press, 1986.
Goodman, P. S., L. S. Sproull, et al. *Technology and Organizations.* San Francisco: Jossey-Bass, 1990.
Scott, W. R., ed. *Annual Review of Sociology*, vol. 14. Palo Alto, CA: Annual Reviews, 1988.
Shapira, Z., ed. *Organizational Decision Making.* New York: Cambridge University Press, 1997.
Sproull, L. S., and P. D. Larkey, eds. *Advances in Information Processing in Organizations: A Research Annual.* Greenwich, CT: JAI Press, 1984.
Van Maanen, J., ed. *Qualitative Studies of Organizations,* Thousand Oaks, CA: Sage, 1998.

Williamson, O., ed. *Organization Theory: From Chester Barnard to the Present and Beyond.* New York: Oxford University Press, 1990.

Youn, T.I.K., and P. B. Murphy. *Organizational Studies in Higher Education.* New York: Garland, 1997.

MARX, KARL (b. May 5, 1818, Trier, Germany; d. March 14, 1883, London, England), social scientist; revolutionary theorist; journalist; philosopher

Marx's theories provide the foundation for revolutionary communism and the democratic socialism that originated in Prussia. The son of a lawyer, he studied law at the University of Bonn in 1835 and soon after transferred to the University of Berlin, where he studied philosophy. There he was influenced by revolutionary student movements that were exploring alternative political philosophies and systems. Later he entered the University of Jena, where he received a Ph.D. in philosophy (1841). Because he was active in antigovernment student organizations, he was not able to secure a teaching job at the university.

He wrote for several radical newspapers and later managed several journals with antigovernment themes. He became the editor of the liberal newspaper *Rheinische Zeitung*, which was backed by Rhenish industrialists. After his marriage, he moved to France, where he met Friedrich Engels. Engels, a German, shared similar views, and together they wrote several articles and books. The most important document that they produced was *The Communist Manifesto* (1948), which was the foundation of socialist movements around the world. They wrote several political and economic columns in daily newspapers and then analyzed their effect on national and international events. They were promoting international unity for the working class in the hope of overthrowing capitalist systems.

After a few years, Marx went back to Prussia, where the revolution was about to begin. The revolution failed, and Marx fled to London, where he developed the majority of his work. He made a living working for the *New York Tribune* and other newspapers. He founded the International Working Men's Association in 1864. This organization concentrated on the conditions of the working class and attempted to develop and transmit his socialist ideas. In his writings, he concentrates on the economic conditions in society and argues that the economy breeds or influences social change. In his view, whomever controls the means of production in society controls economic conditions and therefore social conditions. He believed in an evolutionary pattern in social developments and that societies pass through several stages including primitive communism, Asiatic society, ancient slaveholding society, feudalism, and capitalism.

He argued that the capitalist stage will eventually be overthrown by the working class and will be replaced with a socialist system. He believed that the next stage, communism, will herald the utopian world and final stage of human development (a classless society). He argues that all history is a struggle between the capitalist and the working classes. His ideas on socialism were originally expressed in *The Communist Manifesto*. However, his political, social, and economic views are called *Marxism*, which is the theory of class struggle by which economy is the base of social, political, and legal systems in society.

In Marx's major work *Das Capital*, he analyzes the capitalist system. He contends that the capitalist system is self-destructive and contains its own seeds of destruction. His philosophy is called "dialectic materialism," which includes epistemology (studying and generalizing the original development of knowledge).

He took issue with major political and economic ideas of his time and argued that since the means of production are in the hands of the capitalists, they dominate the fate of the human race. According to Marx, everything else thus falls within their domain—even religion serves their purpose. That is why Marx had a negative view of religion and called it "the opium of nations." In his judgment, human societies are organized for the purpose of production (which is also based on the division of labor and exploitation of the working class [proletariat] by the capitalist [bourgeoisie] class). Here Marx pays close attention to the organizational structure and believes that, owing to the consistent concentration on maximization of profits, humans (working class) are treated as means of production. This treatment of employees causes alienation and depression, and therefore, organizational structure by nature is oppressive and inhumane.

Marx argued that organizations exploit employees and called for the overthrow of this oppressive system and replacement with a fair and more humane system. He believed that all social organizations have similar characteristics and support the system of exploitation of man by man. He even questions the social fabric, customs, and traditions and considers them the support mechanism for the process of exploitation. He calls for public ownership of the means of production and reorganization of social structure in order to bring about a fair, nonexploitative, and classless society.

BIBLIOGRAPHY

Work by Karl Marx

Marx, Karl, and F. Engels. *The Communist Manifesto*. Trans. Samuel Moore, 1888. Moscow: Progress Publishers, 1977.

Works about Karl Marx

Elster, J. *An Introduction to Karl Marx*. New York: Cambridge University Press, 1986.

Hunt, R. N. *The Political Ideas of Marx and Engels*. Pittsburgh: University of Pitts-
    burgh Press, 1974.
McClellan, D. T. *Karl Marx: His Life and Thought*. New York: Harper & Row, 1973.
Thompson, K. W. *Fathers of International Thought: The Legacy of Political Theory*.
    Baton Rouge: Louisiana State University Press, 1994.

MASLOW, ABRAHAM H. (b. April 1, 1908, Brooklyn, NY; d. June 8, 1970, California), founder of the theory of human motivation; father of humanist theory; philosopher; research fellow; college professor; department chair

Maslow was born to a large family (the eldest of eleven). His parents were Russian immigrants, and most of his childhood was spent in a disharmonious environment with a great deal of financial difficulty. Ideologically he leaned toward democratic socialism. He is considered to be the most famous humanist in organizational theory. He attended the City College of New York, Cornell University, and the University of Wisconsin, where he studied philosophy and psychology. He received a Ph.D. from the University of Wisconsin in 1934. He was a research fellow at Columbia University, taught psychology at Brooklyn College, and served as the chair of the Psychology Department at Brandeis University. He also served as a plant manager at the Maslow Coperage Corporation. He is often called the spiritual father of the organizational development movement.

Maslow's major work concerns experimental psychology and social psychology. He participated in cross-cultural fieldwork on a Canadian Indian reservation. That experience led to the use of a psychological approach to analyzing human conditions in organizations. He disagreed with Sigmund Freud in approach to the study of human psychology. He argued that in analyzing human psychology one needs to approach it in a more positive manner. He criticized Freud's psychological approach as negatively oriented and concentrating on man's shortcomings rather than his potential to perform positively. He emphasized man's positive aspects and believed that they can be used to motivate employees. In other words, if one only studies humans through their abnormalities, one is ignoring positive qualities that can contribute to the life of the organization. In developing his theories, Maslow relied on his patients' case histories and did not use employees as the subjects of his experiments. He disagrees with the stimulus-response theory of motivation and developed his own human motivation theory. The basic assumption of his theory is that individuals are meant to satisfy unfulfilled needs; it is often called the "hierarchy of needs."

He concerned himself mostly with the relationship between human needs and motivation. His theory is based on a hierarchy of needs in which there are several different levels. The five levels of innate need that are responsible for human motivation are ranked from the lowest to highest in hierarchical order. After a lower need is satisfied, the next level need will arise. Therefore, employees can only be motivated through higher levels of need. Otherwise, they are not motivated to work harder. With "basic needs" at the bottom of the hierarchy (physiological needs), the needs necessary to sustain the conditions are basics such as food, water, and health. The second level is "safety needs," which demands security, clothing, protection, stability, and relief from fear and anxiety. The third is "belongingness and love," which appears after previous needs are satisfied. These needs can manifest themselves in the need for friendship, intimacy, affection, belonging, and group activity. The fourth level is "esteem needs," which directly relates to the desire of individuals to be recognized. Individuals seek respect for themselves through status and recognition for accomplishment and achievement, a sense of freedom, and reputation and prestige. Finally, the last need is "self-actualization," which is considered the highest need. It deals with the need to reach one's full potential and capabilities. Those who reach this level cannot be motivated further, have exceptional abilities, and are self-motivated. They are satisfied with what they are doing and have a sense of perceiving reality, spontaneity, and problem-solving ability.

Maslow argues that the lower the need is in the hierarchy, the easier it is to motivate, and a need might not be satisfied in its fullest before the next level of need arises. Some needs can be only partially satisfied before the next level of needs arise. In addition, he believes that the higher the need, the stronger is its relation to environment. In other words, the higher needs are more circumstantial and depend on their environment for support and sustenance.

Maslow perceives the human mind as an evolving pattern toward a maturation stage. Therefore, needs undergo fundamental changes. He developed the concept of the "ideal organization" (eupschia) in which a supporting environment is created for the realization of high-level needs (meta-values).

BIBLIOGRAPHY

Works by Abraham H. Maslow

Maslow, A. H. *Motivation and Personality*. New York: Harper & Row, 1954.
———. *New Knowledge in Human Values*. New York: HarperCollins, 1959.
———. *Dominance, Self Esteem, Self Actualization: Germinal Papers of A. H. Maslow*. Ed. R. Lowry. Monterey, CA: Wadsworth, 1973.
———. *Journals of Abraham Maslow*. Ed. R. Lowry. Lexington, MA: Lewis, 1982.
———. *Future Visions*. Ed. E. Hoffman. London: Sage Publishing, 1996.

Works about Abraham H. Maslow

Frick, W. *Humanistic Psychology: Interviews with Maslow, Murphy and Rogers*. Ed. C. Rogers and W. R. Coulson. Columbus, OH: Merrill, 1971.

Schultz, D., and S. E. Schultz. *Theories of Personalities*. Pacific Grove, CA: Brooks/ Cole, 1992.

Shafritz, J. M., and S. Ott. *Classics of Organization Theory*. Bemont, CA: Wadsworth, 1996.

MAYO, GEORGE ELTON (b. December 26, 1880, Adelaide, Australia; d. September 1949, Surrey, England), psychologist; behavioral scientist; pioneer of human relations school

George Mayo's career path led him to be recognized as one of the pioneers of the human relations approach to organizations. He is considered one of the first behavioral scientists due to his deviation from traditional scientific approaches to organization administration and industrial management research. Interestingly enough, Mayo, a native Australian, studied medicine and philosophy and traveled throughout West Africa before settling into a research career that culminated with the legendary "Hawthorne Studies" of 1920s–1930s Chicago. Mayo earned his M.A. degree in logic and philosophy from St. Peter's College, Adelaide, in 1899. He lectured in logic, ethics, and philosophy at Queensland University from 1911 to 1919, during which time he conducted the first psychotherapeutic treatments of soldiers shell-shocked from the war. In 1919 Mayo chaired the Department of Philosophy at Queensland and departed for the United States in 1922. Mayo's focus on working behavior is traced back to his academic study of Pierre Janet and Sigmund Freud and may be generally applicable to considerations of human cooperation in general.

After emigrating to the United States, Mayo joined the University of Pennsylvania faculty in the Wharton School of Finance and Commerce; in 1926, Mayo joined Harvard University's faculty and was tenured as professor of industrial research at the Graduate School of Business Administration. During these posts in America, Mayo conducted the research for which he is now famous. Between 1927 and 1947, when Mayo worked at Harvard, he collaborated with Fritz Roethlisberger and their Business School colleagues to launch the Hawthorne Studies at the Western Electric Company in Chicago, Illinois.

The Hawthorne Studies were conducted at the Western Electric Company's Hawthorne plant in Chicago to test the effects of worker fatigue on production. The project was predicated on the Taylorian hypothesis that workers would respond like machines to changes in working conditions, an issue tested by altering the lighting conditions in the work environment of the subjects. Mayo's and his colleagues' hypothesis was not, however, upheld. They found instead that production climbed, even as the lights dimmed to darkness. Overall, the research group concluded that social and psychological factors could more significantly affect morale and productivity than economic considerations alone.

The Hawthorne Studies left a considerable academic and professional legacy. First, the famous term "Hawthorne effect" is used to describe "the tendency of people to change their behavior when they know that they are being observed." Second, and more important, the studies provided the basis for the human relations school of organization theory (emphasizing, for example, motivation as a social and psychological aspect of the labor environment). Finally, applications of this basis led organization theorists to prioritize and develop methods for evaluating and meeting workers' needs, that is, workers' social and psychological job satisfaction.

When Mayo set out to study social issues in industrial civilizations, he considered that between the eighteenth century and the twentieth century society has shifted from "the apprenticeship system," in which workers learn to "live into" prescribed routines, to "the adaptive society," in which collaborations are aggravated by a continual thrust toward technical advancement. Currently, more recent explorations of the human relations school seek to address issues unanticipated during the early twentieth century, such as how productivity is affected by workers socially alienated by advanced technology, and the long-term differences harbored between workers and managers.

BIBLIOGRAPHY

Works by George Elton Mayo

Mayo, G. E. *The Human Problems of an Industrial Civilization*. New York: Viking Press, 1933.
———. *The Social Problems of an Industrial Civilization*. English ed. London: Routledge and Kegan Paul, 1952.

Works about George Elton Mayo

Bramel, D., and R. Friend. "Hawthorne, the Myth of the Docile Worker, and Class Bias in Psychology." *American Psychologist*, 36, 8, August 1981, 867–878.
Trahair, R. *The Humanist Temper: The Life and Work of Elton Mayo*. New Brunswick, NJ: Transaction Books, 1984.

McGREGOR, DOUGLAS (b. 1906, Detroit, MI; d. October 1964, Boston, MA), social psychologist; public servant; college president; pioneer of industrial relations

McGregor primarily attended high school in Detroit, received his Ph.D. from Harvard University and taught there before he moved to Massachusetts Institute of Technology (MIT) in 1937. He also received an honorary L.L.D. degree from Wayne State University (1949). While at MIT he initiated the development of a program called Industrial Relations. Later he became president of Antioch College. After a few years, he returned to MIT to continue his teaching work. At MIT, he was known for his innovative ideas concerning decision making and participation and for creating a sense of community by initiating the "Goals Discussions" program, which involved the entire university community.

He became a member of Harvard's Psychology Department in 1960 and continued until his death in 1964. He was also a fellow at the National Training Laboratories for Group Development and the Academy of Arts and Sciences. In 1957, he delivered his famous "The Human Side of Enterprise" speech at the fifth Anniversary Convocation of MIT's Alfred P. Sloan School of Management. In that historical speech, he introduced his "Theory Y," which is the hallmark of his work.

McGregor was the founder and president of the Massachusetts Community Nursery School and worked for the U.S. Department of Labor during World War II. His major task was the analysis of labor disputes and arbitration matters. The main thrust of his work was in the social psychology of work. He argues that the main function of management is to predict and control the behavior of employees. He believes that "every managerial act rests on the theory" and contends that what managers practice, and their overall behavior, exhibits their underlying philosophy of management. He developed his famous "Theory X and Theory Y" to explain the nature of management and organizational behavior. His Theory X held certain assumptions about human nature by which individuals are perceived as lazy, unwilling to work, and uncooperative. According to this theory, managers should use control, fear, and punishment (force) to get employees to accomplish their tasks. Theory Y assumes that people are naturally inclined to work and achieve their goals. It maintains that employees like to accept responsibility and will cooperate and be creative only if they are motivated properly. According to Theory Y, work has the therapeutic effect of satisfying many needs including achievement, self-esteem, and curiosity. He rejects the basic assumptions of Theory X and emphasizes the importance of using motivational skills to accomplish organizational tasks.

McGregor criticized dominant management practices that relied on close supervision, rules and regulations, reward, and promises to control workers. This theory uses self-commitment and rewards to motivate employees to achieve their goals. He argues that because of improper management, a good portion of employees' energies and potential are not utilized in organizations.

McGregor's Theory Y revolutionalized the concept of management and the understanding of human nature. He introduced humanistic values into management theory and practice and believed that those values will help managers improve efficiency within organizations. He believed that in order for managers to be successful they need to understand human nature. He argues that control exists only within the confines of human nature. Competent management must accede to basic realities in order to assure acceptable results.

He developed a new paradigm in employee motivation that was the foundation of many theories to come. His main goal was to emphasize human potentials and the inner needs that have to be tapped and directed to achieve the best results. In his judgment, individual needs and organizational goals should be integrated, and employees should be trusted and granted the power to motivate and believe in themselves.

BIBLIOGRAPHY

Works by Douglas McGregor

McGregor, D. "Getting Effective Leadership in the Industrial Organization." MIT, Department of Economics and Social Science, 1944.
———. "The Consultant Role and Organizational Leadership: Improving Human Relations in Industry." *Journal of Social Issues*, 4, 3, 1948.
———. "Management Development: The Hope and the Reality." 24th Midyear Meeting of the American Petroleum Institute's Division of Refining, New York, May 28, 1959.
———. *The Human Side of Enterprise*. New York: McGraw-Hill, 1960; Harmondsworth, UK: Penguin, 1985.
———. "New Concepts of Management." *Technology Review*, 63, 4, February 1961.
———. *The Professional Manager*. Ed. C. McGregor and W. G. Bennis. New York McGraw-Hill, 1967.

Works about Douglas McGregor

Bennis, W. G. "Leadership Theory and Administrative Behavior." *Administrative Science Quarterly*, 4, 1957, 27–45.
Knickerbocker, I. "Leadership: A Conception and Some Implications." *Journal of Social Issues*, 4, 1948, 14–25.
Zimbardo, P., and F. Ruch. *Psychology and Life*. Glenview, IL: Scott, Foresman, 1977.

MERTON, ROBERT K. (b. July 1910, Philadelphia, PA), educator (sociology); sociologist; historian; university professor
Merton attended South Philadelphia High School and won a scholarship to attend Temple University in 1927 to study sociology. He received an A.B. in 1931. He later attended Tulane University Graduate School in New Orleans and received an M.A. in 1932. He obtained a Ph.D. from Harvard in 1936, and an L.L.D. in 1980. He also received an honorary doctoral degree in social science from Yale University in 1968. Merton taught at Harvard from 1936 to 1939 and continued his teaching career at Tulane University from 1939 to 1941. He taught at Columbia University from 1941 until 1963. He also taught at other universities, including Emory University, 1965; Loyola University Chicago, 1970; Kalamazoo College, 1970; Cleveland State University, 1977; University of Pennsylvania, 1979; Brandeis University, 1983; SUNY Albany, 1986; and Oxford University, 1986. Since 1979, he has been professor emeritus at Columbia University.

Merton served as the associate director in the Bureau of Applied Research at Columbia from 1942 to 1971. His decision to choose sociology as his major area of study was influenced by his work on some "content analysis" projects while he was working for George E. Simon at Temple University as a graduate assistant. Later he was also influenced by Talcott Parson, historian E. F. Gay, and C. R. Wright, who were functionalists in pursuing sociology. He wrote several books and articles and was awarded a prize for "Distinguished Accomplishment in Humanistic Scholarship" by the American Council of Learned Societies in 1962. He has helped to establish several research institutions including the Center for Advanced Study in the Behavioral Sciences, the Russell Sage Foundation, and the Columbia University Bureau of Applied Social Research. He was the associate director of Burlington Applied Social Research from 1942 to 1970. He is the recipient of the prize for distinguished scholarship in humanities by the American Council of Learned Social Scientists in 1968. In addition, he received the Commonwealth Award for distinguished service to society in 1979.

Merton has worked in the areas of empirical and theoretical research in sociology. He was interested in analyzing social problems and believed that social problems are the manifestation of a social order that is in violation of accepted norms. He argued that social problems have strong relationships with each other and are relevant to the subjective state of minds, as well as the subjective state of affairs. He concentrates on aggregate social behavior and how people's behavior affects the formation of cultural norms. He believes that because of the differing locations of people within the opportunity structure in society, a gap will develop between people's aspirations and the actual possibility of achieving those aspirations. This disparity between aspirations and achievements causes the social breakdown of the system of control that previously existed. Social disorder is eminent when social behavior cannot be controlled. Therefore, he argues that material success will eventually cause despair and deviance within the system, which he calls the "sociology of deviance." He believes when society emphasizes prosperity, with little attention to the means of reaching the goals, it will create structural pressure and stress on society. This is because there are few means available to reach social goals, and, therefore, social deviance will occur between people in different social locations. They have different motivations and different means that are compatible with their location in society. Although he is a functionalist, he developed his own understanding of functionalism and made some modification to functionalist theory. He believed that not all factors (items) in the system contribute to the functions of the system; for example, different items might have similar functions, or some might even be dysfunctional and have negative effects on the system. He argued that empirical research should focus on the outcome of functional interactions. His work coincided with the recognition and attention to cultural relativism and with the emergence of a new field of social inquiry that combines sociology and psychology—social psychology.

He also contributed to the sociology of science, which includes the contemporary empirical investigations and theories concerning the internal workings of science. He investigated the relationship between science and its environment, the other areas of society. He contributed to the methodology and sociology of acquiring knowledge, including data gathering, analysis, and theory building. He investigated the mutual effects of science and environment on each other and how technical problems and moral dilemmas are related. He conducted several inquiries into issues concerning scientific arenas, including the effect of nonscientific institutions on scientific work and scientists' motivations in conducting scientific work. His major contribution was concerning the sociology of organizations. He studied how changing curriculum would affect students and the effects of social structures on the socialization process in organizations. With regard to the relationship of values and their role in social inquiry, Merton argues that the development of a sound sociological understanding should supersede moral judgments. He believes in a meritorious society in which the means of achieving goals are clear and by which those who achieve them receive proper compensation.

BIBLIOGRAPHY

Works by Robert K. Merton

Merton, R. K. *Social Theory and Social Structure*. New York: Free Press, 1949.
———. *On the Shoulders of Giants*. Chicago: University of Chicago Press, 1993.
Merton, R. K., and P. M. Blan, eds. *Continuities in Structural Inquiry*. Beverly Hills, CA: Sage Publications, 1981.
Merton, R. K., M. Fiske, and A. Curtis, eds. *Mass Persuasion: The Social Psychology of a War Bond Drive*. New York: Harper and Brothers Publishers, 1946.
Merton, R. K., and R. Nisbet, eds. *Contemporary Social Problems*. 3rd ed. Riverside, CA: Harcourt Brace Jovanovich, 1971.

Works about Robert K. Merton

Cohen, B., et al. *Puritanism and the Rise of Modern Science: The Merton Thesis*. New Brunswick, NJ: Rutgers University Press, 1990.
Crothers, C. *Robert K. Merton*. New York: Tavistock Publications, 1987.
Hill, R. B. *Merton's Role Types and Paradigm of Deviance*. New York: Arno Press, 1980.
Sztompka, P. *Robert Merton: An Intellectual Profile*. New York: St. Martin's Press, 1986.

MILLS, C(HARLES) WRIGHT (b. August 28, 1916, Waco, TX; d. March 20, 1962, Nyack, NY), sociologist; political theorist; university professor

Regrettably, little has been published about the life and contributions of the man who warned over a century ago of the coalescing of an elite class of Americans and its affect on society. While teaching at Columbia University in the 1950s, Mills published *The Power Elite* (1956), the tone of which has done nothing to ameliorate an academic reputation of "dark pessimist" that has survived him for over thirty years. Critical opinion varies with regard to how well Mills documented this study of the economic, political, and military influence of the elite class. However, because of its bent toward social criticism, critics of *The Power Elite* did not consider it orthodox sociology at the time of its release.

Mills presents elite theory as a countertheory to the pluralist model of policy making. In contrast to pluralism, Mills argues that public policy making in the United States is a centralized exercise carried out by a small elite group. According to Mills, three groups—corporate chiefs, military leaders, and principal governmental leaders—comprise the governing elite. According to Mills, the three groups, once independent in political thought and autonomous in political behavior, have mostly coalesced into a single political entity. The "power elite" is how Mills terms the group that dominates public policy formulation the United States. He explains that these legislated values mirror elite beliefs and priorities.

Mills's study revealed that common elite values were rooted in similar backgrounds among elites, such as attendance at the same educational and religious institutions. He argues that these common experiences among the groups' members facilitate the movement of members from one group to another, further clouding the once distinctive characteristics of each.

Mills's analysis of national decision making in the United States is criticized for its disregard of institutional influences on decision making and for its lack of evidence of an elite group's control of major decision making in America.

BIBLIOGRAPHY

Works by C. Wright Mills

Gerth, H., and C. W. Mills. *Character and Social Structure: The Psychology of Social Institutions*. New York: Harcourt, Brace, 1953.

Mills, C. W. *The New Men of Power: America's Labor Leaders*. New York: Harcourt, Brace, 1948.

———. *White Collar: The American Middle Classes*. New York: Oxford University Press, 1953.

———. *The Causes of World War Three*. New York: Simon and Schuster, 1958.

———. *The Power Elite*. 1956. New York: Oxford University Press, 1959.

———. *Images of Man: The Classic Tradition in Sociological Thinking*. New York: G. Braziller, 1960.

———. *Listen Yankee: The Revolution in Cuba*. New York: Ballantine, 1960.

———. *The Marxists*. New York: Dell, 1962.

Works about C. Wright Mills

Boyle, C. "Imagining the World Market: International Political Economy and the Task of Social Theory." *Millennium*, 23, 2, Summer 1994, 351–363.

Frost, M. "The Role of Normative Theory in International Relations." *Millennium*, 23, 1, Spring 1994, 109–118.

Gilliam, R. "White Collar from Start to Finish: C. Wright Mills in Transition." *Theory and Society*, 10, 1, January 1981, 1–31.

Halliday, F. "Theory and Ethics in International Relations: The Contradictions of C. Wright Mills." *Millennium*, 23, 2, Summer 1994, 377–385.

Horowitz, I. L., ed. *Power, Politics and People: The Collected Essays of C. Wright Mills*. New York: Ballantine Books, 1963.

Rosenberg, J. "The International Imagination: International Relations Theory and Classic Social Analysis." *Millennium*, 23, 1, Spring 1994, 85–108.

Tillman, R. "The Intellectual Pedigree of C. Wright Mills: A Reappraisal." *Western Political Quarterly*, 32, 4, December 1979, 479–496.

———. *C. Wright Mills: A Native Radical and His American Intellectual Roots*. University Park: Pennsylvania State University Press, 1984.

MOONEY, JAMES D. (b. February 10, 1861, Richmond, IN; d. December 22, 1921, Washington, DC), anthropologist; teacher; organizer

Mooney's father died when he was only eight months old, and his mother raised him and his two sisters. After he graduated from high school, he became a teacher and later worked for a local newspaper. He became associated (through friendship) with Earlham College where he became interested in Indian Affairs. Although Mooney never received any formal education in anthropology, he conducted an impressive study of American Indians. He studied the life and identity of many Native American tribes and conducted intimate and accurate studies on their lives. He joined the Bureau of Ethnology in 1885 and is often called the "Indian Man." Although most of his writing is in anthropology, he also conducted research and wrote several books concerning administration and organization.

Mooney deals with the questions of law, economy, and capitalism and provides solutions to economic problems by presenting an ideal economic system. According to Mooney, the most important factors to the production of wealth are natural resources, hard work, and utilization of machinery. He also indicates that an ideal economic condition does not adhere to the redistribution of wealth to bring about general prosperity in a society, but, rather, it comes about through "the increase in total sum of wealth." In his approach to "organizations," he follows a paradigm similar to other classical theorists. In cooperation with Alan Reiley, he develops specific principles that they believe are fundamental essentials in administering organizations. Their principles were derived from personal experiences at General Motors. They also used organizations such as the military and the Catholic Church as primary sources in the discovery of their principles. They include functional principle, scalar principle, coordination, and finally, staff principle (which emphasizes communication between the line and staff in an organization). He argues that those principles of administration are universal and can be used at any time and any place. In other words, they are generic.

They emphasize the importance of formal organizational structure and reliance on formal authority to accomplish organizational goals. They relate authority and coordination together, in the sense that authority becomes an important coordinating factor. In order for authority to function well, the implementation of rules and regulations is of paramount importance. Therefore, discipline becomes another important factor that is directly related to authority and coordination. Scalar principle is also related directly to the exercise of authority within organizational structure. The two argue that this principle determines different grades in the organization according to authority and responsibility. In this context, leadership becomes an important factor that determines the overall vision and direction of the organization and the vital force for organizational coordination.

Mooney also deals with the question of delegation of responsibility within the organizational hierarchy and is associated with the concept of organizational authority. He argues that delegation is the determinant factor in regulating the relationship between superior and subordinate.

Functional principle mainly distinguishes among different functions in each organization, regardless of position (a horizontal division of labor). In other words, the main emphasis is on the nature of the job and how it should be performed. For example, the function of an accountant is different than that of a secretary. The functional principle involves the setting of proper goals and the making of relevant decisions in order to relate specific functions to the general goals of the organization. This principle must be closely applied in conjunction with other principles. Finally, Mooney argues that communication between line and staff is very critical in setting organizational goals and implementation of public policies that help facilitating those goals. According to Mooney, only through the use of those principles can organizations successfully manage themselves. Mooney's writings on organizational principles have greatly influenced later classical theorists. His approach to management is categorized as "generic management" and is based on the closed system model.

BIBLIOGRAPHY

Works by James D. Mooney

Mooney, J. D. *The New Capitalism*. Princeton, NJ: Princeton University Press, 1934.
Mooney, J. D., and A. Reiley. *Onward Industry*. New York: Harper & Brothers, 1931.
————. *The Principles of Organization*. New York: Harper & Brothers, 1939.

Works about James D. Mooney

Buan, C. M., ed. *The First Duty: A History of the U.S. District Court for Oregon*. Portland: U.S. District Court of Oregon Historical Society, 1993.

Colby, W. M. *Routes to Rainy Mountain: A Biography of James Mooney, Ethnologist*. 1977.

Ellison, G. *James Mooney's History, Myths, and Sacred Formulas of the Cherokees: Containing the Full Texts of Myths of the Cherokee, (1900) and The Sacred Formulas of the Cherokees (1891)*. Asheville, NC: Historical Images, 1992.

Forman, M., and J. Mooney, eds. *The Race to Recruit: Strategies for Successful Business Attraction*. Dubuque, IA: Kendall/Hunt, 1997.

Johnson, F. R., ed. *Stories of the Old Cherokees: Based on Reports and Collections of James Mooney and Others*. Murfreesboro, NC: Johnson, 1975.

McClain, C., ed. *Chinese Immigrants and American Law*. New York: Garland, 1994.

Moses, L. G. *The Indian Man: A Biography of James Mooney*. Urbana: University of Illinois Press, 1984.

———. *James Mooney, U.S. Ethnologist: A Biography*. 1977.

"Plains Indians." *Heritage of the Great Plains*, 30, 1, Spring/Summer 1997.

Powell, J. W. Seventh Annual Report of the Bureau of Ethnology: To the Secretary of the Smithsonian Institution, 1885–86. Washington, DC: U.S. Government Printing Office, 1891.

———. Fourteenth Annual Report of the Bureau of Ethnology: To the Secretary of the Smithsonian Institution, 1892–93. Washington, DC: U.S. Government Printing Office, 1896.

———. Seventeenth Annual Report of the Bureau of American Ethnology: To the Secretary of the Smithsonian Institution, 1895–96. Washington, DC: U.S. Government Printing Office, 1898.

———. Nineteenth Annual Report of the Bureau of American Ethnology: To the Secretary of the Smithsonian Institution, 1897–98. Washington, DC: U.S. Government Printing Office, 1900.

Tedlock, D., and B. Tedlock, eds. *Teachings from the American Earth: Indian Religion and Philosophy*. New York: Liveright, 1992.

Wilson, R. Review of *The Ghost-Dance Religion and the Sioux Outbreak of 1890*, by James Mooney. *Kansas History*, 15, 3, Autumn 1992.

MOSHER, FREDERICK (b. July 1913, Oberlin, OH; d. May 1990, Virginia), editor; university professor

Mosher received a Master of Science from Syracuse University in 1939 and a Doctorate in Public Administration from Harvard University in 1953. He taught public administration and political science at two institutions of higher learning including the University of California at Berkeley (1959–1968) and Syracuse University (1947–1958). He also taught theories of administrative science at the University of Virginia in 1968. In 1980, he retired from academia. He served in different capacities with several public agencies, including the United Nations, the U.S. Department of State, the Tennessee Valley Authority, and the City of Los Angeles. He became a major in the U.S. Air Force and received the Legion of Merit Award (1942–1945). He also served as the editor of the *Public Administration Review Journal* for a few years.

Mosher's writings and ideas were heavily influenced by his experiences at different public agencies and by the social events of his time. His life in the public sector coincided with major changes in the economic and political system in this country including the world wars, the Great Depression, and the civil rights movement. Although Mosher contributed significantly to the general discipline of public administration, his main area of concern was in personnel administration. He studied public administration from a historical perspective and developed a scientific analysis concerning the evolutionary pattern in personnel administration. According to Mosher, history can provide us with valuable practical guidelines that will aid in solving current public administration problems. He believed that public employees must meet the requirements of professionalism to qualify to work in public institutions. He contends that professions are social mechanisms that transform knowledge and put it to work. In his judgment, professions have certain characteristics: They are (1) clear-cut occupations, (2) require higher degrees of education, and (3) offer a tenure career for the person. Therefore, he believes that the public sector's role is changed from static, routine orientation to a dynamic, change-oriented sector.

He developed three merit systems: the career system, the general service system, and the political appointment system. The first category includes white-collar and tenured professional employees with emphasis on person rather than position. The general civil service is an example of white-collar tenured personnel with emphasis on position rather than person. Finally, political appointees are named to office with no tenure to serve elected officials. For example, public managers are supposed to plan and foresee future changes and future developments that might effect their workforce and should use innovative ways to deal with changes around them.

Mosher's attention to historical underpinnings in approaching public administration is the hallmark of his work. In addition, his practical experience in the public and private sectors has influenced his writings. He is one of the proponents of separation of politics and administration. He perceives public administration to be a scientific field that can be explored and is in favor of the development of public administration as a profession. Therefore, he believes that public administration should stay away from politics and concentrate on developing managerial skills to implement the policies. He also emphasized the importance of developing efficiency in the public sector. His ideal bureaucracy is one that is run on businesslike principles. Those principles are scientific and generic and can be applied in any setting regardless of their publicness or privateness. He advocates ideas similar to those of Frederick Taylor, in the sense that he believes there is only one best way to do things in organizations and that the main purpose of a manager is to find the "one best way."

He was also in favor of positivist orientation to research and emphasized the use of reasoning to solve organizational problems. Therefore, his emphasis was on objectivity and approaching public service with no specific value, other than efficiency in mind. In line with his belief in a positivist approach to research and management, he perceives subjectivity as a major problem in the proper functioning of public organizations. He believes that objectivity will prevail through strict application of constitutional laws and organizational rules and regulations. He emphasizes the importance of education as the most powerful means of making bureaucracy responsive to the needs of the public. He draws a close affinity between the public needs, education, and bureaucracy and perceives education as the means by which the will of the public can be realized through bureaucratic action. In short, he believes that the more educated the bureaucracy, the better service it provides to the public. In his judgment, the educational system shapes the structure of the public sector and the behavior of public officials. He perceives the public sector as a powerful force that has to be controlled by its political masters. He argues that there is a tendency by the bureaucracy to seek autonomy from political interference because of the nature of professionalization of public service.

He uses the Constitution as a guide for determining the relationship between politics and administration. He believes that public servants are composed of a nonelected body that should be controlled and educated in order to serve the public interest. In his judgment, democratic values are dominant in the Constitution and should prevail in our bureaucratic systems as well. He refers to the importance of the survival of the government "of the people, by the people, for the people." He refers to professionalism as the most efficient way to translate knowledge into action. He contends that the possibility of a democratic public sector depends on the quality of those who are inspired to work for public agencies. He also emphasizes the importance of the kind of education that public servants will receive and emphasizes the role of universities in influencing the values of public officials. In order to guarantee a quality government, he holds education as the main contributor. He argues that the university system exerts the strongest influence on all aspects of the public sector. He argues that there is a basic and strong intrinsic dislike between professions and politics and considers politics, at its best, amateur and at its worst, corrupt. He argues that professionalism relies on such values as rationality and scientific inquiry. In his judgment present and future leaders function under the influence of knowledge absorbed during the university experience.

BIBLIOGRAPHY

Works by Frederick Mosher

Mosher, F. C. *Programming Systems & Foreign Affairs Leadership*. New York: Oxford University Press, 1970.
———. *Implications for Responsible Government*. New York: Basic Books, 1972.
———. *The GAO: The Quest for Accountability in American Government*. Boulder, CO: Westview Press, 1979.
———. *Democracy and the Public Sector*. New York: Oxford University Press, 1982.
———. *A Tale of Two Agencies: A Comparative Analysis of the General Accounting Office and the Office of Management*. Baton Rouge: Louisiana State University Press, 1984.
———. *Presidential Transitions and Foreign Affairs*. Baton Rouge: Louisiana State University Press, 1987.
———, ed. *Governmental Reorganizations*. Indianapolis, IN: Bobbs-Merrill, 1967.
Mosher, F. C., and O. F. Poland. *The Costs of American Governments*. New York: Dodd, Mead, 1964.

Works about Frederick Mosher

Kaufman, H. "Fear of Bureaucracy: A Raging Pandemic." *Public Administrative Review*, January–February 1981, 225–243.
Stephen, M. O., and J. F. Plant. "The Legacy of Frederick C. Mosher." *Public Administration Review*, March–April 1991, 97–113.
Sylvia, R. D. *Public Personnel Administration*. Belmont, CA: Wadsworth, 1994.

OSTROM, VINCENT (b. September 1919, Nooksack, WA), schoolteacher; university professor; political scientist; director; practitioner

Vincent Ostrom was born to Alfred and Alma (Knudson) Ostrom in 1919. He attended the University of California at Los Angeles (UCLA), receiving a B.A. in political science in 1942, an M.A. in political science in 1945, and a Ph.D. in political science in 1950. While matriculating at UCLA, he taught at Chaffey Union High School in Ontario, California, from 1943 to 1945. From 1945 to 1948 he served as an assistant professor of political science at the University of Wyoming. At the University of Oregon he held assistant and associate professorships from 1954 to 1958 and 1958 to 1964, respectively. He became professor of political science at Indiana University in 1964 and remained in this position until 1990. One of Ostrom's most distinguished academic positions was the Arthur F. Bentley Professor Emeritus of Political Science at Indiana University at Bloomington.

In addition to his professorial experience, Ostrom's career also includes a number of research appointments: The Hooker Distinguished Visiting Scholar at McMaster University from 1984 to 1985; associate director of Pacific Northwest Cooperative Program in Educational Administration from 1951 to 1958; and in 1973, codirector of the Workshop in Political Theory and Policy Analysis at Indiana University. He also held positions in the Budget Officer's School, the Wyoming League of Municipalities, and the Tennessee Water Policy Commission in 1956. He also received fellowships at the Social Science Research Council from 1954 to 1955 and at the Center of Advanced Study in the Behavioral Sciences from 1955 to 1956.

In *The Intellectual Crisis in American Public Administration*, Ostrom identifies a "crisis of confidence" in American public administration and challenges the intellectual pillars of public administration. The crisis becomes the difficulty of scholars to forge a new theoretical direction in the discipline, even against a backdrop that Ostrom equates to a natural science revolution.

Arguing for a departure from the bureaucratic model advanced by classical theorists, such as Max Weber and Woodrow Wilson, he proposes a more democratic framework consisting of a number of decision points that cross organizational lines as an alternative to the hierarchal and centralized bureaucratic model.

Reiterating the democratic beliefs that guided the founding of the United States, Ostrom calls for a return to a public administration system built on the public choice model, which offers citizens more choices through a fragmented network of government activities—a network that fosters negotiation and policy-making discretion on all levels of government in the United States.

Ostrom's support for citizen participation in public policy decisions is further asserted in *The Meaning of American Federalism*. Recalling Hamilton, Madison, and Jay's warnings against centralization of authority in *The Federalist Papers*, and the writings of de Tocqueville, he argues for a strengthening of government fragmentation, which facilitates citizen involvement.

BIBLIOGRAPHY

Works by Vincent Ostrom

Bish, R., and V. Ostrom. *Understanding Urban Government: Metropolitan Reform Reconsidered*. Washington, DC: American Enterprise Institute for Public Policy Research, 1973.

Ostrom, V. *The Political Theory of a Compound Republic: A Reconstruction of the Logical Foundations of American Democracy as Presented in the Federalist*. Blacksburg, VA: Public Choice, 1971.

———. *The Political Theory of a Compound Republic: Designing the American Experiment*. Lincoln: University of Nebraska Press, 1987.

———. *The Intellectual Crisis in American Public Administration*. 1973. Tuscaloosa: University of Alabama Press, 1989.

———. *The Meaning of American Federalism: Constituting a Self-Governing Society*. San Francisco, CA: ICS Press, 1991.

Ostrom, V., and R. Bish, eds. *Comparing Urban Service Delivery Systems: Structure and Performance*. Beverly Hills, CA: Sage Publications, 1977.

Ostrom, V., D. Feeny, and H. Picht, eds. *Rethinking Institutional Analysis and Development: Issues, Alternatives, and Choices.* San Francisco: International Center for Economic Growth, 1988.

Work about Vincent Ostrom

Peterson, P. "Federalism at the American Founding: In Defense of the Diamond Theses." *Publius*, 15, 1, Winter 1985, 23–30.

PERROW, CHARLES (b. February 9, 1925, Tacoma, WA), sociologist; university professor

Charles Perrow, professor of sociology at Yale University, is well known for organizational study at the macrolevel. His contributions to public administration are key, such as his acknowledgment that early institutionalists overlooked the role of power, and the manipulation of social values on the part of institutions. In addition to power, Perrow is concerned with the intricacies of strategy development. First, he privileges knowledge technology over production technology. Second, he describes the two interrelating aspects of technology: "task variability," that is, the number of exceptions workers encounter; and "problem analyzability," that is, the search procedures workers follow to rectify the exceptions.

In 1970, Perrow published *Organizational Analysis*, a structuralist "how-to" purportedly for "those who need to know something about organizational behavior in order to manage, or survive in, organizations." Addressing specific aspects of both industrial and correctional institutions, the five chapters of Perrow's text cover "Perspectives," "Variety of the Species," "Bureaucracy, Structure and Technology," "The Environment," and "Organizational Goals." At the time of publication, *Organizational Analysis* was considered by some critics the best available coverage of organizational legitimation, time, culture, reciprocity, and utilization of environment. Other critics questioned the abstract quality of the five organizational goals Perrow outlines: societal, output, system, product, and derived. Two years later, Perrow published *Complex Organizations: A Critical Essay* (1972), which takes a decidedly non-Weberian approach to organizations and includes a review of the Hawthorne Experiments and a tribute essay to Perrow's mentor, Philip Selznick.

Perrow's seminal works on organizations (which customarily correlate theory and pragmatism) are widely applied across disciplines into theological research and military studies. The interdisciplinary benefit of Perrow's research is apparent in his own contemporary work, including *The AIDS Disaster: The Failure of Organizations in New York and the Nation,* coauthored with Mauro F. Guillen. Echoing conclusions Perrow reached in *Normal Accidents: Living with High-Risk Technologies* (1984), that the "interlocking complexity" of organizations directly contributes to "accidents," Perrow argues that specific aspects of "organization" contributed to the spread of AIDS during the 1980s.

BIBLIOGRAPHY

Works by Charles Perrow

Jenkins, C., and C. Perrow. "Insurgency of the Powerless: Farm Workers Movement (1946–1972)." *American Sociological Review*, 1977, 429–468.

Perrow, C. "The Reluctant Organization and the Aggressive Environment." *Administrative Science Quarterly*, 10, 1965–1966, 238.

———. "A Framework for the Comparative Analysis of Organizations." *American Sociological Review*, 32, 1–6, 1967, 194.

———. *Organization Analysis: A Sociological View.* Belmont, CA: Wadsworth, 1970.

———. *Complex Organizations: A Critical Essay.* 1972. Glenview, IL: Scott, Foresman, 1979.

———. "Disintegrating Social Sciences." *Phi Delta Kappan*, 63, 9, June 1982, 684–688.

———. "The Organizational Context of Human Factors Engineering." *Administrative Science Quarterly*, 28, 4, December 1983, 521.

———. *Normal Accidents: Living with High-Risk Technologies.* New York: Basic Books, 1984.

———. "Comment on Langton's Ecological Theory of Bureaucracy." *Administrative Science Quarterly*, 30, 2, June 1985, 278.

Perrow, C., and M. F. Guillen. *The AIDS Disaster: The Failure of Organizations in New York and the Nation.* New Haven, CT: Yale University Press, 1990.

PORTER, LYMAN W. (b. 1930, Lafayette, IN), educator (administration and psychology); publisher; university professor; dean; fellow

Porter received a B.S. from Northwestern University in 1952 and later attended Yale University, where he received a Ph.D. in 1956. He was awarded an honorary doctorate from De Paul University (Chicago). He taught at the University of California at Berkeley from 1956 to 1967. He later continued his teaching career at the University of California at Irvine, where he taught administration and psychology and became dean of the Graduate School of Administration. He was a fellow and president of the division of industrial and organizational psychology at the American Psychological Association from 1975 to 1976.

His work is in management education and training, as well as human resource management, organization development, and organizational psychology. He believes that organizations are influenced by political considerations and factors. He notes that organizations are composed of many individuals and groups who are trying to accomplish specific goals. In the process of achieving organizational objectives, according to Porter, everyone affects everyone else, regardless of position in the organization. He conducted several studies with Edward Lawler concerning organizational psychology and employee motivation. He argues in favor of a fair and effective reward system. According to Porter, there are two different types of rewards, intrinsic and extrinsic. Mostly organizations are able to determine and control extrinsic rewards, whereas intrinsic rewards are difficult to control and depend on many complicated variables. He argues that the system of rewards plays an important role in determining the success or failure of an organization. In one of his studies (conducted in cooperation with James Perry), they studied different factors that affect employee motivations in organizations. They conclude that environmental factors have a strong effect on employees' level of performance. Role perceptions also constitute an important factor in determining motivation levels. They note that such factors as "self-worth and personal significance can be expected to be affected by environmental factors."

Porter and Edward Lawler developed a model of motivation with variables such as effort, performance, reward, and satisfaction. They argued that there is a direct relationship between individual levels of activity (effort) and rewards. They believed that two factors affect an employee's level of activity. The first is how much the employee values the reward system and his perception of the relationship between the effort that he makes and performance of the task (in their words, if the individual is capable of performing the job in the first place). The second factor that affects the "effort" factor is the "expectation" that the employee has about receiving the reward for performing the job. They demonstrated this relationship in a formula as follows: $E \to P$, which indicates the relationship between effort and intended performance; and $P \to O$, which determines the relationship and expectancy that performance will result in a certain reward (outcome). Therefore, in their view, a combination of these two factors determines an individual's level of motivation. They argue that if the employee is capable of performing the job and receives appropriate rewards for completing it, he or she will be motivated enough to perform. In addition, they believe that other external and internal factors might influence the performance of employees. For example, self-esteem and the cooperation that employees receive from other members of the organization will positively or negatively affect their performance.

BIBLIOGRAPHY

Works by Lyman W. Porter

Porter, L. W. *Organizational Patterns of Managerial Job Attitudes*. New York: American Foundation for Management Research, 1964.

Porter, L. W., and R. W. Allen. *Organizational Influence Processes*. Glenview, IL: Scott, Foresman, 1983.

Porter, L. W., M. Haire, and E. E. Ghiselli. *Managerial Thinking: An International Study*. New York: John Wiley and Sons, 1966.

Porter, L. W., and E. E. Lawler III. *Managerial Attitudes and Performance.* Homewood, IL: Richard D. Irwin, 1968.

------. *Managerial Attitudes and Performance.* New York: McGraw-Hill, 1988.

Porter, L. W., E. Lawler, and R. Hackman. *Behavior in Organizations.* New York: McGraw-Hill, 1975.

Porter, L. W., and J. L. Perry. "Factors Affecting the Context for Motivation in Public Organizations." *Academy of Management Review,* 17, 1, 1982, 114–135.

Porter, L. W., and R. Steers. *Motivation and Work Behavior.* New York: McGraw-Hill, 1975.

------. *Organizational, Work and Personal Factors in Turnover and Absenteeism.* Irvine: University of California, 1972.

Works about Lyman W. Porter

Farnsworth, P. R., ed. *Annual Review of Psychology, 1966.* Palo Alto, CA: Annual Reviews, 1966.

McGuire, J. W., ed. *Contemporary Management: Issues and Viewpoints.* Englewood Cliffs, NJ: Prentice-Hall, 1974.

"Motivation." Boston: Graduate School of Business Administration, Harvard University, 1964–1981.

Organ, D. W., ed. *The Applied Psychology of Work Behavior: A Book of Readings.* Homewood, IL: Irwin, 1991.

RAWLS, JOHN B. (b. 1920, Baltimore, MD), philosopher; university professor; fellow

Rawls graduated from Kent High School in 1939 and completed graduate and undergraduate work at Princeton University. He taught at Princeton for a few years and later joined Oxford University on a Fulbright Fellowship (1952–1953). He taught at Cornell University for six years (1953–1959), then went back to Harvard to teach philosophy in 1962. He also served as the coeditor of the *Philosophical Review* (1956–1959).

He is well known for his philosophical views and specifically his understanding of social theories of "justice." His ideas on justice were influenced by Locke, Kant, Rousseau, and Hobbes, who were major theorists of social contract. However, he presents his theory of justice at a different level. He expresses his thoughts in the context of political theory with the underpinning of social contract tradition and uses an analytical approach. He takes into consideration moral and political philosophy and utilizes decision theory in his analysis. Among his writings, *A Theory of Justice* has provoked the most interest and caused a great deal of controversy. He argues in favor of "justice as fairness." He deals with justice in the context of social institutions and argues that injustice (unbalanced) occurs when, for the sake of the greater good to society, some members lose their freedom. Therefore, in a just society the most important priority is securing the rights of individuals. Therefore, those rights should be guaranteed and cannot be tampered with in any political deal. He believes that public policy decisions should be made based on a disregard for any political gains or under the "veil of ignorance." This approach, according to Rawls, guarantees justice and fairness in policy decisions because resources will be allocated based on social needs rather than political considerations. He believes that the most important task in a just society is to define and guarantee basic rights and duties, as well as each member's contribution to society and his or her share from social wealth.

Rawls argues that society is composed of both cooperation and competition, conflict and mutual interest. Therefore, there have to be certain principles to deal with different social arrangements (cooperative setting), bring about social justice, and distribute social benefits. He argues that the principles of justice must have social acceptability and that basic social institutions must adhere to those principles. He explains that the reason most societies are in a state of conflict is that there is confusion regarding what is just or unjust.

He argues that rational persons are willing to exercise their rights in societies in a context of equality. This principle will then direct all different aspects of life and behavior in societies, including political and social organizations. Here he emphasizes the idea of "fairness" and extends his vision into the role of values and morals and their role in designing organizational structure. This, according to Rawls, will guarantee the full participation of members of society. It also guarantees fairness in the decision-making process because everyone in society is able to have input into the decisions that are made.

BIBLIOGRAPHY

Works by John B. Rawls

Rawls, John B. *A Theory of Justice*. Cambridge, MA: Belknap Press of Harvard University, 1971.
————. *Political Liberalism*. New York: Columbia University Press, 1993.

Works about John B. Rawls

Martin, R. *Rawls and Rights*. Lawrence: University Press of Kansas, 1985.
Norman, D. *Reading Rawls*. New York: Basic Books, 1971.
Pogge, T. *Realizing Rawls*. New York: Cornell University Press, 1982.
Wellnak, J. H., D. Smook, and D. T. Mason. *John Rawls & His Critics*. New York: Garland, 1982.
Wolff, R. *Understanding Rawls*. Princeton, NJ: Princeton University Press, 1977.

RIGGS, FREDERICK WARREN (b. July 3, 1917, Kuling, China), international relations specialist; research associate; university professor; ecologist

Frederick Riggs was born to Clara-Louise Mather and Charles Henry Riggs, who ran an agricultural station in China where Frederick was born and received his early education. Even from this early point, mediating dichotomies has been important to Fred Riggs's development.

Riggs attended the University of Illinois and was awarded a B.A. in 1938; his Ph.D. in international relations was awarded in 1948 from Columbia University. Riggs was not a formally trained public administrator.

From 1947 to 1948, Riggs lectured in international relations at City College of New York City. He worked as research associate at the Foreign Policy Association in New York from 1948 to 1951. From 1951 to 1955, Riggs acted as assistant to the director of the New York City Office of Public Administration Clearing House. He returned to academia in 1955 when he joined the faculty of Yale University for a year. After this tenure ended, Riggs taught comparative administration at Indiana University, Bloomington, until 1960. Despite ties to the American Academy, Riggs lectures in Korea and around the world. Riggs was honored by the Thai government for his work in Thailand.

From a public administration standpoint, Riggs is recognized as an ecologist; this standpoint is perhaps his greatest contribution to public comparativist methodology. He compared political and administrative institutions. Overall, Riggs's approach afforded a reconciliatory approach to theory and statistics.

As a pioneer in model building, Riggs took particular interest in the public administration of developing countries. He is both founder and first chairperson of the comparativists, the Comparative Administration Group formed during a time when public administrators widely believed that American models could be applied in other countries without first considering the specific structures and behaviors of the country. His famous "prismatic" methodology sought negotiation of U.S. practice with indigenous phenomena; he preferred this to the previous dichotomy "traditional" and "modern." Riggs is therefore credited with, and at times critiqued for, inaugurating new social science vocabulary in contexts American and abroad.

Riggs's professional membership reflects a diverse interest in international affairs—public administration, social science, Asian studies, political science, and information science.

BIBLIOGRAPHY

Works by Frederick Warren Riggs

Riggs, F. W. *Pressures on Congress: A Study of the Repeal of Chinese Exclusion.* New York: King's Crown Press, 1950.

———. *Formosa under Chinese Nationalist Rule.* New York: Macmillan, 1952.

———. *The Ecology of Public Administration.* New York: Taplinger, 1961.

———. *Convergences in the Study of Comparative Public Administration and Local Government.* Gainesville: University of Florida Public Administrations Office, 1962.

———. "Trends in the Comparative Study of Public Administration." *International Review of Administrative Sciences*, 28, 1, 1962, 9–15.

———. *Census and Notes on Clintele Groups in Thai Politics and Administration.* Bloomington: Department of Government, Indiana University, 1963.

———. *Models and Priorities in the Comparative Study of Public Administration.* Chicago: Comparative Administration Group, American Society for Public Administration, 1963.

———. *Administration in Developing Countries: The Theory of Prismatic Society.* Boston: Houghton, 1964.

———. "Relearning an Old Lesson: The Political Context of Development Administration." *Public Administration Review*, 65, 1965, 70–79.

———. *Thailand: The Modernization of a Bureaucratic Polity.* Honolulu: East-West Center Press, 1966.

———. *The Political Structures of Administrative Development: Some Tentative Formulations.* Stanford, CA: Center for Advanced Study in the Behavioral Sciences, 1967.

———. *Administrative Reform and Political Responsiveness: A Theory of Dynamic Balancing.* Beverly Hills, CA: Sage Publications, 1970.

———. "Prismatic Societies and Public Administration." *Administrative Change*, 1, 2, December 1973, 12–24.

———. *The Prismatic Society Revisited.* Morristown, NJ: General Learning Press, 1973.

———. *Legislative Origins: A Contextual Approach.* Pittsburgh, PA: International Studies Association, 1975.

———. "Organizational Structures and Contexts." *Administration and Society*, 7, 2, August 1975, 150–190.

———. "The Prismatic Society and Development." *Administrative Change*, 2, January–June 1975, 127–135.

———. *Applied Prismatics: A Development Perspective.* Kirtipur, Nepal: Centre for Economic Development and Administration, Tribhuvan University, 1978.

———. "On Reviewing International Studies: Some Comments." *Journal of Higher Education*, 52, 2, March–April 1981, 143–154.

———. "The Rise and Fall of 'Political Development.' " *Handbook of Political Behavior*, 4, 1981, 289–348.

———. "Research Note: A New Kind of Glossary for Ethnic Studies." *Ethnic and Racial Studies*, 7, 4, October 1984, 551–552.

———. "What is Ethnic? What Is National? Let's Turn the Tables." *Canadian Review of Studies in Nationalism*, 13, 1, Spring 1986, 111–124.

———. "Bureaucratic Politics in the U.S.: Benchmarks for Comparison." *Governance*, 1, 4, October 1988, 343–379.

———. "The Survival of Presidentialism in America: Para-Constitutional Practices." *International Political Science Review*, 9, 4, October 1988, 247–278.

———. "The Political Ecology of American Public Administration: A Neo-Hamiltonian Approach." *International Journal of Public Administration*, 12, 3, 1989, 355–384.

———. "Public Administration: A Comparativist Framework." *Public Administration Review*, 51, 6, November–December 1991, 473–477.

————. "Bureaucracy and the Constitution." *Public Administration Review*, 54, 1, January–February 1994, 65–72.

————. "Ethnonationalism, Industrialism, and the Modern State." *Third World Quarterly*, 15, 4, December 1994, 583–611.

————. "Modernity and Bureaucracy." *Public Administration Review*, 57, 4, July–August 1997, 347–353.

————. "Public Administration in America: Why Our Uniqueness Is Exceptional and Important." *Public Administration Review*, 58, 1, January–February 1998, 22–31.

————, ed. *International Studies.* American Academy of Political and Social Science, 1971.

————. *The Tower of Babel: On the Definition and Analysis of Concepts in the Social Sciences.* Pittsburgh, PA: International Studies Association, 1975.

Works about Frederick Warren Riggs

Chapman, R. A. "Prismatic Theory of Public Administration: A Review of the Theories of Fred W. Riggs." *Public Administration*, 44, Winter 1966, 415–433.

Krishma, D. "Shall We Be Diffracted? A Critical Comment on Fred W. Riggs' Prismatic Societies and Public Administration." *Administration Change*, 2, 1, June 1974, 48–55.

————. "Towards a Saner View of 'Development': A Comment on Fred W. Riggs' Comment." *Administration Change*, 3, 2, January–June 1976, 19–26.

Prasad, V. S., and K. M. Manohar. "Fred W. Riggs." In *Administrative Thinkers*, ed. D. R. Prasad, V. S. Prasad, and P. Satyanarayana. New Delhi: Light and Life Publishers, 1980, 197–226.

ROSENBLOOM, DAVID H. (b. August 1943, New York, NY), editor; political scientist; university professor; fellow

Rosenbloom received a Ph.D. in political science from the University of Chicago in 1969. He also obtained an A.B. from Marietta College in 1964 and an M.A. from the University of Chicago in 1966. He taught political science at the University of Kansas from 1961 to 1971; Tel Aviv University, from 1971 to 1973; and the University of Vermont, Burlington, from 1973 to 1975. He is currently teaching public administration at the American University. He was a fellow at the U.S. Civil Service Commission from 1970 to 1971 and chaired the Percival Wood Clement Prize Essay competition in Constitutional Law in 1977. He became the editor in chief of the *Public Administration Review* in 1991 and one year later received the Distinguished Research Award of the National Association of Schools of Public Affairs and Administration and the American Society for Public Administration. His major areas of expertise are public administration, law, the Constitution, politics, representative bureaucracy, comparative public administration, personnel administration, and labor relations. He has also written extensively on the role of the Civil

Service Commission in the Federal Equal Employment Opportunity program.

Rosenbloom argues in terms of a changing orientation for public administration from management to law. This would make it more responsive to social needs and creates sensitivity toward such issues as constitutional rights, participation, and representation. He contends that the old approach in public administration had repressive characteristics. For example, the classical approach is criticized for emphasizing such principles as hierarchy and unity of command, which undermines constitutional commitment to freedom of expression. In addition, it denies the individuals freedom of expression and participation. In his judgment the most important task of a democratic government is to balance the rights of the individuals and the authority of governments. That is why, he argues, public administration should abandon the traditional approach of emphasizing hierarchical authority with less attention to the rights of the individuals and minorities.

Rosenbloom takes on the issue of the dichotomy of politics and administration and indicates that public institutions, by adopting "businesslike" approaches to administration, go against the major tenets of their nature, which is "publicness." His work in public personnel administration is indicative of the same philosophy of the uniqueness of public institutions. He argues that there are four sources that affect the nature and identity of the public sector and make it different from the private sector. The first source is the Constitution. It provides a great deal of control over bureaucracy through the executive and legislative branches. Constitutional controls affect the operation of government. However, due to the fragmentation of authority over the personnel matters, it is very difficult to bring about substantial change to the conduct of personnel administration. He also indicates that the Constitution provides every individual with unalienable rights and holds personnel administration responsive to those rights. He emphasizes that in application of those rights, the values of efficiency and liberty come into conflict with each other. Therefore, "businesslike" personnel administration cannot be responsive to the needs of the public sector. The second source of the difference between the public and private sector is the final product. The private sector is involved with a competitive market that determines the source of its support. But the public sector's output is monopolistic and service-oriented. The third factor is the source of revenue for each sector. The public's source of revenue is mainly taxes paid by the citizens, which can be affected by politics. The private sector sells its products to the public to generate revenue. According to Rosenbloom, the fourth factor that makes the public sector different from the private is the "public interest." In other words, public institutions should always keep the interest of the public in mind while business firms serve their own interests. In fact, government is responsible for defending and protecting the public from the abusive behavior of private corporations.

He also admits that public administration is suffering from the lack of paradigm and conceptual framework. He believes that this lack of identity is the consequence of the vast areas of human concern with which public administration has to deal. Therefore, these areas are difficult to cover under one paradigm or coherent entity. He contends that public administration can be divided into several subfields, including health, developmental, regulatory, and welfare administrations. In his judgment, the future of public administration is less managerial than a combination of political, economic, legal, and scientific factors at both macro- and microlevels. Therefore, future public administrators are going to deal with political compromises among the different forces that shape policies. His emphasis on the process of administration leads him to believe that public administrators need to be familiar with legal issues and be held responsible for their individual actions. He perceives public administration as being more legalistically oriented in the future. He rejects the idea of outside oversight over the operation of government and believes in reliance on the hierarchical chain of command to provide accountability. Therefore, the ultimate responsibility lies with individual administrators who should adhere to legal principles. (It is important to emphasize that his legal approach advocates strict adherence to the laws not only because they are rules and regulations but because they are the reflection of common social values.) In his view, public employees should take personal responsibility for their actions. This will enhance their participation and their commitment to serve the interest of the public.

Rosenbloom also contends that public administration of the future should have less emphasis on technical matters in favor of sensitivity to the needs of the public. He advocates a public administration that emphasizes not only the values of efficiency, effectiveness, and economy but also representation and individual liberty. He believes that the public should be given the chance to participate in the bureaucratic decision-making process in order to manifest the true representative nature of bureaucracy. In his opinion this will bring more effectiveness to the work of public agencies, because the actions of the administration are the reflection of public needs.

In addition, he believes that in order to bring about public representation in bureaucracy there has to be a formal structure to facilitate this function. For example, he argues that the public should be able to respond and participate in promulgation of administrative rules. In order for the public to make informed decisions, he advocates the dissemination of information and easy access to public documents. He argues that this, by itself, is a means to improve the quality of administrative behavior in public organizations. He also advocates democratization of

governmental institutions for the same reason that government is supposed to represent the core values of society including democracy. This
would encourage participatory management by creating a new administrative culture.

BIBLIOGRAPHY

Works by David H. Rosenbloom

Carrol, J. D., and D. H. Rosenbloom. *Toward Constitutional Competence: A Casebook
    for Public Administrators*. Englewood Cliffs, NJ: Prentice-Hall, 1990.
Rosenbloom, D. H. *Federal Service and the Constitution: The Development of the
    Public Employment Relationship*. Ithaca, NY: Cornell University Press, 1971.
———. *Federal Equal Employment Opportunity: Politics and Public Administration*.
    New York: Praeger, 1977.
———. *Public Administration: Understanding Management, Politics, and Law in the
    Public Sector*. New York: McGraw-Hill, 1993.
———. *Public Administration and Law*. New York: Marcel Dekker, 1997.
———, ed. "Symposium on Public Personnel Administration and the Law." *Re-
    view of Public Personnel Administration*, 2, 1981, 1–61.
Shafritz, J. M., and D. H. Rosenbloom. *Essentials of Labor Relations*. New York:
    Reston, 1985.

Works about David H. Rosenbloom

Compbell, A. "Civil Service Reform: A New Commitment." *Public Administration
    Review*, 38, 1978, 99–103.
Goldman, D. D. "Due Process and Public Personnel Management." *Review of
    Public Personnel Administration*, 2, 1981, 19–28.
Nachimas, D. H. *Public Administration and Law*. New York: Marcel Dekker, 1997.
U.S. Office of Personnel Management. *Civil Service 2000*. Washington, DC: Office
    of Personnel Management, 1988.

SCHICK, ALLEN (b. 1934), educator (public budgeting and finance); editor;
economist; budget expert; university professor; journal founder

Allen Schick received his B.A. from Brooklyn College in 1956 and three
years later his M.A. from Yale University. He completed his Ph.D. from
Yale University in 1966. Schick's main contribution is in public budgeting
and finance. He presently teaches at the Urban Institute of the University
of Maryland. He has taught at Tufts University and has worked with the
Brookings Institution and the Congressional Research Service for several
years. He is also the founder of *Public Budgeting and Finance*, which is
the most prestigious journal in public finance. He is the recipient of the
Waldo Prize from the American Society of Public Administration for his
contribution to the public administration discipline (1989). He also received the Hardeman Prize for his book on the U.S. Congress and the
Brownlow Award for his book on American political institutions.

He argues that budgets are the primary instruments used by governments to direct the affairs of nations. He claims it is the major tool for

bringing about change and implementing certain policies. Schick considers the budget a powerful tool to control bureaucracy. He contends that budgeting is a process that relates the availability of funds to the goals of an organization. He believes that budgeting is a field by itself and has a great influence on public policy making in terms of utilization of public resources. He argues that the American budgeting process is facing substantial crisis because of its inability to face its national challenges by developing major deficits. He also believes that in order to secure majority support the budget process has been modified drastically. He explores the hidden politics of the national budgets and asks for many changes to secure the proper functioning of the process.

According to Schick, historically speaking, the best example of the American budgeting system was during the New Deal period. In his judgment, during that period the federal budget played a major role in determining the future of the country by expanding the scope of the financial role of government. Several programs were created to solve major social problems. Even today, many social programs such as social security, unemployment insurance, housing programs, and public assistance are legacies of the New Deal. The most significant result of the New Deal was overcoming the economic depression of its time. By emphasizing the role of national budget in determining the economic condition of the country, Schick is a strong supporter of reducing the budget deficit through cooperation between the executive and legislative branches.

Schick has conducted extensive studies on the Planning Programming Budgeting Systems (PPBS). This system of budgeting was experimented with during the 1960s and was abandoned in the 1970s. However, many aspects of PPBS are still in use by state, local, and some federal agencies. He believed that PPBS was not very successful with the federal government (referring to its failure and abandonment by the Office of Management and Budget in 1971) because of the budgeting process. He explains that determinations regarding the annual budgets are generally made without benefit of careful planning and systems analysis, much as they were prior to the PPBS. Therefore, he is advocating major modifications of the budgeting process in order to make it more rational.

Schick also conducted studies on the usage of ZBB (Zero Base Budgeting) with Hary Harty. In their studies of four different cities and states, they found that most managers were in favor of the effects of ZBB on their cost-cutting activities. Schick and Harty argue that in using ZBB managers concentrate on cutting their costs because they want to avoid the consequences of assessing their services against the cost of delivering them. This cost cutting is essential because they want to protect themselves, especially when they do not have acceptable ways to measure productivity. Schick also examined the implementation of PPBS in several states and concluded that the reason PPBS was not used as a primary approach to budgeting was political and bureaucratic. He argued that there are three main approaches in budgeting: (1) the emphasis on control, which is a more traditional approach to budgeting; (2) the work load and performance measurement; and (3) the most recent, which emphasizes planning and program analysis. He defends PPBS and argues that it failed because the budget process is "anti-analytic," with emphasis on budgeting routines. Therefore, he argues that PPBS failed to penetrate "vital budgetary routines."

Schick argues that one of the major problems with the budgetary process is the influence of politics on its formulation and implementation. He believes that if the interrelation between the executive and legislative branches, with respect to their budgetary behavior, can be reformed and modified, we can expect a more effective budgetary process. He argues that politics plays a major role in the process of budgeting, especially when major decisions are at stake. Therefore, he blames the lack of confidence in government, its budgetary problems, and its image in the eyes of the public on the politicians. He believes that in order for budget reform and innovation to be successful, officials should change the principle elements by which budgetary decisions are made. Otherwise, according to Schick, reforms will fail and become victims of political pitfalls.

BIBLIOGRAPHY

Works by Allen Schick

Schick, A. L. "The Stage of Budget Reform." *Public Administration Review*, December 1966, 243–258.

———. *Budget Innovation in the States*. Washington, DC: Brookings Institution, 1971.

———. "A Death in the Bureaucracy: The Demise of Federal PPB." *Public Administration Review*, March–April 1973, 146–156.

———. *Congress and Money: Budgeting, Spending, and Taxing*. Washington, DC: Urban Institute, 1980.

———. *Perspectives on Budgeting*. Washington, DC: American Society for Public Administration, 1980.

———. *The Capacity to Budget*. Washington, DC: Urban Institute Press, 1990.

———. "Omnibus Legislation: Lawmaking in an Age of Political Fragmentation." Manuscript. In progress.

———. "Taking Public Budgeting Seriously: What the U.S. Can Learn from Other Countries." Manuscript. In progress.

Schick, A. L., and H. Harty. "Zero Base Budgeting: The Manager's Budget." *Public Budgeting & Finance*, Spring 1982, 86–98.

Work about Allen Schick

Mikesell, J. L. *Fiscal Administration: Analysis and Application for the Public Sector.* 4th ed. Belmont, CA: Wadsworth, 1995.

SCHULTZ, ALFRED (b. 1899, Vienna, Austria; d. 1959, USA), philosopher; lawyer; lecturer; professor

Schultz spent most of his adult life in Austria before migrating to the United States in 1939. His early occupations were law and banking. While he was involved with business activities and law, he lectured at the New School for Social Research in New York in 1943. He received his professorship in 1952. His major work has been on the methodology of the social sciences and critical discussions of the philosophy of Edmund Husserl (his former professor), William James, Max Weber, and Jean-Paul Sartre. His major contribution is in the realm of philosophy and social science and its interconnection between works in both disciplines. He tries to establish a connection between Weber's ideas on sociology and Husserl's understanding of phenomenology. His writings approach sociological foundations with phenomenological orientations, often referred to as "interpretive social theory" or "action theory." He mastered phenomenological philosophy, as well as sociology, economics, and law. He wrote over thirty articles and essays in different languages, including German, English, Spanish, and French.

Schultz concentrates on a variety of topics, including social action, methodology of social sciences, language, and acquisition of knowledge. He argues that knowledge is acquired through everyday experiences (piece-by-piece education) and rejected the notion of any "primordial experience." As far as the relevancy of the knowledge acquired is concerned, he believes that there are three kinds of relevancy: motivational, thematic, and interpretational. He argues that the motivational relevancy is unique to the individual's personal interest and depends on the time and the situation. Accordingly, if motivation is suspended, the situation changes and problems arise, and the individual involves himself with solving the problem at hand. He then turns to thematic relevance, which is a continuation of the first stage (recognition of the problem and efforts to solve it). Thematic relevance concentrates on solving the problem by utilizing the cognitive and investigative abilities of an individual. Schultz argues that interpretational relevance has as its prerequisite the recognition of the problem and the placing of said problem in a larger context. He also talked about the "absolute relevance" by which the knowledge at hand has no use in solving the problem. He contends that there is a "basic" relevance" imposed on people that has a great effect on life as a whole. This imposed reality is the environment in which one is born and other conditions that surround an individual.

He attempts to make sense of the daily life by understanding and using common sense of knowledge. He perceives the social world as a composition of a multitude of realities. He believes people relate to those realities differently and therefore that people "conduct" differently according to their subjective understanding of reality (either inner-life [covert] or "thinking" or outer-life [overt] or "doing"). Overt actions are geared to the outer world. According to Schultz, action takes place only when the covert precedes the overt.

Schultz deals with the question of motivation at length and argues that there are two sets of concepts that are related to motivation: one is the "in-order-to" and the other is the "because" motive. In the first category, the person has an "end" in mind before embarking on any action. But in the second, the person conducting the act is doing it spontaneously due to or "because" of certain circumstances beyond his or her control. He also recognizes the inner components of human communication and concerns himself with the question of "ego." He believes that interchanges between individuals' egos create the shared reality. He engages in the concept of a world of cognitive and conative awareness and the recognition of different levels of egos.

BIBLIOGRAPHY

Works by Alfred Schultz

Schultz, A. Collected Papers: The Problem of Social Reality. Ed. M. Natanson. Netherlands: The Hague Publishing, 1962.
———. On Phenomenology and Social Relations. Ed. H. R. Wagner. Chicago: University of Chicago Press, 1970.
———. Reflection on the Problem of Relevance. Ed. R. M. Zaner. New Haven, CT: Yale University Press, 1970.
Schultz, A., and T. Luckmann. The Structure of the Life-World. Trans. R. M. Zaner and H. T. Engelhardt, Jr. Evanston, IL: Northwestern University Press, 1973.

Works about Alfred Schultz

Bierstedt, R. Power and Progress: Essays on Sociological Theory. New York: McGraw-Hill, 1974.
Sciambra, J. C. From Herbert Spencer to Alfred Schultz: Jack London, His Library, and the Rise of Radical Racialism in Turn-of-the-century America. 1997.

SEIDMAN, HAROLD (b. July 2, 1911, Brooklyn, NY), public administrator; consultant; lecturer; municipal administrator

Harold Seidman is primarily known for his studies of federalism, his research on government-owned corporations, and his federal coordination of Alaska and Hawaii to statehood. His expertise is grounded in consulting work he completed during the 1950s and early 1960s when he served as consultant to the United Nations, Guatemala, Vietnam, the Economic Commission for Africa, and the President's Council on Executive Organization. Nonetheless, Seidman's professional career also required involvement on the city level with the New York City Department of Investigation from 1938 to 1943. He did not begin teaching on the university level until 1952, when he lectured at George Washington University for a year. The teaching career continued when Seidman lectured in 1962 at the University of Southern California and taught as visiting professor (in 1969 at Syracuse University, in 1971 at University of Connecticut, and from 1972 to 1975 at the University of Leeds, England).

From 1968 to 1971, Seidman was scholar-in-residence at the National Academy of Public Administration in Washington, DC, during which time he produced the seminal *Politics, Position, and Power: The Dynamics of Federal Organization* (1970) from his "inside view" of federal administration and the "institutional history, ideology, values, biases, symbols and folklore" that it mirrors.

Specifically, Seidman's book outlines a number of organizations—including departmental structures, regulatory agencies, government corporations, and independent agencies—and describes the distinct "cultures" or "ecologies" of administrative agencies. Unlike previous works, Seidman's project "presents an inside view of Federal Administration as it affects and is affected by the continuing contest . . . for power, position and political advantage" and concludes with a radical call for new analyses leading to "reorganization of the Congressional Committee structure." Seidman contextualizes his core argument with distinct material. He presents significant background detail that historicizes administrative organization from Hoover's presidency through Nixon's. He describes organization theory and most important, initiates his study with an overview of presidential study commissions on administrative organization in order to explain how these previous works have not determined administrative reality and diversity.

In particular, Seidman targets the role of congressional committees in administrative process and the relationship between these committees and administrative agencies, exposing contentions between parallel couples—congressmen and senators, and governors and local politicians. Seidman concludes that the informal (not the formal) lines of power more significantly determine bureaucratic output. As Seidman explains, the misunderstanding of "institutional culture" has affected politicians and has led to "White House distrust of bureaucracy" as well. Privileging resolution over polemic, Seidman recommends a strategy of balanced power among agencies, committees, and sections of government.

BIBLIOGRAPHY

Works by Harold Seidman

Seidman, H. *Labor Czars: A History of Labor Racketeering.* New York: Liveright Publishing Corporation, 1938.

———. *Politics, Position, and Power: The Dynamics of Federal Organization.* New York: Oxford University Press, 1970.

Seidman, H., and R. Gilmour. *Investigating Municipal Administration: A Study of the New York City Department of Investigation.* New York: Institute of Public Administration, Columbia University Press, 1941.

SELZNICK, PHILIP (b. 1919, Newark, NJ), professor; expert on public agency institutionalization

Selznick's contribution to the open model of organizational theory and behavior is "co-optation," a concept advanced in his study of the Tennessee Valley Authority (TVA), entitled *TVA and the Grassroots* (1949). Co-optation is a twofold process. In the first part, formal co-optation, an organization undergoes "the process of absorbing new elements into [its] leadership or policy-determining structure . . . as a means of averting threats to its stability or existence." Informal co-optation is the process of response to formal co-optation. Overall, co-optation is the process by which a larger agency is controlled by a secondary (perhaps subordinate) organization that is vital to its operations. The former process is public, the latter private, in order to secure the public's belief in its claim on sovereign power. The two types of co-optation that can exist are fundamental to Selznick's development of the co-optation theory.

Selznick illustrates the relationship through the example of the decision-making bodies of Tennessee agriculture (local farm bureau organizations, land grant colleges, and fertilizer associations) achieving conservative leadership of the Tennessee Valley Authority. The institutionalization of the TVA culminated in a locally entrenched grassroots group determining development for an entire eight-state, mid-South region. Co-optation in this context was successful because citizen involvement was minimal and opposition was voiceless; that is, it projected "the illusion of a voice without the voice itself." In the case of the TVA, then, co-optation granted social control. The intent of co-optation is to quell opposition to agency initiatives by allowing opposing groups and individuals to participate in various degrees in the agency's policy decision making.

Selznick's study of co-optation in the Tennessee Valley introduces two additional key concepts for studies of institutionalization: environment and leadership. The case of the TVA suggested to Selznick the importance of the "relationship" between a public organization and its environments. Moreover, Selznick suggests that leadership was the crucial force in the institutionalization of the TVA.

Ideas of shaping the "environment" and determining "leadership" reach full potential in Selznick's *Leadership in Administration: A Sociological Interpretation* (1957), an application of organizational theory and behavior. Selznick first differentiates the organization (temporary) and the institution (adaptive and long lasting). The latter, he explains, is a social organism that prevails under the leadership of an executive who is able to effectively alter the environment. Unlike the "administrator" who wastes time on bureaucratic and technical chores, the "executive" is a

128 SIMON, HERBERT

leader who shapes social elements at the "institutional level." The co-alescing of the institutional environment takes many forms: defining the mission, defending institutional integrity, negotiating power with intra-institutional parties, recruiting and training staff, and determining new directions. In the case of the TVA for example, Selznick compares the effective executive to the statesman. In the context of institutional lead-ership in general, Selznick suggests that, like a statesman, the executive knows how to protect the distinctive autonomy of institutional elites.

Attention to emotional and symbolic factors in an organization draws Selznick's comparison of human experience and organic institutions closer together. Selznick's *Leadership in Administration* is in fact known for its attack on the argument that determinants of efficiency can be universalized. According to Selznick, contrary to the teaching of admin-istrative managers, an institution's "human" dimensions are idiosyn-cratic; therefore, no one body of measures is both widely applicable and consistently productive. Selznick's theory is that the most institutional aspect of administration is also its most personal—the highly contingent loyalty and purpose generated by employees. These are characteristics of Selznick's doctrine of "value infusion." The employees of a value-infused work setting not only act upon common premises in the local (work) context, but they also aspire to the institution's code of produc-tivity and not simply their own concept of personal gain.

BIBLIOGRAPHY

Works by Philip Selznick

Selznick, P. *TVA and the Grassroots: A Study in the Sociology of Formal Organization*. Berkeley and Los Angeles: University of California Press, 1949.
———. *Leadership in Administration: A Sociological Interpretation*. New York: Row, Peterson, 1957.
———. *Law, Society, and Industrial Justice*. New York: Russell Sage Foundation, 1969.
———. *The Moral Commonwealth: Social Theory and the Promise of Community*. Berkeley: University of California Press, 1992.
———. "Thinking about Community: Ten Theses." *Society*, 32, 5, July–August 1995, 33–37.
———. "Ten Theses: Thoughts on Communitarianism." *Current*, 378, December 1995, 11–14.

Work about Philip Selznick

Weatherley, R. *Approaches to Cutback Management. Human Services at Risk: Admin-istrative Strategies for Survival*. Lexington, MA: Lexington Books/D. C. Heath, 1984.

SIMON, HERBERT (b. June 15, 1916, Milwaukee, WI), university profes-sor; consultant; principal architect of the bounded rationality theory; No-bel Prize winner (1978)

Simon received his Ph.D. from the University of Chicago in 1943 and taught at the University of Chicago and served as the head of the Department of Social Sciences in 1947. He also worked for the local governments in Illinois and lectured at many other universities including Harvard University, Massachusetts Institute of Technology, and Princeton University. In addition to consulting for the Rand Corporation and Cowel Foundation for Research in 1952, Simon served as the chair of the division of behavioral sciences at the National Research Council during the 1968–1972 period, and he was a member of the President's Science Advisory Committee (1968–1972). In 1978, Simon received a Nobel Prize in economics. He taught computer science and psychology at the Carnegie-Mellon University at Pittsburgh after 1949 for several years. He developed his ideas in management and operation research during his years of formal education and work experience.

Simon advocates an administrative theory based upon scientific analysis and positivism. He is also popular for his strong departure from the classical theory of administration and his advocacy of the rational approach in the decision-making process in organizations. He equates administration with decision making and believes in developing an administrative science based on logical positivism.

In 1947 he published his doctoral dissertation at the University of Chicago (*Administrative Behavior*). In this book, Simon launches his first critique of the classical principles of management and questions the notion of "principles" in administration, which he calls "proverbs" of administration. He convincingly posits that those so-called principles often conflict with each other and will not hold up to scientific inquiry. Thus, they are not applicable in complex circumstances and cannot be called "principles." He then demonstrates how every principle in administration can be nullified by using logical reasoning. For example, one principle suggests a manager should delegate authority and responsibility, whereas another advocates unity of command, which implies selecting a few subordinates for each supervisor in order to facilitate organizational control. His approach is based upon a positivist approach of knowledge acquisition and examination of "factual propositions." He believes that facts and values can be separated; moreover, by concentrating on facts, organizations increase rationality. He argues that facts are empirical and can be scientifically verified, whereas values are not verifiable and deal with certain ideals—for example, what it is versus what it should be.

Simon cites the main job of an administrator as separating facts from values and setting a desired realistic goal for the organization and constructing an efficient means to reach it. Therefore, there is a scientific process that has to be followed in order to secure the attainment of organizational goals. This approach is called the rational comprehensive method of decision making. The main function of the decision maker is to secure and select the best alternatives among different options by comparing the consequences of them all. In this context, Simon presents his "bounded rationality" theory. According to this theory, the "rational comprehensive" model is practically constrained due to limitations of time, resources, and information; therefore, most decisions *"satisfice"* rather than *"maximize."*

Simon also focuses attention on the social psychology of decision making and believes that decision making is the heart of any organization. He emphasizes communication as a means of making rational decisions. In other words, in order for the subordinates to make good decisions, they need to have access to adequate information. In sum, he emphasizes development of "rationality" in organizations. Simon qualifies this idea in 1958, within a book coauthored with James March. Simon and March argue that in reality most decisions are not made rationally due to the limitations in information gathering, example, "bounded rationality," by which decision makers are hastily satisfied with the first acceptable solution. They call this process "satisficing decision making," for most of the time the decision maker's main goal is not to make the most efficient decision but to reach a compromise and agreement with other decision makers in the organization.

Once decisions are made, they have to be implemented through the hierarchical structure of the organization. Simon emphasizes the essential role authority plays to ensure an organization's proper functioning. He recognizes authority as the engine that ensures organizational responsibility to project completion and facilitates coordination of different functions.

Simon believes that public administrators must focus on the decision-making process and try to make this process as scientific as possible. Positioning organizational efficiency as a universal goal, Simon advocates bifurcation of facts and values to facilitate a rational decision-making process based on acquisition of facts through objective scientific inquiry.

BIBLIOGRAPHY

Works by Herbert Simon

Simon, H. A. *Administrative Behavior*. New York: Free Press, 1947.
———. *Administrative Behavior*. 2nd ed. New York: Macmillan, 1957.
———. *Models of Man: Social and Rational*. New York: John Wiley & Sons, 1957.
———. *The New Science of Management Decision*. New York: Harper & Row, 1960.
———. *The Shape of Automation*. New York: Harper, 1965.
———. "Organization Man: Rational or Self-Actualizing." *Public Administration Review*, July–August 1973, 346–53.
———. *A New Scientific Management Decision*. Englewood Cliffs, NJ: Prentice-Hall, 1977.
———. *The Sciences of the Artificial*. 2nd ed. Cambridge: MIT Press, 1981.

Simon, H. A., and J. G. March. *Organizations*. New York: John Wiley & Sons, 1958.

Simon, H. A., and A. Newell. *Human Problem Solving*. Englewood Cliffs, NJ: Prentice-Hall, 1972.

Simon, H. A., D. W. Smithburg, and V. A. Thompson. *Public Administration*. New York: Alfred A. Knopf, 1950.

Works about Herbert Simon

Baker, R.J.S. *Administrative Theory and Public Administration*. London: Hutchinson University Library, 1972.

Hoselitz, Bert F., ed. *A Reader's Guide to the Social Sciences*. New York: Free Press, 1970.

Little, J. H. "Administrative Man Faces the Quality Transformation: Comparing the Ideas of Herbert A. Simon and Edward Deming." *American Review of Public Administration*, 24, 1994, 67–85.

Schumann, D. and D. W. Oluf III. *Public Administration in the United States*. Lexington, MA: D. C. Health, 1988.

TAYLOR, FREDERICK WINSLOW (b. March 20, 1856, Germantown, PA; d. March 28, 1915, Philadelphia, PA), engineer; consultant; editor; father of scientific management

Frederick Taylor is considered the father of the Scientific Movement and the editor of its mouthpiece, *Shop Management*. By 1911, the Scientific Movement, which had evolved into the Society to Promote Scientific Management, developed into the Taylor Society. "Conservative radical" Frederick Taylor continues to be known for his "radical" association with the Progressive movement and distrust of big business yet "conservative" opposition to unions and disinterest in labor concerns outside of the shop level of industry. Researching and writing during the day of "systemizer" engineers bent on man-to-machine labor efficiency, Taylor claims that he was one of a few who addressed the labor problem in a way that was human centered (on the ordinary worker), although the man-machine interface was his primary focus. A unique set of contradictions abounded in what we know of the life and career of Frederick Taylor, including whether or not he is a public administrator.

Woodrow Wilson set the precedent that "private sectors" like engineering and "public sectors" like policy be separate. As he put it, administrators ought to deal exclusively in "the detailed and systematic execution of public law." Scientific management, a field directly concerned with efficiency, was considered a useful source of information for administrators in American government and constitutional systems. Today, in Taylor's work and research, scholars believe to own a legacy of increased efficiency in public business management. Taylor himself heralded the "mental revolution" ignited by scientific management. The scientific management philosophy contains four basic components: (1)

creating science; (2) scientifically selecting workmen; (3) scientific education and shaping of workmen; (4) amicable, close cooperation between management and workers.

Increasing polarities abound in aspects of Taylor's early life. His parents are a case study in opposites. Emily Winslow Taylor, a devout Puritan, abolitionist, linguist, and feminist, instilled in young Frederick the urge to interrogate, revolt, and work diligently and consistently. These are traits that propelled him to Philips Exeter Academy and later to Harvard (where he passed entrance exams but left due to failed eyesight). Frederick's father, Franklin Taylor, a Philadelphia attorney, was as influential on his children's upbringing as he was on the world of law, preferring instead to devote his energies to literature and history. (After completing his master's degree from Princeton University, he practiced law rarely and on his inherited wealth lived primarily as a gentleman of leisure.) The married couple's home served as something of a socially radical salon during the seasons that they were not in Germany or France. Taylor's early education took place in Europe, for which he did not care much.

Parting company with his socially elite, radically inclined parents, Frederick Taylor served as an apprentice at Enterprise Hydraulic Works of Philadelphia from 1874 to 1878. Afterward, Taylor served as a laborer, time clerk, machinist, gang boss, and eventually chief engineer of the Midvale Steel Company over a period of six years. Scholars attribute Taylor's rapid professional advancement to his parents' networks and acknowledge that Taylor's identification with laborers shifted dramatically once he became the "authoritarian" manager who condemned informal output restrictions imposed by work group, or what he called "systematic soldiering," that is, loafing. Based upon what he experienced at Midvale, Taylor was able to identify seven main defects of management, including its (1) lack of understanding worker-management responsibilities, (2) ineffective work standards, (3) restricted output due to soldiering, (4) failure to offer jobs and incentives that discourage soldiering, (5) unscientific approach, (6) need for research on departmental divisions, and (7) job placements that were not based on aptitude or interest of workers.

Also during his time at Midvale, Taylor earned a degree from Stevens Institute of Technology in Hoboken, New Jersey; although never officially enrolled, he was able to take and pass the school's exit examinations. Another interesting aspect of Taylor's development is that as a laborer and researcher he readily adopted the mores of the laboring class, which included making "cold-blooded" references to and coming to blows with laborers. Finally, Taylor cautioned against paying workers excessively in case it demoralized them.

With regard to the labor class, Taylor is known for having divided it into two types: the first-class and the second-class workman. The second-class worker is lazy and, although physically able, refuses to work to full potential. Taylor believed that everyone is capable of being a first-class worker (willing and able) at some task. According to Taylor, the management should be responsible for locating and developing first-class workers. Overall, Taylor promoted a scientific rather than rule-based or spontaneous approach to labor efficiency: (1) developing a science of management, (2) selecting and training workmen, (3) interfacing science and workmen, and (4) equally dividing work and responsibility between management and workers.

Scientific management's two components (time and motion studies and piecework incentive plan) address systematic soldiering as a problem. At Midvale, working as a tool clerk, Taylor's job was to keep the time records and watch the men work. He would time with a stopwatch, then record the length of time a worker took to complete elementary motions, such as locating and lifting tools and materials. By 1890, when Taylor left Midvale, his time and motion studies had helped administrators reorganize the company. Taylor presented some early findings in "A Piece Rate System," a paper presented to the American Society of Mechanical Engineers. Taylor officially introduced public administration to scientific management in 1906 when he attempted to lend his services to government arsenals and navy yards. His attempt resulted in full-scale strikes and resistance on the part of workers and the government's eventual ban of stopwatches in government-run factories.

Taylor's professional career includes numerous opportunities for consulting and publishing. Between 1890 and 1893 Taylor served as manager of the Manufacturing Investment Company. Over the following five years, he worked as a management consultant to different companies. From 1898 to 1901, Taylor was consultant to Bethlehem Steel Company and was spokesman and propagandist for the "movement" from 1901 to 1915. Taylor wrote and presented many papers during his career. His published works include *Shop Management* (1903), *The Principles of Scientific Management* (1911), and *Scientific Management* (1947). In *Principles*, Taylor examines what causes inefficiency in modern organizations and how to reconstruct them using a scientific approach.

BIBLIOGRAPHY

Works by Frederick Winslow Taylor

Taylor, F. W. *The Principles of Scientific Management.* New York: Harper and Brothers, 1911.
———. *Shop Management.* New York: American Society of Mechanical Engineers, 1903; New York: Harper and Brothers, 1911.
———. *Scientific Management.* New York: Harper and Brothers, 1947.

———. "On the Art of Cutting Metals." In *Scientific Management*, ed. C. B. Thompson. Easton, PA: Hive Publishing, 1972, 242–67.

———. "A Piece Rate System." In *Scientific Management*, ed. C. B. Thompson. Easton, PA: Hive Publishing, 1972, 636–683.

Works about Frederick Winslow Taylor

Copley, F. B. *Frederick W. Taylor: Father of Scientific Management*. New York: American Society of Mechanical Engineers, 1923.

Fry, B. *Mastering Public Administration: From Max Weber to Dwight Waldo*. New York: Chatham House Publishers, 1989.

Kanigel, R. *The One Best Way: Frederick Winslow Taylor and the Enigma of Efficiency*. New York: Viking, 1997.

Nelson, D. *Frederick Taylor and the Rise of Scientific Management*. Madison: University of Wisconsin Press, 1980.

Prasad, D. R., V. S. Prasad, and P. Satyanarayana. *Administrative Thinkers*. New Delhi: Light and Life Publishers, 1980.

Schachter, H. L. *Frederick Taylor and the Public Administration Community: A Reevaluation*. Albany: State University of New York Press, 1989.

———. "Frederick Winslow Taylor and the Idea of Worker Participation: A Brief against Easy Administrative Dichotomies." *Administration and Society*, 21, 1, May 1989, 20–30.

Spender, J. C. *Scientific Management: Frederick Winslow Taylor's Gift to the World?* Boston: Kluwer Academic Publishers, 1996.

Wrege, C. D., and R. Greenwood. *Frederick W. Taylor, the Father of Scientific Management: Myth and Reality*. Homewood, IL: Business One Irwin, 1991.

THOMPSON, JAMES D. (b. January 11, 1920, Indianapolis, IN; d. September 1973, Nashville, TN), professor; sociologist; university administrator; U.S. army lieutenant

James Thompson was born in, and received secondary education in, Indiana. After attending Indiana University (and earning his Bachelor of Science degree in 1941 and Master's in 1947), he went on to become an educator, researcher, and administrator who contributed to several American universities, including Cornell University, University of Pittsburgh, Vanderbilt University, and alma maters Indiana University and University of North Carolina at Chapel Hill, where he completed his Ph.D.

Thompson's first teaching position began in 1947 when he was assistant professor of journalism at the University of Wisconsin. During his lifetime, Thompson was an associate professor of sociology, director of an Administrative Science Center, and professor of business administration as well. Part of the behavioral revolution in public administration theory, Thompson's most lasting contribution is widely recognized as a systems or sociological perspective of organizational theory.

Like other organizational systems theorists, Thompson focuses on explaining the underlying rationality of organizations. Thompson has schematized the multiple elements grounding the complex organization; he dedicates much of *Organizations in Action: The Social Science Bases of Administrative Theory* (1967) to identifying the "interdependent parts" of the system, given that "a system contains more variables than we can comprehend at one time." Thompson's work classifies and categorizes organizational parts.

According to Thompson, organizational rationality consists of three interrelated activities (input, technological, and output) and three technologies (long-linked, mediating, and intensive) that correlate with three variables of change and adaptation (cost, interdependence, and coordination). Stability and homogeneity are the two environmental factors affecting organizations, which Thompson refers to as "crucial contingencies" for structure. Thompson has also contributed to public administration a systematic approach for evaluating the efficacy of the organization; output is deemed clear or ambiguous, and technology is deemed complete or incomplete.

BIBLIOGRAPHY

Works by James D. Thompson

Thompson, J. D. *Approaches to Organizational Design*. Pittsburgh: University of Pittsburgh Press, 1966.
———. *Organizations in Action: The Social Science Bases of Administration*. New York: McGraw-Hill, 1967.
———, ed. *Comparative Studies in Administration*. Pittsburgh: University of Pittsburgh Press, 1959.
Thompson, J. D., and D. R. Van. *The Behavioral Sciences: An Interpretation*. Menlo Park, CA: Addison-Wesley, 1970.

Works about James D. Thompson

Rushing, W. A., ed. *Organizations and Beyond: Selected Essays of James D. Thompson*. Lexington: Lexington Books, 1976.
Van De Ven, A., A. Delbecq, and R. Koenig, Jr. "Determinants of Coordination Modes within Organizations." *American Sociological Review*, 41, 2, April 1976, 322–338.

THOMPSON, VICTOR A. (b. September 1912, Hannah, ND), consultant; university professor; department chair

He received a B.A. (1939) and an M.A. (1941) from the University of Washington and a Ph.D. from Columbia University in 1949. During the early 1940s, he served as the assistant director of the Division of Fuel and Automotive Rationing at the U.S. Office of Price Administration (OPA) (1942–1946). He left the OPA in 1945, joined the University of Texas at Austin to teach political science (1946–1947), and later taught at the Illinois Institute of Technology (1947–1962). He became the chair of the Political Science Department at the Institute.

He taught political science at Syracuse University from 1962 to 1966 and later at the University of Illinois (1966–1968). He served as chair of the Department of Political Science at the University of Illinois from 1968 to 1971. Since 1971, he has been a faculty member in the Department of Political Science at the University of Florida at Gainesville.

During his tenure at the University of Chicago, he worked closely with Herbert Simon in the public administration discipline, specifically on bureaucratic innovations and organizations. He is the recipient of the Social Science Research Council Demobilization Award. In 1945, he received a grant from the Social Science Research Council to conduct a study on the regulatory process and price rationing. While in Chicago, he also worked as a consultant for the National Security Resources Board. His first book was the result of this study, which dealt mostly with the decision-making process as it relates to governmental price control. His emphasis was on the rational decision-making process. He argued that the rational method of decision making required several steps, including gathering of information, generating proper alternatives, and finally, choosing the best alternative.

In 1950, Thompson coauthored *Public Administration* with Herbert A. Simon and Donald W. Smithburg, which brought them a great deal of recognition in public administration. In 1961, he worked for the University of Chicago at the Center for Programs in Government where he conducted research on executive development programs. He conducted a great deal of research on modern organizations and wrote several books on the subject. He argued that modern societies are inevitably becoming more bureaucratic, which is a direct result of specializations in carrying out their social functions. He argues that although bureaucracy is useful by itself, it sometimes hinders individual innovation and creativity when there is too much emphasis on hierarchy. He attempts to provide a moral and philosophical basis for analyzing organizations. In his analysis of social organizations, Thompson holds that there are two main concerns that dominate the operations of social organizations. One is maintenance of the organization itself, and the other is the achievement of organizational goals. He believes that, in general, organizations sacrifice organizational goals in favor of the means of achievement. He believes that organizations are becoming more impersonal and insensitive toward the particular needs of citizens. In other words, organizations are not responding to the basic sociopsychological needs of individuals. He favors a more compassionate and personalized treatment of people by bureaucratic organizations.

Thompson believes that organizations can be healthy and productive by creating a supportive atmosphere and open communication to facilitate working for a common goal. Thus, he is in favor of T-Group training, which was developed by the practitioners of organization development. The main objective of those groups is to promote full inter-personal communication among group members.

In his judgment, in order for innovations to take place, a creative process must evolve. This includes preparation, incubation, illumination, and verification. In his later books, Thompson entertains several questions relevant to different aspects of organizations, including organizational development, employee sensitivity training and organizational change. He states that an organization is a logical, non-individualized mix of experts who come together to accomplish a mutually understood goal. He objects to the idea of empowering bureaucrats and administrators and argues that major achievements are made by specialists and that bureaucrats and administrators are nothing but a hindrance and parasites to organizational development and growth. He believes that bureaucrats survive in organizations because of the usage of "dramaturgy" and manufacturing "snow jobs" to cover their inability to truly contribute to the overall purpose of the organization. He claims superficial acts and gestures such as personal aloofness and a firm handshake create the image of usefulness in organizations. He advocates the elimination of administrators so that the specialists are able to communicate with each other and contribute to overall organizational goals.

BIBLIOGRAPHY

Works by Victor A. Thompson

Simon, H. A., D. W. Smithburg, and V. A. Thompson. *Public Administration*. New York: Alfred A. Knopf, 1950.

Thompson, V. A. *The Regulator Process in OPA Rationing*. New York: Kings Crown Press, 1950.

———. *Modern Organization*. New York: Alfred A. Knopf, 1961.

———. *Toward a Communication Theory of Organization*. Princeton, NJ: Princeton University Press, 1963.

———. *Without Sympathy or Enthusiasm: The Problem of Administrative Compassion*. Tuscaloosa: University of Alabama Press, 1975.

———. *Bureaucracy and the Learning World*. New York: General Learning Press, 1976.

Work about Victor A. Thompson

Peterson, J. W., L. M. Allen, and N. J. Argyle. *Political Science: An Overview of the Fields*. Dubuque, IA: Kendall/Hunt, 1997.

WALDO, (CLIFFORD) DWIGHT (b. September 1913, Nebraska), political scientist; director; university professor; fellow

Waldo grew up in a small town in Nebraska and attended the Nebraska Wesleyan University. After two years, he transferred to a smaller college in Peru, Nebraska (Nebraska State Teachers College) and received a B.A. in 1935. After graduation he received a scholarship to attend the University of Nebraska (1935) and obtained an M.A. in 1937. Originally, he wanted to become an English teacher, but he changed his mind and studied political science. Later he attended Yale University and received a Ph.D. in 1942. He taught at Yale University from 1944 to 1946 and later moved to California to become the director of the Institute for Government Studies and to teach at the University of California at Berkeley from 1946 to 1967. He then became the Albert Schweitzer Professor of Humanities at Syracuse University (New York) until 1979, when he became emeritus.

Waldo was a Carl Hatch Professor of Law and Public Administration at the University of New Mexico from 1984 to 1986 and a resident fellow at Woodrow Wilson International Center for Scholars, Smithsonian Institute, in Washington from 1979 to 1981. He conducted extensive studies in bureaucracy, politics, and city management.

Waldo contributed a great deal to public administration. Some of his major themes include public administration identity and definition; the relationship between public administration, political philosophy, and other areas of knowledge and experience; public administration and its linkage with theory, practice, and teaching; and the study of change and uncertainty and its effect in public administration. He analyzed the development of government through historical perspective and argues that the major mission of civil service reform was moral rather than economic. He emphasizes the importance of public morality and argues that government should be administered not only with knowledge but with integrity. He tries to locate a place for the study of public administration within a large political and social perspective. He argues that understanding of organizations is not only a sociological but also a psychological and legal endeavor.

Waldo believes that public administration is the utilization of public resources to accommodate the goals of state. He believes that public administration combines and utilizes elements of management to conduct state affairs. Therefore, he contends that politics and administration are not separate. He argues that "the function of politics is primarily the expression of the state will, secondary with the execution of that will. The problem is to exert essential but not excessive control over the organization through politics.

He believed that American public administration has been fascinated by the concept of "principles" of public administration during the early twentieth century. He criticizes this approach and indicates that those principles are the product of physical laws and laws must be rooted within the bounds of reality or fact. Therefore, he argues that administration cannot be purely scientific because it is fused with "values." He severely criticizes the assumption (which originated from Woodrow Wilson's 1887 argument) that politics and administration should be separated and public organizations should become businesslike. He believes that public organizations should advocate the "founding values" of all citizens and public administration is inherently political in nature.

He emphasized the importance of organizations in general and public organizations in particular, in affecting the life of society as a whole. In his judgment, organizations are the anatomy and management is the philosophy, which must work together to achieve efficiency in organizations. He believed efficiency can only be realized if organizations move toward their goals. He argued in favor of decentralization in organizations because he believed it is more compatible with social needs and would serve the public more effectively. He believed that public administration is a profession that can draw from many different disciplines. He develops a historical analysis of bureaucracies and how they have been used in ancient times to enable rulers to stay in power and expand and protect an empire. However, he argues that those structures were modernized and transformed in Western democracies to serve the common man. Therefore, bureaucracies have been the most powerful tools to achieve objectives by the private or public sectors. In his judgment, bureaucracy helped achieve industrialization, democracy, and nationalism.

In analyzing the political theory of American public administration, he disagreed with its overemphasis on the economic concept of efficiency, the inconsistency and rigidity of administrative principles, and the methodology of determining those principles. He supported the behavioral approach to the study of public administration. He did not agree with uniform and unchanging principles of administration and held that government administration differs from one part of the world to the other. In his judgment, public administration is a response to social needs. He describes how the business sector has influenced the business of public administration. He predicts a movement toward specialization and professionalization in public administration.

BIBLIOGRAPHY

Works by Dwight Waldo

Waldo, D. *The Administrative State.* New York: Ronald Press, 1948.

———. *Ideas and Issues in Public Administration.* New York: McGraw-Hill, 1953.

———. *The Study of Public Administration.* Garden City, NY: Doubleday & Company, 1955.

———. *Perspectives on Administration.* Tuscaloosa: University of Alabama Press, 1956.

———. *The Public Administration in a Time of Turbulence.* Scranton, PA: Chandler, 1971.

———. *Democracy-Bureaucracy, and Hypocrisy.* Novato, CA: Chandler & Sharp Publishers, 1976.

————. *The Enterprise of Public Administration*. Novato, CA: Chandler & Sharp Publishers, 1980.

Works about Dwight Waldo

Avila, P. J. "The Power and the Glory: A Preliminary Investigation of the Effects of Eurocentrism on the Development of Public Administration in the Western Tradition from Plato to Dwight Waldo." Master's thesis. Kutztown University of Pennsylvania, 1992.

Brown, B.E.S., and R. J. Stillman. *A Search for Public Administration: The Ideas and Career of Dwight Waldo*. College Station: Texas A&M University Press, 1986.

Laohavichien, U. "Dwight Waldo: The Leading Light of Public Administration for Three Decades." *Philippine Journal of Public Administration*, 27, 1, January 1983.

WEBER, MAX (b. April 21, 1864, Erfurt, Germany; d. June 1920, Germany), founder of modern sociology; university professor; member of parliament; political sociologist; father of bureaucracy

Weber was born in a politically active family. His father, Max Weber, Sr., was a lawyer and a member of the German Parliament. He studied law, economics, and philosophy at the University of Heidelberg and Göttingen University and taught economics at the University of Freiburg in 1894 and at Heidelberg in 1896. He also worked in an administrative capacity after the war and participated in drafting the Weimar Constitution. In his times he made great contributions in the sociology of religion, political sociology, and the methodology of social sciences. However, his major contribution was in political sociology with emphasis on bureaucracy. In fact, he is often called the "father of bureaucracy."

Weber advocated a historical approach in his social and political analysis. His political philosophy was of a "liberal" tradition, and he fought for his ideas against the conservatives and Marxists of his time. He was also a strong nationalist who believed in the preservation of German culture. His religious beliefs revolved around the Protestantism that significantly shaped his views on economics and politics.

Weber's understanding of human behavior and action manifest itself in his orientation toward rational action. As opposed to Marx, whose basis for social analysis was class conflict, Weber believed that a range of other factors, including religion, nationalism, and ethnicity, can affect social behavior. Although he emphasized the separation of values and facts in his analysis of social and political phenomena, he also realized the role of values in shaping social orientations. He argued that the role of science is to explain social phenomena without making value judgments. He favored a "neutral" science in dealing with social phenomena.

He believed that forces of rationality are responsible for the major economic and social development of the Western world. In addition, he argued that rationalization is the direct effect of capitalism, which is influenced by Protestantism. Therefore, he drew a unilinear relationship between Protestantism, capitalism, and rationality.

Weber believed that "state" is a combination of structure, rules, and bureaucratic behavior that exercises domination over the people through its authority. Authority bases its legitimacy on three sources: charismatic, legal-rational, or traditional. Charismatic authority is based on the personal qualifications of a leader and is a product of crisis and enthusiasm. Followers feel a sense of loyalty and emotional attachment to the leader. Traditional authority, on the other hand, relies on past customs, traditions, and precedent for its legitimacy. Finally, legal-rational authority originates from logical and reasonable procedures and the rule of law. Therefore, in the latter, the rule of law determines the scope of authority and the legitimacy of behavior.

He argued that bureaucracy, as the manifestation of human rationality, has its roots in the authority of the state and is the only logical means of rationalization. The state imposes its compulsory decisions on society through bureaucratic means. Therefore, bureaucracy is a means of domination over society. In addition, he held that bureaucracy is the most logical organization to make aggregate rational decisions for society and that bureaucrats should be the embodiment of rules and regulations in running state organizations.

According to Weber, bureaucracy provides for precise, clear, and rapid decisions that are not possible with other forms of administration. He believed that bureaucracy and capitalism share the same compatible values (efficiency and rationality). This is due to the fact that capitalism is the pursuit of material, rationality, and replacement of personal relationship with the impersonal. Therefore, they are mutually supportive. The scope of authority in a bureaucracy is determined by the rules and regulations that set the stage for performance. Its rationality is based on specific characteristics that he explains in his "ideal type" of bureaucracy. The ideal type is not a normative type but represents a historical and logical pattern of rational organization that cannot be found in present bureaucratic organizations. It provides imperative control on human behavior and procedures in order to accomplish goals.

He believed that justice can only be served through bureaucratic organizations. He realized the weaknesses and shortcomings of bureaucracy in limiting individual freedom and creativity. Therefore, he suggests that using small-scale bureaucratic organizations, instead of large-scale bureaucracies, will help overcome the negative effects of bureaucratic life. Max Weber advocates the supremacy of political masters over the bureaucratic and economic spheres in society. He argues that political leaders should exercise control over bureaucratic behavior. He separates politics from administration and believes that politicians and bureaucrats should perform separate functions. Bureaucrats are simply the executors of the orders of political masters. However, he acknowledges that, due to their knowledge and expertise, bureaucrats are able to protect themselves from effective political scrutiny and become a privileged class of their own. He warns against the bureaucratic influence on public policies and asks for political control of bureaucracy in order to preserve the rule of law. In the extreme case of bureaucratization of society, he hopes for charismatic leaders to come forth and curb bureaucratic power.

BIBLIOGRAPHY

Works by Max Weber

Weber, M. *The Religion of China: Confucianism and Taoism*. Glencoe, IL: Free Press, 1915.

———. *The Religion of India: The Sociology of Hinduism and Buddhism*. Trans. and ed. H. H. Garth and D. Martindale. Glencoe, IL: Free Press, 1917.

———. *Protestant Ethics and the Spirit of Capitalism*. Trans. T. Parson. London: Allen & Unwin; New York: Scribner, 1930.

———. "The Protestant Sects and the Spirit of Capitalism." In *From Max Weber: Essays in Sociology*. New York: Oxford University Press, 1946.

———. *Essays in Sociology*. Trans. and ed. H. H. Garth and C. W. Mills. New York: Oxford University Press, 1948.

———. *On the Methodology of the Social Sciences*. Trans. and ed. E. Shils and H. A. Finch. Glencoe, IL: Free Press, 1949.

———. "The Social Causes of Decay of Ancient Civilization." *Journal of General Education*, 5, 1950, 75–88.

———. *General Economic History*. Trans. F. H. Knight. Glencoe, IL: Free Press, 1952.

———. *The Theory of Social and Economic Organization*. Trans. and ed. A. M. Henderson and T. Parson. Glencoe, IL: Free Press, 1957.

———. "The Three Types of Legitimacy Rule." In *Complex Organizations: A Sociological Reader*, ed. A. Etzioni. New York: Holt, Rinehart and Winston, 1961.

Works about Max Weber

Beetham, K. *Max Weber and the Theory of Modern Politics*. London: Allen & Unwin, 1974.

Daimant, A. "The Bureaucratic Model: Max Weber Rejected, Rediscovered, Reformed." In *Papers in Comparative Public Administration*, ed. F. Heady and S. L. Stokes. Ann Arbor: Institute of Public Administration, University of Michigan, 1962.

Loewenstein, K. *Max Weber's Political Ideas in the Perspective of Our Time*. Amherst: University of Massachusetts Press, 1966.

Marcus, H. "Industrialism and Capitalism in the Work of Max Weber." In *Negations: Essays in Critical Theory*, trans. J. J. Shapiro. Boston: Beacon Press 1968.

Merton, R. K. "Bureaucratic Structure and Personality." In *Reader in Bureaucracy*, ed. R. K. Merton, R. H. Turner, E. H. Sutherland, A. W. Gouldner, and A. D. Lassel. New York: Free Press, 1952.

Reinhard B. *Max Weber: An Intellectual Portrait*. Berkeley: University of California Press, 1960.

Rheinstein, M., ed. *Max Weber on Law in Economy and Society*. Cambridge, MA: Harvard University Press, 1954.

WHITE, LEONARD DUPREE (b. January, 17, 1891, Acton, MA; d. February 23, 1958, Long Pine, CA) scholar; editor; university professor

During his lifetime, Leonard White earned a variety of distinctions. He held honorary degrees from Dartmouth and Princeton and a distinguished professorship from the University of Chicago where he taught until retirement in 1956 after a forty-year tenure in its Department of Political Science. He was the first editor of the *American Society for Public Administration* and its president in 1947. In 1948, White received two honors, one domestic, the other international. The Commander of the Order of Leopold II from Belgium was bestowed upon him, and the American Political Science Association offered him the Woodrow Wilson Award for his publication *The Federalists*, published that same year. In 1954, White was granted the Columbia University Bancroft Prize for his publication *The Jacksonians* (1954). As researcher and author, White is known for two additional seminal works on public administration: *The Jeffersonians* (1951) and *The Republican Era* (1958). Collectively, the four volumes span over 100 years of administrative history of the federal government, based upon public reports, office memoranda, and private letters. The volumes sustain a comparative focus on Federalist administrative mainstays of stability, on the one hand, and Jacksonian doctrines of relative revolution, on the other.

White has been heralded for researching and writing during the world war eras during which he spearheaded academic trends in continuity and collectivity and continued political tendencies toward appraisal and revision of public policies and processes. Like other political scientists of the early twentieth century, White was influenced by the U.S. depression and transition from agrarian to urban ideologies. White maintained an empirical approach to the problems of American government, which he first researched through observation before writing. Two of his earliest influential articles reflect his scientific methodology: "The Status of Scientific Research in Illinois" (1923) and "Evaluation of Financial Control of Research in State Governments" (1924). Nonetheless, White's *Introduction to the Study of Public Administration* (1926) is considered the bumper crop of his career in scholarship and the first textbook on public administration in the field.

Introduction underwent revisions and reprints in 1939, 1948, and 1954. And although in subsequent editions White foregrounds his interest in sharing with his readers how his outlook has developed, the four assumptions recorded in the first edition remain a central aspect of his endeavor: (1) administration is "a unitary process that can be studied uniformly, at the federal, state, and local levels"; (2) management rather than law should initiate administration studies; (3) the scientific approach should be used, although "administration is still primarily an art"; (4) administration is quintessentially "the problem of modern government." In keeping "with reality," *Introduction* primarily ignores politics, targets an audience of practitioners (rather than scholars), and unfolds from Taylor's assertion that the scientific approach is best for study of management. The book's working definition of *public administration* is noteworthy: "the management of men and materials in the accomplishment of the purposes of the state."

After *Introduction*, White continued to publish influential material that reflects his explorations of civics and public service—previously unharvested terrain. *The City Manager* (1927) was the culminating work from a series of field writing White completed while employed as a U.S. Civil Service Commissioner. He contributed to *Trends in Public Administration* (1933) for President Hoover's Research Committee on Social Trends. His noteworthy comparative administration studies include *Whitley Councils in the British Civil Service* (1933) and a submission published in *Civil Service Abroad* (1935). Also in 1935, White published as *Government Career Service* lectures he delivered about public policy conundrums he faced in public office. Finally, it is important to note that White's teaching legacy rivals popular opinion of his scholarship.

BIBLIOGRAPHY

Works by Leonard Dupree White

Gaus, J. M., and L. White. "Public Administration in the United States in 1933." *Political Science Review*, 28, 3, June 1934, 443–456.

Gaus, J. M., L. White, and M. E. Dimock. *The Frontiers of Public Administration.* Chicago: University of Chicago Press, 1936.

White, L. *The City Manager.* Chicago: University of Chicago Press, 1927.

———. "Public Administration: Public Administration, 1931–32." *American Political Science Review*, 27, 3, June 1933, 433–444.

———. *Introduction to the Study of Public Administration.* 1926. New York: Harper & Brothers, 1939.

———. *Defense and War Administration.* New York: Macmillan, 1942.

———. *Civil Service in Wartime.* Chicago: University of Chicago Press, 1945.

———. *The Jeffersonians: A Study in Administrative History: 1801–1829.* New York: Macmillan, 1951.

———. *The Jacksonians: A Study in Administrative History, 1829–1861.* New York: Macmillan, 1954.

———. *The Republican Era: A Study in Administrative History, 1869–1901.* New York: Macmillan, 1958.

————. *The Federalists: A Study in Administrative History*. 1948. New York: Macmillan, 1964.

Works about Leonard Dupree White

Gaus, J. M. "Leonard Dupree White 1891–1958." *Public Administration Review*, 18, Summer 1958.
Storing, H. J. "Leonard D. White and the Study of Public Administration." *Public Administration Review*, 25, March 1965.

WILDAVSKY, AARON B. (b. 1930, Brooklyn, NY; d. September 4, 1993, Oakland, CA), professor; fellow; university dean; war veteran; budgeting expert

Aaron Wildavsky is known as a leader in the fields of public administration, public policy, and political science. He approached teaching and writing as socially conscious endeavors. The third child of Ukrainian émigrés, Wildavsky graduated from Brooklyn's Erasmus Hall High School in 1948 and in 1954 received a B.A. from Brooklyn College. He served in the U.S. Army during the Korean War and studied in Australia on a Fulbright scholarship before completing a Ph.D. at Yale University. Wildavsky was a full member of the university faculty at Berkeley for thirty years and founded the Graduate School of Public Policy for which he acted as dean. He taught at Oberlin College after Berkeley and was the past president of the American Political Science Association.

The breadth of his work reflects the multifaceted quality of his personal experiences. His work in and related to public administration includes fiscal policy, U.S. gas and oil policy, health policy, political culture and community leadership, research methodology and evolution of the social sciences, and the art of policy analysis. Current trends in public administration studies of municipal budgeting continue to appropriate Wildavsky's work in budgeting, for example, zero-based, capital, target-based, and program budgeting.

Wildavsky made his mark in public administration and earned his reputation as a critic of program budgeting with *The Politics of the Budgetary Process*, published in 1964. Written near the end of the descriptive period, Wildavsky's text examines budgetary culture and competition as well as its strategy and power. He describes its process as fragmented, specialized, incremental, and sequential and proposes against its inherent bent toward big government. Citing "reconciliation" as the best type of reform, Wildavsky criticizes federal spending that lacks control. Although the best received book on the politics of administration, Wildavsky's project was not without its critics. In "The Political Economy of Efficiency: Cost Benefit Analysis, Systems Analysis, and Program Budgeting" (1966), he responds to charges with more extensive commentary on economic rationality.

BIBLIOGRAPHY

Works by Aaron B. Wildavsky

Caiden, N., and A. Wildavsky. *Planning and Budgeting in Poor Countries.* New York: Wiley, 1974.

Clark, J., and A. Wildavsky. *The Moral Collapse of Communism: Poland as a Cautionary Tale.* San Francisco: Institute of Contemporary Studies Press, 1990.

Dempster, M. A., and A. Wildavsky. "On Change, or, There Is No Magic Size for an Increment." *Political Studies,* 27, Spring 1979, 371–389.

Douglas, J., and A. Wildavsky. "Big Government and the Private Foundations." *Policy Studies Journal,* 9, 8, 1980–1981, 1175–1190.

————. *Risk and Culture: An Essay on the Selection of Technical and Environmental Dangers.* Berkeley: University of California Press, 1982.

Ellis, R., and A. Wildavsky. *Dilemmas of Presidential Leadership from Washington through Lincoln.* New Brunswick, NJ: Transaction Publishers, 1989.

Golembiewski, R., and A. Wildavsky, eds. *The Costs of Federalism: Essays in Honor of James W. Fesler.* New Brunswick, NJ: Transaction Publishers, 1984.

Heclo, H., and A. Wildavsky. *The Private Government of Public Money: Community and Policy Inside British Politics.* Berkeley: University of California Press, 1974.

May, J., and A. Wildavsky, eds. *The Policy Cycle.* Beverly Hills: Sage Publications, 1978.

Mullins, K., and A. Wildavsky. "The Procedural Presidency of George Bush." *Society,* 28, January–February 1991, 49–59.

Nienaber, J., and A. Wildavsky. *The Budgeting and Evaluation of Federal Recreation Programs: Or, Money Doesn't Grow on Trees.* New York: Basic Books, 1973.

Polsby, N., and A. Wildavsky. *Presidential Elections: Strategies of American Electoral Politics.* New York: Scribner, 1976.

Pressman, J., and A. Wildavsky. *Implementation: How Great Expectations in Washington Are Dashed in Oakland.* Berkeley: University of California Press, 1984.

Wildavsky, A. *The Politics of the Budgetary Process.* Boston: Little, Brown, 1964.

————. "The Political Economy of Efficiency: Cost Benefit Analysis, Systems Analysis, and Program Budgeting." *Public Administration Review,* 26, 4, December 1966.

————. *Budgeting: A Comparative Theory of Budgeting Processes.* Boston: Little, Brown, 1975.

————. "Principles for a Graduate School of Public Policy." *Journal of Urban Analysis,* 4, April 1977, 3–28.

————. "What's in It for Us? America's National Interest in Israel." *Middle East Review,* 10, Fall 1977, 5–13.

————. "Budgetary Futures: Why Politicians May Want Spending Limits in Turbulent Times." *Public Budgeting and Finance,* 1, Spring 1981, 20–27.

————. "The Three-Party System: 1980 and After." *Public Interest,* Summer 1981, 47–57.

————. "The Budget as New Social Contract." *Journal of Contemporary Studies,* 5, Spring 1982, 3–19.

————. "Item Veto without a Global Spending Limit: Locking the Treasury after

the Dollars Have Fled." *Notre Dame Journal of Law, Ethics and Public Policy,*
1, 2, 1985, 165–176.
————. "The Once and Future School of Public Policy." *Public Interest,* Spring
1985, 25–41.
————. *A History of Taxation and Expenditure in the Western World.* Glen Echo,
MD: Simon Publications, 1986.
————. *The New Politics of the Budgetary Process.* Glenview, IL: Scott, Foresman,
1988.
————. *The Beleaguered Presidency.* New Brunswick, NJ: Transaction Publishers,
1991.
————. "Political Implications of Budget Reform: A Retrospective." *Public Ad-
ministration Review,* 52, 6, November–December 1992, 594–599.
————, ed. *Beyond Containment: Alternative Policies toward the Soviet Union.* San
Francisco: Institute for Contemporary Studies, 1983.
Wildavsky, A., and M. Boskin, eds. *The Federal Budget: Economics and Politics.* San
Francisco: Institute for Contemporary Studies, 1982.
Wildavsky, A., and N. W. Polsby. *Presidential Elections: Contemporary Strategies of
American Electoral Politics.* 1984. New York: Macmillan, 1988.
Wildavsky, A., and S. Weiner. "The Prophylactic Presidency." *Public Interest,*
Summer 1978, 3–19.

Works about Aaron B. Wildavsky

Ellis, R., and M. Thompson, eds. *Culture Matters: Essays in Honor of Aaron Wildavsky.* Boulder, CO: Westview Press, 1997.
Forester, J. "The Policy Analysis–Critical Theory Affair: Wildavsky and Haber-
mas as Bedfellows?" *Journal of Public Policy,* 2, 2, 1982, 145–164.
Jones, L. R. "Aaron Wildavsky: A Man and Scholar for All Seasons." *Public Ad-
ministration Review,* 55, 1, January–February 1995, 3–16.
————. "Wildavsky on Budget Reform." *Policy Sciences,* 29, 3, August 1996, 227–
234.
Laitin, D. "Political Culture and Political Preferences." *American Political Science
Review,* 82, 2, June 1988, 589–597.
Lee, F. P. " 'The Two Presidencies' Revisited." *Presidential Studies Quarterly,* 10,
4, Fall 1980, 620–628.
Leloup, L. T. "Congress versus the 'Two Presidencies' Reconsidered." *Social Sci-
ence Quarterly,* 59, March 1979, 704–719.
Whicker, M. L. "Toward a Grander Budget Theory." *Public Administration Review,*
52, 6, November–December 1992, 601–603.

WILLOUGHBY, WILLIAM F. (b. July 1867, Virginia; d. 1960, Washington,
DC), budget analyst; public servant; economist; political scientist; consultant
   Willoughby received an A.B. from Johns Hopkins University in 1888
and was an economist, an expert and lecturer in public service, and a
political scientist. He served as a budget analyst on the Commission on
Economy and Efficiency under President William Taft (1911–1912). He
was also a consultant on economic and educational matters for the U.S.
Commission to Paris Expedition in 1900. His major focus of study was

on the relationship between politics and economic growth and how government can facilitate economic advancement and solve economic problems. He also concentrated on the question of the distribution of power in a political system among different branches, and he addressed major questions of political structure in a single policy and within a colonial structure (colonies and the mother country). He believed in limited function for government and argued that governments should only involve themselves with lawmaking, execution of the laws, and internal and external security.

He entertains the question of individual liberty versus the will of the state and believes that the state is the protector of individual rights and individual freedom. In other words, by "state action," individuals can realize their freedom. Otherwise, their rights would be denied by more powerful individuals than them. Therefore, state action is done through the exertion of collective will. He also believed that government can only interfere in the matter of individual rights insofar as is permitted by the Constitution and that it should restrain itself from matters that are within its jurisdiction. He explains different orientations to political thought, including the anarchist school (which adheres to a society with no government). This school emphasizes the superiority of natural law over others to guarantee the fullest rights for individuals. Closest to the anarchist school is the individualist school, which believes that individual rights are supreme and should be respected to the fullest. This school disagrees with the anarchist in the sense that it sees the existence of government as a necessary evil that guarantees individual rights and freedoms and protects people from each other. The collectivistic school, according to Willoughby, perceives government as a promoter of equality and justice among citizens. According to this school, collective rights take precedent over individual rights. The socialistic school promotes the idea that government is an agent of change and knows what is good for the community. It emphasizes the importance of government as an initiator and facilitator of change through governmental involvement with activities. This school believes that individuals are motivated by greed and exploitation and think only of their own interests. Therefore, government becomes an instrument for bringing about equality and justice. Accordingly, government takes control of the means of production and the redistribution of national wealth to bring about greater equality among its citizens. Finally, the last school is communism (the next step after socialism) by which an ideal society will emerge, and government will be eliminated and people will live in harmony, justice, and equality, running their own affairs.

Willoughby classifies the behavior and functions of different governments according to the degree that they exercise their sovereign powers. In other words, the question of sovereignty, according to Willoughby, is the ultimate determinant of the degree of power that a government is entitled in relation to its citizens. In a democratic system, the people act collectively in the legislation and administration of the affairs of the state. Residents directly involve themselves in determining public policy. He argues that this kind of government has difficulty functioning because of the enormous complexity that might cause. Therefore, he believes that democracy has limitations and can fully succeed only if proper conditions exist.

In a representative democratic system, voters (the electorates) determine the scope of public policy and elect decision makers who determine the public policy-making process. A representative democracy believes in the sovereignty of people. However, people cannot exercise their sovereign power directly and must elect representatives to utilize that power. This system is more the rule of experts as compared to the rule of the people.

He is in favor of specialization and departmentalization of work at the federal and state levels. He also emphasizes the importance of governments that function according to the laws, rules, and regulations. In his emphasis on the legalistic approach to government, he argues that the work of government can be summarized into three functions: to uphold justice, to guarantee individual liberty, and to protect the natural rights of all citizens. He differentiates between the "state" and "government." He believed that government is the collection of instruments that are required to carry out the will of the state (body politics). He argues that the separation of different branches of government is a myth and oversimplification, which he called "traditional threefold classification." He was very critical of the overall functions of government and called for a major overhaul of the administrative function to make it more efficient. He called for the recognition of two more functions including the "electorate" and the "administration."

According to Willoughby, recognition of the electorate and administration gives legitimacy to what really exists and the power that these two bodies have. That is why he favors the dichotomy between politics and administration and believes that lines of separation between these two are very blurry. However, he recognizes that policy making and implementation of the policies call for different functions. According to him, the main function of "administration" is to administer the laws that are decided within the legislative branch and explained by the judiciary. In addition, he argues that administration's most distinctive role concerns the function of the individual divisions and the organization as a whole. In addition, the study of public administration should be concerned with the "operation of the administrative branch" because this approach makes government more efficient. Willoughby contends that administrators should be granted a great amount of authority and power to carry out their functions. This approach makes the executive branch a "single," integrated piece of administrative machinery.

Willoughby favors the application of scientific principles in the conduct of government. He called for several principles that will make government work more efficiently, including departmentalization of government and specialization of services at each level. He also believed that jobs should be grouped together in order to create uniformity of responses. This, in his opinion, will bring more efficiency to government. He also offered several remedies to improve the administration of laws in the judicial system. He made many suggestions concerning the reorganization of the court system, the promulgation of proper rules and regulations, and the development of a more workable system of hiring and retaining good judges. The electorate function is simply representative of the shifting of power from the leader to the people.

BIBLIOGRAPHY

Works by William F. Willoughby

Willoughby, W. F. *The Government of Modern States*. New York: D. Appleton-Century, 1919.

———. *The Reorganization of the Administrative Branch of the National Government*. Baltimore, MD: Johns Hopkins University Press, 1923.

———. *The Legal Status and Function of the General National Accounting Office of the National Government*. Baltimore, MD: Johns Hopkins University Press, 1927.

———. *Principles of Public Organization*. Baltimore, MD: Johns Hopkins University Press, 1927.

———. *Principles of Judicial Administration*. Washington, DC: Brookings Institution, 1929.

———. *Principle of Legislative Organizations and Administration*. Washington, DC: Brookings Institution, 1934.

Works about William F. Willoughby

Ramsey, E. C. *William F. Willoughby, a Progressive in China, 1914–1916*. 1976.

Shafritz, J. M., and A. C. Hyde, eds. *Classics of Public Administration*. Pacific Grove, CA: Brooks/Cole, 1992.

WILSON, (THOMAS) WOODROW (b. December 28, 1856, Staunton, VA: d. February 3, 1924, Washington, DC), rhetorician; teacher; university president; state governor; twenty-eighth president of the United States; Nobel Prize recipient (1919)

Wilson sustained a tenuous connection between professional practice and theoretical premise. Such praxis is exemplified by the legislative application of ideas he developed in *The Study of Administration* (1887), one of his most significant (indeed celebrated) scholastic developments. Originally, the piece was an address Wilson delivered at Cornell in 1886 during his term as assistant professor of history at Bryn Mawr College

(1885–1888). The two foci of the 1887 essay are efficiency in government and civil service reform, which argues against the "spoils system" and the patronage that grants primary and influential government participation to the well connected. In the essay Wilson interrogates an American system "left at loose ends" and advocates the "dichotomy" of administration, which current interpretation recognizes as the separation of "politics" from "public administration." Using the politics–administration dichotomy, Wilson broadened the acceptance of administrative science study and appropriation. Although the application of the dichotomy to governance (in part two of Wilson's essay) elicits criticism, academicians find sustained value in the 1887 essay as the basis for the reform movement, which reached its full evolution after Wilson's death.

Wilson is the only president whose (accomplished) academic career actualized progression from relative obscurity to the pinnacle of American politics. The third of four children born to pious Scotch-Irish parents, Thomas Wilson experienced the culmination of his career in the service of two presidential terms (1913–1917 and 1917–1921); national political leadership was Wilson's boyhood dream. Current scholarship regarding Wilson's political legacy maintains that his extensive academic training provided the reformist ideology that characterized his administrative success. Wilson's academic experiences began in his childhood home with his father, a Presbyterian minister who exposed young Wilson to English literature, and continued during enrollment in several secondary schools (including University of Virginia law school). Wilson's models would include several English political orators (Gladstone, Burke, Bright, Cobden), several English authors (Sir Walter Scott, Dickens, Wordsworth), and German and Prussian political writers, most noticeably Lorenz von Stein. Most of Wilson's professors were educated in Germany.

The linkage between Wilson's scholastic insight and political performance began in 1879, through his most significant early publication, "Cabinet Government in the United States," a recommendation that America adopt the parliamentary system. Wilson's study of Walter Bagehot's *The English Constitution* (1867, revised 1872) directly contributed to composition of this essay. Although the proposition seemed logical to Wilson in theory (election of the legislature followed by extraction of a cabinet and prime minister, a bipartite process resulting in a jointly legislative-executive, administrative arm of "partisan neutrality"), he quickly found the institutional logistics problematic. There is noticeable conflict between Wilson's German-inspired thrust that politics and administration be separate (articulated in 1887) and his British-inspired view that legislative and executive power be unified (described in 1879). In response to the slippage, Van Riper surmises that at such times Wilson's "innate good sense" led the scholarly statesman to occupy an intermediate position.

Congressional Government: A Stay in American Politics (1885) reveals that Wilson is critical of American democracy. Wilson used this work to interrogate American governmental institutions (including the presidency) he believed ill-designed because they could neither "foster" nor "manage" effective administration. Next, Wilson's 1887 study of administrative science (during graduate work completed at Johns Hopkins) concluded that developing an administrative arm would create the conscious, effective government necessary for an evolved and modern American democracy. Wilson's publication of *The State* (1889), a treatment of comparative government, is considered the first of such textbooks in the country. He completed this work during tenure as a Wesleyan University professor (1888–1890). The courses in administration that Wilson taught at Princeton and Johns Hopkins were unique; only two other schools in the United States also offered courses in this area. Wilson's additional scholarship includes *Division and Reunion* (1893), *History of the American People* (1902), *Constitutional Government in the United States* (1908), and numerous articles within popular and academic journals. Wilson's was an exceptional position; few scholars of political science and public administration have occupied the high political positions necessary to actually test and apply the theoretical knowledge produced academically.

Wilson was a prolific administrative reformer from 1910 to 1916. As governor of New Jersey (1910–1912), he adopted several new measures, including a primary election law, a corrupt-practices act, a public-utilities act, and an employer's liability law. He also passed several laws for school-reform and a law allowing cities "to adopt the commission form of government." In October 1913, Wilson spearheaded the congressional passage of the Underwood Tariff Act, which generally reduced import rates and specifically removed tariffs from goods including wool, sugar, iron ore, steel, and rails. The Federal Reserve Act, passed by Congress in December 1913, was based upon the banking and currency law reform program developed by Wilson six months prior. During his second year of office, Wilson met continued success in the establishment of the Federal Trade Commission and the passage of the Clayton Antitrust Act. The next series of reforms were developed in 1916—adoption of the Adamson Act and the Child Labor Act and institution of a "Tariff Commission." During 1916 America also witnessed Wilson's reforms in foreign affairs. He led Congress to repeal the Panama Tolls Act and aided passage of the Jones Bill. Although less scholastic, the basis of these two final measures were motivated by Wilson's democratic convictions of "peace and goodwill."

His was a progressive intellect, which he characterized as "swimming upstream" during a moment of reflection toward the end of his life. Indeed, prior to his extensive achievement—high political offices, prolific publication, doctoral work at Johns Hopkins University, completion of the undergraduate curriculum of the College of New Jersey (now Princeton University), and successful completion of freshman year at Davidson College—Thomas Woodrow Wilson the child struggled with dyslexia. Determination proved to be a central conviction of Wilson the football coach, who told his players at Wesleyan University, "Go in to win. Don't admit defeat before you start." Wilson's travel across the Atlantic during presidency was unprecedented, as was conversation with a pope by an American president serving office, before he met with Pope Benedict XV in Rome during his second administrative term. During his life, Wilson's energy and high ideals won him the loyalty and friendship of family as well as colleagues. Wilson enjoyed two successful marriages, first to Ellen Louise Axson, with whom he shared marriage from 1885 until her death in 1914, and second to Edith Bolling Galt, herself a widow, with whom he shared marriage from 1915 until his death.

Occasionally, conservative critics were disdainful of Wilson's theoretical idealism. This was the case during his position as president of Princeton University (1902–1910). Curricular, fiscal, structural, and administrative reforms proposed during these years marked Wilson as partial to "the common" and staunchly critical of "the rich and powerful." Extensive reportage of controversy gained Wilson a public awareness that boosted his political appeal. Coincidentally, the socioeconomic politics of the Princeton situation provide a thematic precursor to Wilson's refusal of an inaugural ball in 1913, evidence of his (and the first lady's) dislike for "large social affairs." Wilson scholars have also recognized that there are noticeable similarities between the eight years of Wilson's tenure as president of Princeton and the eight years of his U.S. presidential term. Comparison reveals that the initial years of both tenures were successful, but the later years were disastrous.

Additional anti-Wilson sentiment took the form of the accusation during World War I that he was a "human icicle," a critique launched by some Americans for his "calm" when 128 American casualties resulted from the German's torpedo of the *Lusitania*, a British passenger liner. Yet Wilson's overwhelming popularity as a great leader of war, juridical scholar of integrity, and eloquent spokesman of solid principle prevailed. Through the "practice" of his leadership tenures, Wilson enacted his convictions. He is the humanitarian who achieved presidential reelection in 1916 because popular opinion celebrated that "He kept us out of war." He is as well the humanitarian president who developed "Fourteen Points," the guide for peace settlement during World War I. And in 1920, Wilson was the recipient of the 1919 Nobel Peace Prize for his work toward founding the League of Nations. Wilson is the only American president interred in Washington, DC.

BIBLIOGRAPHY

Works by Woodrow Wilson

Wilson, W. *Constitutional Government in the United States.* 1908. New York: Columbia University Press, 1921.
———. *The Road Away from Revolution.* Boston: Atlantic Monthly Press, 1923.
———. *The New Freedom: A Call for the Emancipation of the Generous Energies of a People.* Garden City, NJ: Doubleday, Doran, 1933.
———. *The Study of Administration.* 1887. Washington, DC: Public Affairs Press, 1955.
———. *Congressional Government: A Study in American Politics.* 1885. Boston: Houghton Mifflin, 1913; New York: Meridian Books, 1956.
———. *The State: Elements of Historical and Practical Politics.* 1889. Boston: D. C. Health, 1998.

Works about Woodrow Wilson

Bimes, T., and S. Skowronek. "Woodrow Wilson's Critique of Popular Leadership: Reassessing the Modern-Traditional Divide in Presidential History." *Polity,* 29, 1, Fall 1996, 27–63.
Buckingham, P. H. *Woodrow Wilson: A Bibliography of His Times and Presidency.* Wilmington, DE: Scholarly Resources, 1990.
Caiden, G. E. "In Search of an Apolitical Science of American Public Administration." In *Politics and Administration: Woodrow Wilson and American Public Administration,* ed. J. Rabin and J. S. Bowman. New York: Marcel Dekker, 1984.
Cooper, P. J. "The Wilsonian Dichotomy in Administrative Law." In *Politics and Administration: Woodrow Wilson and American Public Administration,* ed. J. Rabin and J. S. Bowman. New York: Marcel Dekker, 1984.
Day, D., ed. *Woodrow Wilson's Own Story.* Boston: Little, Brown, 1952.
Eden, R. "Opinion Leadership and the Problem of Executive Power: Woodrow Wilson's Original Position." *Review of Politics,* 57, 3, Summer 1995, 483–504.
Farmer, F., ed. *The Wilson Reader.* New York: Oceana Publications, 1956.
Golembiewski, R. T. "Ways in Which 'The Study of Administration' Confounds the Study of Administration." In *Politics and Administration: Woodrow Wilson and American Public Administration,* ed. J. Rabin and J. S. Bowman. New York: Marcel Dekker, 1984.
Heckscher, A, ed. *The Politics of Woodrow Wilson.* New York: Harper, 1956.
Lynch, T. D., and M. H. Rahimi. "Woodrow Wilson and the Revolution in Public Budgeting." In *Politics and Administration: Woodrow Wilson and American Public Administration,* ed. J. Rabin and J. S. Bowman. New York: Marcel Dekker, 1984.
Martin, D. W. "The Fading Legacy of Woodrow Wilson." *Public Administration Review,* 48, 2, March 1988, 631–636.
Miewald, R. D. "The Origins of Wilson's Thought: The German Tradition and the Organic State." In *Politics and Administration: Woodrow Wilson and*

American Public Administration, ed. J. Rabin and J. S. Bowman. New York: Marcel Dekker, 1984.

Morrow, W. L. "Woodrow Wilson and the Politics of Morality: The 1980s and Beyond." In *Politics and Administration: Woodrow Wilson and American Public Administration*, ed. J. Rabin and J. S. Bowman. New York: Marcel Dekker, 1984.

Mulder, J. M., E. M. White, and E. S. White. *Woodrow Wilson: A Bibliography*. Westport, CT: Greenwood Press, 1997.

Ninkovich, F. A. *The Wilsonian Century: U.S. Foreign Policy since 1900*. Chicago: University of Chicago Press, 1999.

Padover, S. K. *Wilson's Ideals*. Washington, DC: American Council of Public Affairs, 1942.

Rohr, J. A. "The Constitutional World of Woodrow Wilson." In *Politics and Administration: Woodrow Wilson and American Public Administration*, ed. J. Rabin and J. S. Bowman. New York: Marcel Dekker, 1984.

Saunders, R. *In Search of Woodrow Wilson: Beliefs and Behavior*. Westport, CT: Greenwood Press, 1998.

Schwabe, K. *Woodrow Wilson, Revolutionary Germany, and Peacemaking: 1918–1919 Missionary Diplomacy and the Realities of Power*. Chapel Hill: University of North Carolina Press, 1985.

Stid, D. D. "Woodrow Wilson and the Problem of Party Government." *Polity*, 26, 4, Summer 1994, 553–578.

———. *The President as Statesman: Woodrow Wilson and the Constitution*. Lawrence: University Press of Kansas, 1998.

Thayer, F. C. "Woodrow Wilson and the 'Upstairs/Downstairs' Problem." In *Politics and Administration: Woodrow Wilson and American Public Administration*, ed. J. Rabin and J. S. Bowman. New York: Marcel Dekker, 1984.

Thorsen, N. *The Political Thought of Woodrow Wilson, 1875–1910*. Princeton, NJ: Princeton University Press, 1988.

Van Riper, P. "The Politics–Administration Dichotomy: Concept or Reality?" In *Politics and Administration: Woodrow Wilson and American Public Administration*, ed. J. Rabin and J. S. Bowman. New York: Marcel Dekker, 1984.

Waldo, D. "The Perdurability of the Politics–Administration Dichotomy: Woodrow Wilson and the Identity Crisis in Public Administration." In *Politics and Administration: Woodrow Wilson and American Public Administration*, ed. J. Rabin and J. S. Bowman. New York: Marcel Dekker, 1984.

Walker, L. "Woodrow Wilson: Progressive Reform and Public Administration." *Political Science Quarterly*, 104, 3, Fall 1989, 509–525.

Zentner, S. "Liberalism and Executive Power: Woodrow Wilson and the American Founders." *Polity*, 26, 4, Summer 1994, 579–600.

WRIGHT, DEIL (b. June 18, 1930, Three Rivers, MI), political scientist; lecturer; consultant; adviser; university professor

Deil Wright was born to William Henry and Gertrude Wright in 1930. He received A.B., M.P.A., and Ph.D. degrees from the University of Michigan. His teaching career began as an assistant professor at Wayne State University in Detroit in 1956. Wright also held professorial aca-

demic positions at the University of Iowa in Iowa City and the University
of California at Berkeley. He currently teaches at the University of North
Carolina (UNC) at Chapel Hill, having joined the faculty in 1967 and
serving as professor of political science and director of the graduate Public Administration Program. He became the Alumni Distinguished Professor at UNC in 1983.

Wright has served in a number of advisory capacities. Among these
are the Director's Advisory Committee of the National Institutes of
Health, the North Carolina Council on State Goals and Policies, the
North Carolina State Internship Council, and the Tax Policy Round Table
of the Lincoln Institute of Land Policy. His international lecture and consulting experiences include Europe, Australia, Indonesia, Thailand, Japan, Korea, and Africa.

The author of over ninety-nine books and monographs, Wright's focus
in public administration research gives special attention to state and local
executive behavior, organization theory, and federalism. In *Understanding Intergovernmental Relations*, he asserts that intergovernmental relations
involve "all the permutations and combinations of relations among the
units of government" in our governmental system and that "the individual actions and attitudes of public officials are at the core of intergovernmental relations."

Wright brings clarity to the three conceptual bases of federal, state,
and local governmental relationships—federalism, intergovernmental relations (IGR), and intergovernmental management (IGM). According to
Wright, five characteristics distinguish IGR from federalism. Unlike federalism, IGR involves all units of government, whereas federalism's focus is primarily on national and state governments. Second, while
federalism relies more on formal and legalistic relations, IGR encom-
passes both formal and informal relations, as well as personal relations.
Third, IGR encourages more frequent and regular contacts than federalism. A fourth distinguishing factor points to the types of actors involved in governmental activities. Wright believes that public
administrators dominate intergovernmental relations, whereas elected
officials command activities relating to federalism. A final difference between IGR and federalism concerns focus. For IGR, according to Wright,
the focus centers on formulating and implementing public policy; federalism's focus, on the other hand, identifies government jurisdiction and
function.

Wright argues that a newer concept, intergovernmental management,
which emphasizes problem solving, considers activities that intergovernmental relations do not. In contrast to IGR activities that are carried out
by generalists in administration, IGM activities are carried out by program professionals whose specializations are on policy, management,
and implementation.

In his historical account, Wright notes that while the study of federalism and IGR span 200 years and 60 years, respectively, IGM's evolution covers only a decade. He further argues that unlike federalism and IGR, IGM is unique in its linkage of "strategy" and "operations" in governing.

Appreciation of Wright's work is evidenced in his awards for distinguished scholarly contributions to the field of federalism and intergovernmental relations from the American Political Science Association and the American Society for Public Administration.

BIBLIOGRAPHY

Works by Deil Wright

Haas, P., and D. Wright. "Administrative Turnover in State Government: A Research Note." *Administration and Society*, 21, August 1989, 65–77.

Hebert, F. T., and D. Wright. "State Administrators: How Representative? How Professional?" *State Government*, 55, 1, 1982, 22–28.

Mowitz, R., and D. Wright. *Profile of a Metropolis: A Case Book.* Detroit: Wayne State University Press, 1962.

Wright, D. *Intergovernmental Relations in the United States: Selected Books and Documents on Federalism and National-State-Local Relations.* Philadelphia: Center for the Study of Federalism, Temple University, 1973.

————. *Understanding Intergovernmental Relations: Public Policy and Participants' Perspectives in Local, State and National Governments.* North Scituate, MA: Duxbury Press, 1978.

————. "Administrative Reform in Japan: Politics, Policy and Public Administration in a Deliberative Society." *Public Administration Review*, 47, March–April 1987, 121–133.

————. "The Origins, Emergence, and Maturity of Federalism and Intergovernmental Relations: Two Centuries of Territory and Power." In *Handbook of Public Administration*, ed. J. Rabin, W. B. Hildreth, and G. J. Miller. New York: Marcel Dekker, 1989.

————. "Federalism, Intergovernmental Relations and Intergovernmental Management: Conceptual Reflections, Comparisons, and Interpretations." In *Strategies for Managing Intergovernmental Policies and Networks*, ed. R. Gage and M. Mandell. Westport, CT: Praeger, 1990.

————. "Federalism, Intergovernmental Relations, and Intergovernmental Management: Historical Reflections and Conceptual Comparisons." *Public Administration Review*, 50, March–April 1990, 168–178.

————. "Policy Shifts in the Politics and Administration of Intergovernmental Relations, 1930s–1990s." *Annals of the American Academy of Political and Social Science*, 509, May 1990, 60–72.

————. "The United States: Intergovernmental Relations." In *Intergovernmental Relations and Public Policy*, ed. B. Galligan, O. Hughes, and C. Walsh. Sydney: Allen and Unwin, 1990.

————. "Explaining Administrative Reform(s)—The U.S.A. and Beyond." *Korea Public Administration Journal*, 3, Spring 1994, 209–219.

———. "Understanding and Securing Local Government Autonomy: The Case of the United States of America." *Korea Public Administration Journal*, 3, Winter 1994, 153–193.

———. "Democracy and Federalism in the United States of America: Intergovernmental Patterns, Policies, and Perspectives." In *Local Government in Nigeria and the United States: Learning from Comparison*, ed. O. Aborisade and R. J. Mundt. Department of Local Government Studies, Obafemi Awolowo University, Ile-Ife, Nigeria, 1995.

Wright, D., and A. Bullard. "Circumventing the Glass Ceiling: Women Executives in American State Governments." *Public Administration Review*, 53, May–June 1993, 189–202.

Wright, D., and P. Haas. "Public Policy and Administrative Turnover in State Government: The Role of Governor." *Policy Studies Journal*, 17, Summer 1989, 788–803.

Wright, D., T. Hebert, and J. Brudney. "Political Challenges in State Governments: Policy and Administrative Leadership in the American States in the 1990s." *Public Productivity and Management Review*, 16, Fall 1992, 1–21.

Wright, D., and S. Jenks. "An Agency-Level Approach to Change(s) in the Administrative Functions of American State Government(s)." *State and Local Government Review*, 25, Spring 1993, 78–86.

Wright, D., and J. Jun, eds. *Globalization and Decentralization: Institutional Contexts, Policy Issues, and Intergovernmental Relations in Japan and the United States*. Washington, DC: Georgetown University Press, 1996.

Wright, D., and C. Miller. "Gubernatorial Leadership and State Administration: Institutional Orientations in a Changing Political Environment." In *Executive Leadership in the Public Service*, ed. R. Denhardt and W. Steward. Tuscaloosa: University of Alabama Press, 1992.

Wright, D., and J. Yoo. "The Evolving Profile of State Administrators." *Journal of State Government*, 64, January–March 1991, 30–38.

———. "Public Policy and Intergovernmental Relations: Measuring Perceived Change(s) in National Influence—The Effects of the Federalism Decade." *Policy Studies Journal*, 21, Winter 1993, 687–699.

———. "Public Administration Education and Formal Administrative Position: Do They Make a Difference? A Note on Pope's Proposition and Miles' Law in an Intergovernmental Context." *Public Administration Review*, 54, July–August 1994, 357–363.

INDEX

About the Authors

PATRICIA MOSS WIGFALL is Associate Professor and former Acting Director of the Public Administration Program in the Department of Political Science at North Carolina Central University. She has published in the areas of school choice, tuition tax credits, and demographic influences and intergenerational differences in school finance.

BEHROOZ KALANTARI is Associate Professor of Public Administration at Savannah State University. His articles have appeared in the *International Journal of Public Administration, International Third World Studies—Journal and Review,* and *Journal of Business Ethics.*

CPSIA information can be obtained
at www.ICGtesting.com
Printed in the USA.
JSHW031420310121
11377JS00001B/3

9 780313 302039